INVINCIBLE

HOW CAN YOU INSPIRE OTHERS WITH YOUR INDOMITABLE THOUGHTS AND ACTIONS?

DR. AMIT DAS

Made with ♥ on the Notion Press Platform
www.notionpress.com

To

All my bosses and mentors who made a difference in my professional career.

" A hero is not someone who does extraordinary physical feats. Perhaps we respect those individuals because they possess the discipline to succeed, but it is their discipline—not only their physical prowess but also their moral fervor—that empowers them to move beyond their prior experiences. But to be a hero, you don't have to be a professional athlete. In truth, ordinary folks like you and me perform some of the most amazing acts of excellence."

- Dr. Amit Das, Motivational Speaker, Leadership Coach , Counsellor, and Mentor.

Contents

Foreword

Dear Reader,

Thank you for taking the time to learn more about "**INVINCIBLE**" and the rewarding outcome of bolstering your self-confidence. This is a book is packed with inspirational sayings and tried-and-true advice on utilising optimism to build your life .

It's crucial for college students, recent grads, and anybody else who either hates their job or needs a change to become a more significant and real version of themselves. Are you already there? Do you understand the meaning of life? Have you figured out your passions and what you love to do? The two concepts that most define and affect the direction of your life are purpose and passion. You get enthused about life when you are passionate. Your purpose illuminates the way ahead and gives you confidence and courage.

We were all made to provide solutions to the world's numerous problems and challenges and make it a more pleasant and safe place to live. All men must abandon selfish, avaricious, haphazard, fruitless, and evil lifestyles in order to live intentionally and make wise choices regarding our everyday activities in order to produce a lot of fruits. There are many abilities, spiritual gifts, and skills that may be used to improve the world and bring glory to almighty. Everyone has the ability to solve at least one specific problem for someone, and this should be realised. One is set to be directed, ideally, to discover his or her purpose or at least become highly fruitful by reading " **INVINCIBLE.**"

The only way you think that will define how best you have created your legacy in this life, regardless of where you are from, how educated you are, or the situations you find yourself in. This book will make you question your ability to overcome obstacles, achieve your goals, and have a fulfilling life. You'll realise what all really successful individuals have in common after reading this book.

This book will hold your hand as you embark on this incredible adventure of self-transformation and self-growth, and personality development is a trip worth taking. This book is with real-life quotes from business leaders from all walks of life who used the science of successful planning to perfect their trade and rise to the top of their profession will inspire and amuse readers along the way. Even when life gets wilder, even crazier, learn how to develop fresh and correct plans.

The author of this book talked about the importance of energy management for your professional success and how to create an energy investment strategy for expansion and sustainability. He offers advice on how to focus on the things that matter most, prepare your brain for sleep, eat sensibly, and plan a seven-day recharging sprint. He concludes by explaining how to instill a high-energy work atmosphere by invigorating time management and looking for quiet areas and recharge stations nearby.

Reading about successful people's lives may have a profound impact on readers and their own. There are several things you may learn from such individuals, from their challenges to their dedication to building tremendous reputations. You will have a clear understanding of two questions after reading this book, such as:

How do you cultivate a winning mindset, keep it, and use it to experience tremendous personal growth?

The author has demonstrated to you how you may start to influence the world by altering the way you feel, think, speak, and act. You will discover what it takes to build the life you want in this straightforward, quick-paced book. It is a comprehensive approach that offers some realistic, scientific, easy-to-implement, but extremely powerful tactics to assist you in realising your actual potential and achieving the happiness and prosperity of your dreams! So train yourself to be in command of yourself and let the world see your unique brightness! You can now choose. Clicking the order button now can either transform your life for the better or worse for the foreseeable future compared to doing nothing.

All those points have been captured in this part of the book to show what his mentors and well-wishers feel about this book and have shared their thoughts to make it an effective piece of advice for your success.

Once again, thank you for taking the time to learn more about how you would reframe your mental attitude towards everyday situations to find a positive perspective in your life? Thank you for taking the time to read this book.

Carpe diem.

Dr. Amit Das

Leadership Coach , Counsellor, and Mentor.

Preface

"Fear, uncertainty, and worry are common characteristics of successful individuals. They just do not allow these emotions to stop them. Because they are invincible."

Some people find it impossible to imagine leaving their safety bubble, especially if you are confident that you will experience anxiety. Having said that, we all occasionally need a little more incentive to face our fears and leave the safety of our comfort zones.

Why are so many of us scared to leave our comfort zones, although it has long been believed that life begins at the other end? I'll tell you why: being in your comfort zone reduces worry and tension. This makes it quite simple to never cross the line since, let's face it, being in your own safety bubble is pretty darn comfortable.

Success is never permanent; failure lasts for a long time.

Failure is rather simple to comprehend. We adore success and rejoice in it. We despise and avoid its opposite, failure, as a result. But it isn't actually sound reasoning. It all depends on how you define the terms. Stop seeing success and failure as chronic conditions, please. Viewing success as a feat in one specific area is a far more fruitful viewpoint.

The failure to recognise the inevitable nature of both pleasure and suffering is the problem. Recognising that change is inevitable will make it easier for you to be more prepared for when unforeseen difficulties arise in your life that, in some ways, may obstruct or undermine your happiness and that instinctive need for safety, security, and stability.

How can you then expose yourself and work even harder to achieve your goals? Where can you go today to try your luck? Look for chances to push yourself a little bit harder. One more question, please. Establish one additional link. Even if there is a chance of rejection, introduce yourself in a new setting. Growth produces opportunities, which are simply another word for luck.

I will demonstrate to you all how you may start to influence the world by altering the way you feel, think, speak, and act. Instead of merely existing, begin to grow! I will cover many aspects including the human condition, discovering your purpose in life, and the secret to long-lasting happiness. I will take you on a memorable trip with some priceless insights on these aspects of life, whether you're wanting to realise your full potential, learn how to succeed at business, or even how you may give back to the world.

Alter begins at the end of your comfort zone; you never change your life until you move out of your comfort zone. Instead of telling ourselves lies and making up reasons to stay in our comfort zones, we must be honest about what we want and take risks.

This book primarily discusses the fundamental mental skills required as a basis for the reader to construct a successful, happy, and fulfilling life. If you approach the book with this in mind, you may rapidly see how the recommendations presented can help you become the person you really want to be and get personally connected with them.

Making your own growth zone workouts is a fantastic way to build your confidence, acquire new knowledge, and increase your experience. And you may start doing that in whichever parts of your life you'd like by adhering to the straightforward procedures I'm about to share with you. The first step is to pick an area of your life where you want to gain more confidence. Create activities that get harder and harder in stage two. They should span the gamut from the most important thing you want to feel secure doing in the future to what you can do now if you just push yourself a little bit. After that, in step three, you begin working out in your growth zone. You repeat the process once the exercises become simple enough.

However, this power is what allows us to operate. And our time management reveals where we put our efforts in order of importance. We can't always offer our best if we aren't deliberate about how we show up in our time. Any encounter or conversation should begin with an honest energy exchange. Like expressing your gratitude, sharing a humorous anecdote, or developing relationships via enjoyable events that have absolutely nothing to do with business. People will remember it if you promptly make the most of your available time.

All the chapters serves as a roadmap for readers who are pursuing their ambitions. Sometimes the path and the destination are both very far away. I will provide the everyday strength and drive that people need at different phases of life. Instead of focusing on how far away the destination is, one could consider how much ground has already been covered and feel deserving and optimistic. This book is the result of my life's work and personal experiences. My mind is buzzing with inspiration and zeal.

We are all aware of how valuable time is. We truly worry about it and are preoccupied with the idea that we don't have enough. I'm advocating that we put energy first so that we may use our time more effectively and feel better and happier while doing so. In this book, I will urge my readers to try some tried-and-true workouts, suggestions, and tactics that may transform their lives in unimaginable ways!

Most likely, since you're reading this, you do. It's not just you. In clarity, the only piece in a range of pieces where spirituality navigates the landscape shaped by the human mind's wanderings is the book's straightforward writing and transparent presentation tackle contentious spirituality-related issues with a certain sense of newness that will excite the mind and drive one to reconsider and relearn. I will demonstrate how to lower stress, sharpen attention, unleash extraordinary creativity, increase productivity exponentially, and restore equilibrium based on the crucial idea that winning begins at the start of the day. Your life may undergo a life-changing makeover in as little as 30 minutes every day.

Have you ever physically visited a place without intellectually or emotionally experiencing it? We all occasionally do it, after all. In reality, we have 60 to 80,000 ideas every day. And the majority of those are unrelated to the current situation in front of us. In fact, it's estimated that humans think about the past around 40% of the time and the future roughly 50% of the time. So we don't truly find ourselves in the present very frequently.

Have you ever noticed how rushed everyone seems to be these days? So it feels somewhat unexpected but amazing when someone gives you their whole focus and attention. Getting this kind of energy boost might significantly impact your work. We can really do more in less time because it truly wakes up the brain and gets you ready to perform at your best without causing all the stress-related wear and tear. You will realise that at first it may seem like a waste of time given everything else on your to-do list or the packed schedule of your meeting, but please bear with me.

If you ask anyone, especially young children, what they want to be, they will tell you those inspirational names of people who have been indomitable in their approach to life, bounced back despite all odds in their lives, and finally inspired us with their invincible thoughts and actions. Isn't it true? It's fascinating to see how people can have an impact on both children and adults.

How to cultivate a winning mindset, keep it, and use it to experience tremendous personal growth?

I will disclose your surest route to success and assist you in bringing your hidden brilliance to light. This book covers a variety of disciplines, including new-age spirituality and methods for emotional emancipation. In order to let readers pick the approach they might like to try out to solve their current difficulties, I have given sufficient information. You may learn how to deal with the daily barrage of irritation with the help of how to reduce workplace conflict and stress without letting your confidence, mood, or momentum suffer.

In this book, I'll show you how to change the way you see and respond to failures in your life. You may enhance your perspective on failure, the lessons you acquire from it, and the methods you use failure to create advancements, guaranteeing that failure always results in improvement.

Each of us was made for a reason, but if we don't know what that reason is or what we want, our unrealised potential remains dormant.

Avoid negative ideas and beliefs, and you will observe changes in your life. Your desires may be realised and a life with a happily ever after can be created just by using basic healing practises. This book will provide you with detailed instructions on how to discover the meaning and purpose of your life in order to feel fulfilled and like you're on the right track.

Your life will essentially become more useful to you, the people around you, and eventually the world, if you have a feeling of purpose and meaning in it. This book, which is extremely encouraging and inspirational, wants its readers to realise that a sunrise and a beautiful day always follow a long and gloomy night. By teaching you how to strive, understand, create, condition, envision, and savour, this book demonstrates how to find your life's purpose and then begin living it. It gives you options so you can go your own way, believe in your progress, and be confident enough to move forward. Your own dreams are the key; all you need is this book. It will show you how to develop positive thinking that will enable you to realise your full potential. You will achieve beyond your wildest expectations thanks to it.

Be deliberate. Be inspired.

We were all made to provide solutions to the world's numerous problems and challenges and make it a more pleasant and safe place to live. All men must abandon selfish, avaricious, haphazard, fruitless, and evil lifestyles in order to live intentionally and make wise choices regarding our everyday activities in order to produce a lot of fruits. There are many abilities, spiritual gifts, and skills that may be used to improve the world and bring glory to almighty. Everyone has the ability to solve at least one specific problem for someone, and this should be realised. One is set to be directed, ideally, to discover his or her purpose or at least become highly fruitful by reading this book.

When individuals have a sense of purpose, productivity rises because this fosters job satisfaction and creates an internal drive for excellence that is considerably stronger than monetary rewards or the prospect of punishment. People who have a strong sense of purpose are also more equipped to adjust and recover in the face of a disaster. Any person who is motivated by their work's purpose is better able to stay motivated and actively engaged in it even in the face of adversity than those who are not.

In order to inspire and direct readers to want, pursue, and fulfil their earthly purposes—or to strive to yield abundant fruit and be a benefit to almighty, mankind, and all of creation—this book discusses methodical ideas. It aims to instil a lifestyle of purpose in the reader so that, by almighty's grace , they may live by a plan, desire to be productive, and ultimately fulfil the almighty's purpose.

If you modify your way of thinking, everything may be healed. Your body will then be healthy and fit.

There is a fix for each issue. The chance of resolving the issue also arises when you discuss it someplace. I will offer simple procedures that may be used to assess the feasibility of novel concepts. In this book, I have also included guidelines and strategies to prevent burnout. The wonderful part about all the concepts discussed in this book, "**INVINCIBLE**" is that they are written and presented in such a way that they can be applied to nearly any circumstance.

The only way you think that will define how best you have created your legacy in this life, regardless of where you are from, how educated you are, or the situations you find yourself in.

Even better, you'll have a personal insight into how you really compare and what needs to change in you in order to alter the trajectory of your personal life. This book is a collection of brief talks on your life's critical factors to accomplishing your pursuits and thriving in life.

You'll discover a number of things, including a little-known technique for how to step beyond your comfort zone in a way that most people have never done before—comfortably and safely. You'll discover how to eliminate the imposter syndrome, stop people-pleasing, reduce self-doubt, understand where it actually comes from, how to read people more effectively, overcome the need for acceptance, stop people-pleasing, and much more.

This book will inspire you to create more precise goals, become a mind-master today, and accomplish any objectives you set for yourself. This book offers tried-and-true methods for developing self-control so you may transform your life and accomplish any objective you set for yourself. You will re-vision and re-cast your life's tale as explorers in your own lives by discovering your deepest inspiration, your happiest emotions, and expressing your ambitions. You'll discover how to eliminate the imposter syndrome, stop people-pleasing, reduce self-doubt, understand where it actually comes from, how to read people more effectively, overcome the need for acceptance, stop people-pleasing, and much more.

Many of us just float through life doing jobs we don't like while accruing massive amounts of debt from college loans and pursuing things we aren't particularly interested in. We completely stop caring about the things that really make us feel alive.

If you're seeking a means to protect yourself against these unpleasant features of modern life, look no further. You can now choose. Clicking the order button now can either transform your life for the better or worse for the foreseeable future compared to doing nothing.

I advise individuals to make decisions with confidence, expect success, and promote their talents, which emphasises humility and an awareness of failure. Nearly everyone I spoke with in India downplayed their accomplishments. When I asked them to briefly describe their achievements, I was met with utter silence and blank looks. This wasn't because they didn't know or because their accomplishments were secret, but rather because they were uncomfortable answering such a basic icebreaker question. I had heard that they were modest about their achievements, but I never anticipated that humility to be so obvious. So let's take a trip down memory lane and examine things from a different angle! I view obstacles as stepping stones.

A person's character and optimism are often put to the test by obstacles on their journey.

Why are we more afraid of failure than success? Your negative ideas will gradually disappear if you form a successful habit, and you'll start to think that success will come through hard work and optimism. The goal of human life is to escape the suffering of a material existence and find happiness. Happiness is something we strive for all the time, yet we frequently fall short. Happiness may appear for a moment, but it is fleeting. We cannot avoid suffering, even when we may not desire it. We need to comprehend what is causing our difficulties in the first place so we can fix them. Since the beginning of time, we have been stuck in this material world, and the enjoyment we seek here is fleeting and deceptive.

"Excellence is an art won by training and habituation. We do not act rightly because we have virtue or excellence, but we rather have those because we have acted rightly. We are what we repeatedly do. Excellence, then, is not an act but a habit." -Will Durant

This book is a wonderful illustration of how you might occasionally truly "find" your purpose? When you are exhausted, it is much simpler to sit on the sofa and watch a feel-good programme than it is to go out to dinner with your family, but what good is it to do that? We all squander much too much time on pointless activities. It is preferable to create lasting friendships now. There are also millions of lonely people in the world who would kill to have a dinner companion. maximising life's happiness to the fullest. I have to go home, but I have a choice between taking the five-minute subway ride underground or taking a 30-minute leisurely stroll through a park and through streets lined with trees. Living with purpose produces lasting happiness.

Many individuals underrate their potential and what they are capable of. The gap between where we are now and our potential is what we call potential. Potential frequently results in success for that person. This is not always about success (although for many, this is exactly what it is). Finding tranquilly is important to some people. Some people place more value on "being" than on "having" or "doing." Others care more about relationships and having the freedom to be themselves in order to meet the appropriate partner. Some claim that if we need to "unleash your potential," it suggests that something is wrong with us or that we are insufficient just as we are.

“Happiness is the art of never holding in your mind the memory of any unpleasant thing that has passed.”

The power you possess is something you yourself are unaware of. You may use your strength to get what you deserve in life by focusing all of your energy in the appropriate directions. You must use the power inside you to do it. Most of the time, you concentrate on difficulties rather than what may go well. You should perform a few rituals in order to focus your energies in the direction of your dreams. You may employ your entire potential and become alive by engaging in these rituals. We underrate our capacity to do more in life.

Everyone aspires to lead a meaningful life. It's a trait of humanity that stems from our dislike of feeling motionless. We must continue to advance toward a target or objective. Without it, we are less content. However, it's simpler said than done. What does living a life with meaning entail? Living with purpose entails pursuing a significant goal that aligns with your beliefs and passions and makes you happy.

There's always a way to do it better.

What do we define as the purpose of our lives? Purpose must begin with each of us as an individual. What is the mission we see for ourselves? Let's start by discussing purpose in terms of human psychology. While some could contend that each of us has a distinct mission, the bulk of us have two characteristics and will identify with them. Development is the first. Being the best version of ourselves is our top priority as humans, along with actualizing our potential and growing to our fullest potential.

Our eagerness to trust life outweighs our capacity for reason as long as we maintain this awareness. So, effortless living is the readiness to let go of our urge for desired results and accept the flow experience. We release situations that no longer benefit us rather than frantically grasping at life. To let go means to mentally and emotionally distance oneself from circumstances that are out of our control. Instead of moving with the flow, energy is wasted fighting against life. The egoic mind asserts that it is far more intelligent than that which directs the stars and planets. Given that we are a minor component in a carefully planned process, we are aware of the fallacy of that assumption.

Positive thinking has a beneficial impact on your health as well, reducing stress and enhancing your general welfare. Even when you are sick, your body heals more quickly. By adopting a positive outlook, you can establish emotional equilibrium, which really aids the brain's healthy operation. You develop the ability to maintain attention, which enables you to make wise choices in difficult circumstances. You'll start to feel better about yourself after you adopt an optimistic outlook. Your confidence and inner strength will increase as a result of treating yourself with more love and respect. You'll overcome your self-limiting beliefs and take on fresh tasks.

In today's world, people are attempting to extend their horizons, which could lead to social success but not actual success. You must be able to perceive things clearly and without distortion if you want to be genuinely successful. A hero is not someone who does extraordinary physical feats. Perhaps we respect those individuals because they possess the discipline to succeed, but it is their discipline—not only their physical prowess but also their moral fervor—that empowers them to move beyond their prior experiences. But to be a hero, you don't have to be a professional athlete. In truth, ordinary folks like you and me perform some of the most amazing acts of bravery.

Personal productivity is the effective completion of tasks that advance your goals while preserving equilibrium in significant spheres of your life. Depending on what's important to you, being more productive on a personal level may imply many things, such as fostering social connections, improving one's health, or boosting one's income. In the end, setting the proper priorities is the key to achieving your objectives while avoiding burnout.

By identifying your views, values, and motives clearly, I'll show you how to truly understand yourself in this book. I'll show you how to make an impact and acquire profound personal understanding by utilising the power of perspective. Additionally, I'll walk you through five tried-and-true methods you may use to improve your own self-awareness. You'll have your own action plan when you finish reading this book to help you put what you've learned into practise and get results. It's time to delve deeper into what you can do to improve your self-awareness so that you may achieve the type of success in both your personal and professional lives that you desire.

Your gifts, your passions, and your abilities are the three components that make up your strength, as I'll use the word in this book. What are you still holding out for? You can create and sustain it by using the resources you already have. Join me on this adventure to discover what true happiness is. You can create and sustain it by utilising the resources you already have. This book would assist you in addressing and finding solutions to all of life's most important concerns. It's an expensive game that so many of us play to learn by making mistakes, often again. With the help of this book for the twenty-first century, you'll be able to handle whatever society throws at you and succeed in life. The book delves into the science behind why these processes work and the most effective methods to put them into practise on a daily basis, covering everything from preparing at night to incorporating little life hacks into your morning routine. Examine each of these chapters, then choose one. Before attempting another, give it your complete attention.

There will always be obstacles and challenges that stand in your way. Building mental strength will help you develop resilience to those potential hazards so you can continue on your journey to success.

Acknowledgements

*At the outset, I will thank my family for supporting me throughout the journey of writing my book and encouraging me to live my dreams; my son has always been instrumental in giving his inspiration to complete the writing of this book. Despite the fact that I am listed as the author of this book,"***INVINCIBLE***" would not have been published if I had depended entirely on my own talents. Creating this book required more than anything—it took a family of dedicated and caring people who were always prepared to lend a hand.*

Writing a book while working full-time is no simple task, so I'd want to express my gratitude to my amazing coworkers who act as cheerleaders in equal measure. Thank you, too, to my students and clients for your patience and unflinching support while I worked on this book!

Thank you to everyone who has listened to me argue for doing everything you can to make your life, including your work life, more progressive. I appreciate everyone's assistance throughout the process. This book would not have been possible without each of you having had an impact on my life in some manner.

Lastly, I would like to thank all the people with whom I have been associated. You gave me power. I would like to thank Notion Press for publishing my book. Finally, thank you all for gifting your time to read this book.

I'd want to convey my heartfelt appreciation to the almighty God for bestowing his blessings and being so gracious.

CHAPTER ONE

Your Definition Of Invincibility

"In today's world, people are attempting to extend their horizons, which could lead to social success but not actual success."

As per the Oxford dictionary, "invincible" means impossible to defeat or prevent from doing what is intended. The word "invincible" is derived from the Latin verb vincere, which means "to conquer," and the prefix in- The word vincible, from the Latin vincere, also came to denote "capable of being overcome or subjugated."

Life may be seen as a play or game if you can accept everything as it is. You can play it well and with delight; that much is certain. People will consider you successful if you can play it well. A positive attitude is a way of thinking that resists giving in easily and is not deterred by challenges, problems, or delays. True optimism involves anticipating challenges and thinking about failure in addition to just asserting that everything will be fine.

A positive attitude has to become your daily default mental attitude if you want to make good adjustments and improvements in your life.

It needs to develop into a habit and a way of life. Although it can seem difficult, doing this is a slow and fun process. You can only truly achieve success in life by developing self-mastery, which you may do by using the create your legacy tree paradigm. Then, rather than taking years, your own growth will direct you toward the accomplishment of empowering objectives.

What is success?

Is it your money? Is it your contentment? Is it your fame?

One of the best-known modern authorities on achievement, inspiration, and living a balanced life was the late Zig Ziglar. In his book Born to Win!, he makes the case that success cannot be summed up in a single phrase but rather is made up of a variety of factors. One may contend that each person's concept is unique and that there is no such thing as a universal definition.

Success is a subjective concept. I believe that success is when you achieve your goals and are content. It might be used for both daily activities and life in general. My definition of success is achieving personal goals, whatever they may be.

Your definition of success could contain more of one than the other, or it might be a combination of the two. It may potentially be something completely different. No matter how you currently define success, this short but mighty book called "INVINCIBLE" will undoubtedly change the way you think about and define it. This includes a wide range of remarkable stories and examples. The message will strike a chord with you deeply and leave you feeling deeply responsible for how you decide to accomplish the success you want. These include initiative, enthusiasm, optimism, decision-making, using failure to your advantage, selecting heroes carefully, managing oneself, managing one's boss, managing others, and leading others.

In today's world, people are attempting to extend their horizons, which could lead to social success but not actual success. You must be able to perceive things clearly and without distortion if you want to be genuinely successful. A hero is not someone who does extraordinary physical feats. Perhaps we respect those individuals because they possess the discipline to succeed, but it is their discipline—not only their physical prowess but also their moral fervor—that empowers them to move beyond their prior experiences. But to be a hero, you don't have to be a professional athlete. In truth, ordinary folks like you and me perform some of the most amazing acts of bravery.

I wrote this collection of thoughts with folks who recognise the value of leaving a legacy in mind, but who are unsure of why they are alive or what they should be doing with their life in mind. It is a collection that will inspire both creatives in general and those who have never thought of themselves as creative or as capable of creating something admirable. These concepts should be read and digested as if they were a collection of flashcards.

One of the nicest feelings a person can experience is the knowledge that they are making a good difference in someone else's life. The soul enjoys having a sensation of joy, happiness, and fulfillment. It's the emotion a doctor experiences after saving a patient's life. It is the emotion a teacher experiences when a former pupil informs him during a visit years later that he attended college because of him. It is the emotion parents have when their child returns from active duty wearing a military uniform. There are several methods to motivate others. People are paying attention to what you say, do, and how you act, whether you realise it or not. Your legacy is what others will remember you by when you grow older and depart this planet. It includes the effects you have on other people.

In the free and easily accessible information era, there is no longer a necessity for individuals to overload their heads with knowledge. The war may be lost by those who regurgitate; those who innovate will plough their own path and triumph. Beacuase there is a clear distinction between winners and losers. Don't give up, because if you do, you've already lost. In the end, you have no right to complain to anybody about anything if you're not prepared to stand up for yourself. Hence, living in complaint is not worth it. Utilise it to the fullest. Your final day is unknown to you. Live your life to the fullest, in whatever way you see fit.

Never waver in your commitment to excellence. Excellence is a journey, not a destination. Be prepared to sacrifice everything except persistence, commitment, enthusiasm, diligence, tenacity, self-belief, appreciation, and motivation in order to achieve your goals. Most importantly, commit to lifelong learning and make learning your top priority. As a result, you are now a "student of success." Spend all of your time, effort, money, and resources achieving what you desire in life.

Developing into a "Hero" having a player's mentality doesn't guarantee success. You will exhaust all of your options and again ask yourself, "What can I do?" but some issues simply cannot be resolved. The idea that everything turns out okay in the end is untrue.

You can be invincible; you can leave a legacy because you control your destiny.

You are in charge of your own destiny. You have undoubtedly heard this a lot in your life. Maybe this resonates with you, or maybe you feel that the sentiment condescendingly oversimplifies the difficulties of life that might restrict your alternatives. Whether or not you feel like you have complete control over your destiny, the truth is that you do. Controlling your ideas is a key component in shaping (or influencing) your future. The viewpoint that you have influence over what happens rather than feeling as though something is happening to you is created by viewing problems as opportunities. Because of this, you may take action and affect change as opposed to just accepting your circumstances.

When things do not go as planned or as we had hoped, we frequently blame it on fate. The opposite is also true in that some individuals frequently blame others' success on their fate rather than recognising the effort they put into their accomplishments. In other words, we associate our choices with our future.

We frequently believe that destiny, a great power, governs our lives rather than ourselves. What one should understand, though, is that a man's fate is determined by his mind and the thoughts he puts into action. Thank goodness Walt decided to ignore all of his detractors and pursue his ambitions instead of listening to them, as a result of which we now have the Disney corporation. A determined intellect might lead you to destinations you never imagined.

That is why the phrase "It's all in the head" is so popular. Only the choices we make will determine our future.

"Your destiny is to fulfill those things upon which you focus most intently. So choose to keep your focus on that which is truly magnificent, beautiful, uplifting and joyful. Your life is always moving toward something."- Ralph Marston

You must learn to regulate your ideas, pictures, dreams, daydreams, and actions. Your thoughts, words, and actions must all be deliberate and in line with your mission, beliefs, and objectives. Sometimes you come up with a brilliant concept right away that you can develop and run with. Everything seems to be going great until you have a setback. You get punched in the gut by failure, leaving you with aching wounds and no choice but to whine about what might have been. Change your replies if you don't like the results.

Our ideas are the embodiment of our minds, and our actions are the result of those thoughts. One just cannot sit back, fold his arms, and claim that everything in his or her life is the result of fate. Our way of thinking and the way we see the world directly affect how we live. Only the choices we make will determine our future. For instance, if a person has a strong will and a determined attitude, the decision-making process and how the choice is carried out will eventually establish that person's fate, which will finally determine their destiny.

When compared to the effort we put into achieving success, we frequently have higher expectations and hope that it will arrive sooner rather than later. If it does not, we tend to become upset and eventually sink farther into the pit of inferiority. The majority of individuals have observed this circumstance, when regular and committed efforts are neglected and only failures are celebrated. Such instances may be found anywhere in the world. The majority of famous people have had significant setbacks in their battles with life. Nevertheless, they persisted in their paths to success and eventually experienced enormous success in their specialised industries. They never let their race, religion, or any other distinction stand in the way of their achievement.

Choosing your new way of life when do we truly stop and realise that our behaviours are harming us?

On the basis of events and observations from previous lives, one's conception of man may alter. Your thoughts will get better as you watch and learn more, which will improve how you think and behave. Successful individuals spend a lot of time considering what and how they should act, and it is this way of thinking that has enabled them to change their fate and achieve better things in life. A strong and capable intellect is capable of great things. A man's ability to regulate his thoughts and use willpower is what enables him to achieve so much in life. The mindset that "it was destined to be" brings about disaster because it causes us to give up on our efforts to continuously work toward success and instead to use this as a justification for our failures.

There once lived a very rich and inquisitive king. This monarch ordered a large boulder to be put in the centre of a highway. He then lurked nearby to observe if anyone else would attempt to move the enormous boulder from the path.

Several of the richest merchants and courtiers of the monarch were among the first to pass through. They didn't move it but walked around it. Some who spoke out loudly accused the king of neglecting the roads. They did not even attempt to move the boulder.

A peasant arrived at last. Vegetables filled his arms. The peasant set down his burden and attempted to move the rock to the side of the path when he reached the boulder, rather than simply going past it like the others had done. He put a lot of work into it, but he eventually succeeded.

The farmer had just finished loading up his cart and was getting ready to go when he noticed a pocketbook lying in the road where the boulder had been. The commoner unzipped the purse. A message from the monarch and other gold coins were also inside the bag. The money in the bag was a prize, according to the king's message, for removing the boulder off the route.

The monarch demonstrated to the peasant what many of us never realise: every challenge offers a chance to advance our status.

"Life is not always going to be roses and rainbows. You are going to have uncomfortable moments. It's what we do with those moments that is going to count and determine our destiny."

Considering that everything is temporary, try to avoid being attached to people, places, or events. Dread is the source of clinging, which breeds more fear. Change your thoughts to more powerful ones so that you can easily allow what is required to flow into your experience. Don't hold onto things you don't need anymore. Consider repurposing it if you haven't used it in the past three months. Less tangible possessions free us from having to handle more. I'm not advocating leading a simple existence; rather, you shouldn't look to worldly items to bolster your sense of identity.

Whatever you choose to call it—destiny, fate, karma, serendipity—the notion that life is predetermined by forces outside of our control is an age-old one. It exists in every culture on earth, including ancient Chinese narrative and Greek mythology. But what if fate wasn't actually real? What if you had influence over your future? You have acknowledged your internal centre of control if you think you are in charge of your own destiny. It means that you accept responsibility for your thoughts, actions, and results. This method of thinking can help you become unstoppable. You may learn to take charge of your future. You must first embrace who you are and where you are right now in order to take control of your future. You'll run out of things to do if you trick yourself into thinking that you're further along in your goals than you actually are.

"Your life will be no better than the plans you make and the action you take. You are the architect and builder of your own life, fortune, destiny."

Don't delude yourself into thinking your life is worse than it is, though. Take a step back and consider your situation differently. Increase your awareness of yourself and embrace the truth. If you don't know where you're starting from, you can't develop a strategy to control your fate. Accepting reality does not entail passively accepting your fate without taking any action. It entails taking responsibility for the things you can alter and letting go of the things you can't. You have no influence over what people believe or do. You have no power over the market. Your own mentality is the only thing you have control over. To do that, you must challenge the self-talk you believe in and replace it with an empowering one.

Not everything works out as planned. Sometimes things go wrong.

Owning up to your errors because everyone makes mistakes, but not everyone comprehends the necessity of taking responsibility for them. It's because admitting your faults is actually the first step in recovering from a failure. It involves admitting that you're accountable for all or part of the unfortunate situation that just happened. There are numerous significant reasons to do this, but before that, it could be helpful to discuss why it's so typical for individuals to refuse to accept responsibility for their mistakes. Actually, there are three. First, it's so simple to place the blame somewhere else. Blame, in my opinion, is only an abbreviation for an essentially meaningless justification. Playing the blame game is never beneficial.

Oprah Winfrey was dismissed from her first television job before she became the king of television. Walt Disney launched a number of businesses that were total failures before he succeeded in building the Disney empire. What makes them so unique now? Is it because of their exceptional talent and wisdom? Maybe, but most experts emphasise something else, such as a strong work ethic, persistence, and drive to persevere. They were frequently prepared to fail. After one significant failure, most people would have given up, but they didn't. Instead, they took the path taken by all successful individuals. They accepted the success cycle, which has the following steps: attempt, err, learn, and achieve. Now, the first three steps—try, fail, learn—may occasionally need to be repeatedly carried out in order to provide a specific result.

What's the most crucial initial move to making today successful? Having a productive morning. Boosting your motivation and productivity. This effective morning practise can help you start off on the right foot. Remind yourself to discard, swap, and enhance as soon as you wake up, while drinking your morning coffee, or even while taking a shower. Start your day by letting go of any negative thoughts or issues that have been keeping you down.

The amazing "rags to riches" story of Tushar Jain, co-founder of a firm valued at Rs 250 crore, demonstrates how many people are compelled to give up on their dreams because they are unable to realise them. But this man put a lot of effort into getting what he desired, and he was finally successful.

Tushar Jain is an MD and co-founder of High Spirit Commercial Ventures Pvt. Ltd. Tushar Jain faced several obstacles on his amazing path, but he persisted and is now the boss of a Rs 250 crore company that employs thousands of people. 1992 saw a lot of financial losses due to the infamous stockbroker Harshad Mehta swindle. One of them was Moolchand Jain, a Jharkhandi businessman who lost all of his money in the scam in 1992. According to Yourstory, Tushar Jain started selling bags on the streets of Mumbai with the help of his teenage son after this deception caused his family's financial situation to worsen.

After working hard to enhance his position, Tushar Jain, with grit and persistence, successfully founded a company named High Spirit Commercial Ventures in 2012. Tushar Jain co-founded High Spirit Commercial Ventures, the fourth-largest supplier of bags and backpacks in India. The Rs 250 crore company, in addition to its Mumbai headquarters, has 10 regional offices around India. In order to grow his business throughout India, Tushar Jain founded a firm in 1999 that had 300 stores. In 2002, he moved his operations to Mumbai. His first internal brand was "Priority," which he developed. In 2006, he developed contacts with a number of important clients and delivered them customised bags. By 2007, he had established a foothold in the Indian market. He constructed his plant and started making between three and four thousand bags every day to do this. Tushar Jain's company published Traworld and Hashtag in 2017 as a result of his ongoing success. Due to positive consumer feedback, Bollywood celebrity and fashion icon Sonam Kapoor Ahuja has joined our team as the Traworld brand ambassador.

Tushar Jain always believed that if you work hard and are passionate about your goals, success is never far away. Tushar not only started a business but also produced thousands of jobs. He has also mentored a number of business owners who are now successful and earning up to Rs 50 crores.

To thrive professionally, it is crucial to recognise your strengths. But frequently, we are unsure of our own advantages.

Find out what your biggest strengths are, your natural talents, and your passions. I will provide specific examples to help you identify what to concentrate on doing (and what to avoid doing) to build on your skills and elevate your worth as an employee. These exeamples can also assist you in determining whether or not your present position is a good fit for you and how to handle a mismatch.

Are you supposed to do what you're doing in terms of your career? Are you focusing your attention on the things that make you special? A job does not automatically make you valuable. Additionally, you must continually improve at adding value through what makes you unique, powerful, and distinctive. Your quality of life and professional achievement will be significantly impacted by your capacity to match your skills with your day-to-day job.

You'll advance more rapidly if you concentrate on your strengths rather than try to strengthen your weaknesses. But how can you actually identify your talents, let alone learn how to develop them at work? You will be led along a path of self-discovery through this book. I'll walk you through a process to identify your areas of inherent talent, your areas of deepest interest, and the abilities you've honed through time. I'll also look at how you might involve a friend or two in your self-evaluation process. I'll look at strategies you may employ to capitalise on these advantages and raise your market value. After that, I'll try to match your abilities with the job duties you now have or would like to have. It's critical to know oneself in order to better yourself in the competitive job market of today.

Our world's virtually infinite options are one of its most beautiful aspects. We have a lot of options, particularly when it comes to our professions. Flexibility may be both a benefit and a burden, though. Most of us have trouble deciding where to direct our attention. If a person switches careers frequently, it may be time and energy lost. I personally engaged in it for a long time until I figured out who I was and began concentrating on my abilities. I have a pretty clear notion of strength that I use when I use the word.

Your abilities are your gifts because they have virtually always come to you spontaneously. These are often areas where you excel above others and which have always come naturally to you. What I refer to as "love" is the second component of a strength. Something you enjoy doing, in particular. When you have this sort of employment, time goes by quickly since you are enjoying yourself so much. And lastly, your skills are a representation of the information and abilities you've accumulated through time. Education, mentoring, or on-the-job training are all sources of skills. You develop strength when you bring together your talents, passions, and abilities. One individual you know who is content and successful in their work comes to mind. They probably enjoy what they do, have a natural talent for it, and have worked hard and learned to hone their talents over time. They have discovered their strength, and they are making good use of it in ways that the global market values.

Do what you love, and the money will follow, is an adage that you've probably heard before. If you have the talents and abilities to match your love, there is some validity to this saying. Do what you love, and it's more probable that money will follow if you're good and gifted at it, which is maybe a better way to phrase the original remark. Many people focus their professional decisions purely on financial gain.

However, because they don't enjoy their jobs, they become irritated at work, are less successful overall, and eventually quit or change occupations. When you enjoy what you do, you can put up with the parts of the job you don't like. But because I genuinely enjoy what I do, I'm prepared to put up with that minor discomfort in order to achieve the bigger objective. Simply put, pursuing your passions helps you live a long, healthy life. I've told a straightforward message to you to internalise in order to make this process of understanding easier for you. Before having someone else respond, you will first respond to the following issues.

- Recognise the main distinctions between talents, passions, and skills.
- Look into techniques for figuring out what you enjoy doing.
- Identify your core competencies by reflecting on yourself and receiving input from others.
- By evaluating and rating your job activities, decide which ones are your strongest and most useful.
- Define the steps necessary to improve your strengths and invest in yourself.
- Recall how to match your skills to your tasks and figure out when to advance in your existing job rather than change to a new one.

Don't overthink your response; instead, write down the first thought that occurs to you. And certainly, you should record it. The entire procedure depends on written answers. Now, you can ponder upon the following questions:

First, what aspect of your current employment do you enjoy the most? No matter how tiny, there are aspects of every profession that people enjoy; mention them below. What would you do for a living if money were no object?

Second, what type of employment would you like to undertake if you didn't have to worry about paying the bills? Write down your response.

Third, what types of work activities do you lose yourself in? Perhaps you stay up late working on something you just adore, and others have to tell you to quit. Write down your response. List your interests next, whether they involve fishing, stamp collecting, or anything else. This inquiry prepares you for the following, more significant inquiry.

Fourth, what aspects of those pastimes are transferable to the workplace? Perhaps there is a strong job that would be comparable to collecting stamps; for example, the ability to pay attention to detail, classify things, and evaluate things has value in the workplace. List your interests on paper.

The final question just allows you to pause and take it all in. Take five minutes to reflect in silence. Keeping it simple: What sort of work do you appreciate doing the most? Let your thoughts wander over all the many tasks you've completed since you first remembered. Which type of employment did you like the most? Take notes on any responses you have after five minutes. Your written responses to these inquiries have now prepared you to hear comments about your loves.

"I can't relate to lazy people. We don't speak the same language. I don't understand you. I don't want to understand you."- Kobe Bryant

Kobe Bryant is well-known. He is a basketball superstar who has enjoyed enormous success both on and off the court. But what exactly accounts for Kobe's fame? And how did he get to his current position? His drive, work ethic, and love for the game are unmatched. Kobe is a great icon, and people all around the world are inspired by his life story. Since day one, Kobe has been the most dedicated player I've ever seen. He simply did an amazing job. He arrived, worked out before practise, practised harder than everybody else, worked out again after practise, and kept going the entire trip. Olympic qualification comes first, followed by the games themselves.

Kobe Bryant's accomplishments off the court are just a small part of his overall career. He has achieved great success outside the court as well. Some of the biggest brands in the world, such as Nike, McDonald's, and Coca-Cola, have endorsement agreements with him. His own production business and investment firm have also been established. He has published a number of books, including an autobiography and a book for kids.

Your legacy will be determined by your ability to motivate and inspire others to achieve success in life. For instance, Kobe Bryant did not leave his many followers money and other assets when he passed away. He left them with his motivating words and deeds. His capacity to uplift and encourage people to take action will forever be remembered.

"There are two types of people who will tell you that you cannot make a difference in this world: those who don't want you to try, and those who are afraid you will succeed and outperform them."- Dr. Amit Das

A common definition of success is the capacity to realise your life's objectives, whatever they may be. Success may sometimes be better described as attainment, accomplishment, or advancement. It is a journey rather than a destination that aids in the development of the abilities and assets you need to succeed. For me, living successfully means being able to take care of myself and not constantly relying on others to take care of my needs. It's completing my tasks at my own pace and according to my own conditions.

Success is a nebulous concept. Success, in my opinion, is when you accomplish your goals and are content. It may be utilised for both general life chores and specific life duties. Reaching personal objectives, no matter what they may be, is my measure of success. Some individuals think some goals are tiny, while others think they are vast. It's important that they are individuals; each person has a unique recipe for personal success.

What does "success" mean to you? Is it your income or your investments that matter? Is it the size of each, or the price you paid for your house or car? Is it your track record for promotions or your reputation in the neighbourhood? Is it that you've accomplished more than you ever thought possible or that you've triumphed over really difficult situations that nobody would have believed feasible? Perhaps you think that your success depends on the possessions you have. On the other hand, you can believe that success is dependent on intangible factors like connections like love or friendship. You may achieve success in life if you are given the appropriate direction.

Success is the state of having attained a goal or objective, which is the opposite of failure.

The accomplishment of intended visions and deliberated goals defines success. Success may also refer to a certain social standing that designates an affluent individual who may also have achieved notoriety for a successful conclusion. You may focus on your ambitions and goals once you have determined what is essential to you individually. The definition of success knowing what success means in your own personal life is one of the most crucial first stages to success in life. The definitions of success that are most commonly used, such as having a lot of money, being affluent, possessing many material possessions, and having degrees, are far from the genuine definition of success. While some people may view possessing expensive automobiles and a large home as the ultimate definition of success, others see it as leading a life filled with love and happiness with their family. In this chapter, I will present a clear explanation of the holy rules to succeed in life. Here, I will enable you to develop into the best version of yourself by providing knowledge of the Vedic scriptures and humorous tales that everyone can relate to.

Just as fire has intrinsic heat, so does our drive to improve.

You may make enormous advances by adopting the attitudes of the great, implementing the rituals of the symbols, and practising the habits of the heroes. If so, here I will will share with you a very practical and simple method for letting go of this negative weight. You will experience an increase in your self-awareness and emotional control with a straightforward, step-by-step approach.

- You will discover how to create strong emotions.

- You will discover how to build optimism.
- You will discover how to remove emotional barriers.
- You will discover how to develop mental toughness.
- You will discover how to embrace your fear.
- You will discover how to become unstoppable in cultivating your emotions.

If you want to have better relationships, achieve success at work, have more money, or just get rid of the negative emotions that are accompanying your life, this book will reshape the way you think about your feelings and provide you with the tools and strategies you need to turn your emotions into a powerful ally. Are you sick and tired of being angry, miserable, or afraid? Do you feel powerless and unable to take any action? Do you feel negatively about your friends, coworkers, or life in general?

Although everyone has their own definition of success, most people associate it with things like riches, fame, and power. However, other individuals define success as being a caring and responsible father or a loving and devoted husband. My understanding is discovering your actual self, living your life purposefully, discovering what you love to do, and doing it constantly will lead to success.

"Success is more a function of attitude than of skills, aptitudes, or intellectual prowess. Everyone can develop a success mindset and achieve amazing levels of success."

Success and achievement are not the same things, despite the fact that accomplishment is sometimes connected with success. When you try to achieve particular goals, you call it an accomplishment when you get the desired results. In essence, it refers to the outcomes you anticipate or plan for. Success is the result or benefit of a goal that has been attained. The meaning of achievement with each objective you complete, you move closer to financial security and a prosperous life. Through this book, you will learn from top achievers, established leaders, and individuals who have excelled in their fields. Every day, read just one definition and one chapter. Think about it, eat it up, and accept it. Own it. Allow the revelations to permeate your spirit and give you the insight, drive, and inspiration you need to release the genuinely exceptional performance that is inside you.

"Success does not mean an absence of problems, it is overcoming problems. Success is not measured by how high we go up in life, but how many times we bounce back when we fall down."

Many people think that significant, life-affirming experiences are what characterise success, pleasure, and fulfilment. We may create the life we desire and a life that is worth living by maintaining consistency with key routines and behaviors. I would explain the actions you may follow to achieve your goals in terms of your life, relationships, and job. It all starts with how we begin each day. You'll be on the right track to figuring out exactly what you want from life and how you want to live it after you make some tiny changes to your morning routine. You can improve your morning and increase your productivity, drive, and happiness.

Unfortunately, a lot of us spend our whole lives looking for our true calling and interests since they do not come to us naturally. Additionally, there are occasions when they are right in front of your eyes but you fail to see them. Humans are pleasure-seeking creatures, but if you let pleasure dictate how your life unfolds, you'll never discover your passion and purpose. Do you ever feel as though you don't belong where you are? If that occurs to you, you might want to reconsider your decision. By reading this book, you may change the way you think, uncover your passion and purpose, and locate the place where you belong. Your desire to live can be killed by trying to fit in; you may never find a setting where your abilities and skills are valued and embraced. Also, it feels like life is a never-ending battle to please other people. Here, I will help you to overcome some of your fears; strengthen your mental fortitude; discover your passion and purpose; feel better about yourself; and reframe your life goals.

Earl Nightingale was a personal development expert who lived in the early years of this century. And I've heard him quoted as saying, "Success is the ongoing realisation of a worthy goal." Or sometimes it's quoted as "Success is the progressive realisation of a worthy goal." Now, rejection can make us feel like anything but a success, but let's go ahead and look a little more deeply at that statement. Success is not a destination. It's an unfolding It's a journey. It's a step-by-step realisation. It's a daily embodiment of your values. So if you think of success as not a question of what you are doing or what you achieve, but rather, who are you being? Who is the person? What kind of person do you want to be? This is one kind of odd approach to consider things. When you leave the room, try to picture the impression you want to make on people. He or she has kindness, charity, thoughtfulness, delight, and good humour. Those are admirable objectives, so regardless of any recent setbacks or rejections you may have encountered, take a moment to assess your progress toward achieving them.

Even if it may not seem like it right now, if you are becoming the person you want to be, then congrats! You are successful. So, take a time to list some of your most significant principles and noble objectives. We're not simply discussing things that are material or even concrete objectives, so perhaps my aim is to be more compassionate and peaceful everywhere I go. My objective is to use every opportunity to express my creativity. My mission is to boost, enhance, and support other people's creativity. Investigate your own values and realise that you can apply them to anything and everything you do. Everything from doing the dishes to taking the dog on a walk to looking for a new job to waging a war to rule the free world. If your life is an expression of your noble aims or principles, you can succeed in your daily activities.

Success is not a safe endpoint but rather an exciting journey. It is not a secure harbour; it is a difficult journey. Material advantages make the journey safe, pleasurable, and comfortable. Success has other, more crucial aspects, too. Additionally, it involves having good physical and mental health, boundless energy, zest and excitement for life, meaningful and satisfying relationships, creativity, the development of one's talents, abilities, and aptitudes, emotional stability, and a sense of purpose.

The meaning of success can be elaborated in the following manner: S: Satisfaction U: Understanding C: Confidence C: Contribution E: Effort S: Self-Realisation S: Serenity. Success is discovering your special calling that will enable you to cultivate all the talents that God has given you and leave a legacy of successful service to others around you. We were made for success. The knowledgeable

Creator created us with the capacity to excel. When we refuse to harness the resources of our intellect and heart and unlock the tremendous power buried within us, we defy the great architect of all. Our inheritance is success. Few people really make use of this birthright throughout their lifetime. According to psychologists and scientists, the average human only makes use of a small portion of their mental capacity.

Actually, this proportion ranges from 3% to 10%. To play the role of our own actual value, intrinsic abilities, and talents, we have utterly failed. Realising our full potential is success. Everyone have some inherent power and value. Recognising these assets and perfecting them is success. It results from recognising that we tried our hardest to improve to the best of our abilities.

Those who are brave and take risks; become invincible, they will succeed. Isn't??

There was a farmer who grew bored of having different natural forces dictate the quality of his produce. He contacted Shiva one day and said, "I'm weary of all the natural bullshit happening." You cannot possibly be a farmer. You were a hunter, as I recall from history. Why don't you leave nature in my hands because you have no idea what it takes to farm? I work on a farm. I am aware of all times, including when it is expected to rain and when it is expected to be sunny. You are simply a hunter and an insane ascetic; therefore, you don't know.

You would never make a decent farmer. Everything is happening at the wrong time. You should let me handle it.

Shiva said, "Okay, nature is in your hands," when he was in one of such moods. The farmer then decided on his crop.

He then exclaims, "Rain!" And then it rains. He uses his finger to prod the ground and says, "Okay, it's drenched up to six inches." " Stop!" He then ploughed his field, planted maize seeds, and waited two days before hearing the words "Rain!" and "Sunlight!" He was working in the field one day when "Cloud!" Everything just transpired as he had wished, and a stunning corn harvest appeared. He was ecstatic.

He wanted to make sure that no birds arrived when it was time to harvest. He was taken aback by this since, despite shouting "No birds!" No birds appeared as a result. When he glanced at the crop, there was no grain on the plants, so he returned to his fields instead of harvesting the maize. What on earth is this? he wondered. "What went wrong?" He couldn't figure it out since he had properly handled the rain, water, and sun.

He returned to Shiva, puzzled, having followed all of the instructions. Have you destroyed my crop? Shiva remarked, "I have been observing; I didn't want to get involved because you were in command."

You may learn how to reach the same degree of greatness in your own life by working on incorporating these habits into it, just like previous successful individuals have done.

We all have "a desire to be successful," regardless of where we are from, what we do for a living, or our age. We were all created simply to succeed.

I adore reading the memoirs and biographies of well-known and accomplished people. I enjoy observing how others have overcome challenges, written their own stories, and achieved success. I pick up a lot from them. So become a student of success yourself. A comprehensive study of prosperous individuals might be conducted. Napoleon Hill authored "Think and Grow Rich" in this manner. He conducted interviews with all of these affluent and successful people and discovered what made them successful. So proceed at this time. Write down three of the factors that contributed to your most recent successful endeavour.After that, make notes on how you might replicate that achievement in your next endeavours.

Leonardo DiCaprio was an underprivileged child growing up on the fringes of Los Angeles before becoming one of the biggest stars in Hollywood and starring in blockbusters like Titanic, The Revenant, and The Wolf of Wall Street. The actor thinks that growing up around a lot of poverty, drug use, and violence has given him the ability to represent the darkest aspects of mankind in his works. Following some criticism for his performance in The Wolf of Wall Street, which detractors claimed glorified drug use, prostitution, and other "immoral" behaviours, Leonardo DiCaprio defended the part by drawing parallels between it and his own upbringing. "Who am I to talk about this?" he said in an interview with The Times. It returns to the town center. It sprang from the fact that I had a really difficult childhood and had experienced the other end of the spectrum. DiCaprio is thought to be worth more than $245 million.

You might not be aware of it (yet), but God wants to use your prosperity to win over the unconverted. There are occasions when success does come with some kind of quantifiability in the perspective of the outside world. However, even if your success doesn't come with a lot of money or other tangible belongings, people will still be drawn to you because of the way you live your life.

Life has this peculiar way of giving you what you want if you just won't take anything less than the greatest.

Everyone enjoys analysing why things went wrong. What if, though, we paid just as much attention to everything that goes right? The next time you accomplish anything that truly succeeds, ask yourself and other people how they solved it "Do you know why things went so well?" What went well on our end? Were there any lucky breaks? "What can we do for a similar fantastic outcome the next time?" Additionally, you may utilise this when conversing with other prosperous individuals. Consider asking them why they are so prosperous. Query them: "What practises do you have that you believe have aided your success?" What do you do to prepare? "What exactly is unnoticed invisible labor?" As you listen, make notes.

Another short story of Halle Berry who slept in a homeless shelter for several years before she received an Oscar. The star, a struggling actress with a burning desire to succeed in Hollywood, looked for less expensive housing options. However, she claims that her early acting career's challenges ultimately made her stronger. "It taught me how to take care of myself and that I could survive through any scenario, even if that meant going to a shelter for a short stay," Berry said in a People interview. The current estimated net worth of Halle Berry is $80 million.

"Passion is energy. Feel the power that comes from focusing on what excites you" – Oprah Winfrey

Oprah had a variety of odd occupations as a child before getting a job as the local news anchor at a tiny radio network. She later began her own chat show while working for a TV station. She became a fan favourite thanks to her moving performance in that programme. Her television programme thus became one of the most popular programmes ever. Oprah had a lot of hardship as a child as a result of poverty. So, as she rose to fame, she gave money to the poor in an effort to make the world a better place to live. She is regarded as one of the greatest philanthropists of colour and one of the most powerful people in the world today. She has a $3 billion net worth, placing her among the all-time most prosperous businesswomen. Oprah has been dubbed the most influential woman of her generation by Life magazine. According to Business Week, she is the biggest African American philanthropist in American history.

"Often we don't even realise who we're meant to be because we're so busy trying to live out someone else's ideas. But other people and their opinions hold no power in defining our destiny."- Oprah Winfrey

A few things could occur by accident. However, if you wait for the right moment, nice things could come your way only after you have passed away, since things might take some time. Even according to quantum physics, if you try, you might be able to walk through a wall once in a "zillion" times since there is a pulse of particles taking place. just that you'll have a broken skull before you reach that one billionth time. Living by chance sometimes means living with fear and worry.

Whatever happens or doesn't happen when you live by intent and capacity, at least you have control over what is happening to you. It's a more secure way of living. There is no such thing as failure for a devoted guy. If you trip and fall 100 times in a day, you have learned 100 lessons. Your mind becomes structured if you make such a strong commitment to developing something you genuinely care about. Since the way you think affects the way you feel, once your mind is organised, your emotions will also become structured. Your energy and even your physical body will become organised once your thoughts and emotions are in order. Your capacity to create and materialise whatever you desire is remarkable if all four of these are coordinated in one direction. You can create in a variety of ways.

Clarity, not assurance, is what a person needs. If you want to go through a crowd of people without bumping into anyone, make sure your eyesight is clear and you can see where everyone is. If you have confidence but poor vision, you will walk all over everyone. People believe that confidence is an adequate replacement for clarity because there isn't any. It's just not possible. Consider that you always flip a coin to choose the most important choices in your life. Heads go one way, tails go the other. 50% of the time, it works. If you are correct only half of the time, you can only keep your job as a weatherman or an astrologer. There is no other job on earth that you can keep. We require several identities in order to manage the various situations that arise in our lives. You can play your character to the fullest and yet feel at ease with it if you are fluid in your approach and can switch between roles with ease.

But the personality of the majority of individuals is solid as a rock. They are always under its weight, and everything that does not fall within its purview makes them suffer. If you want to change it, you must choose a different course of action. Teaming up with someone you dislike is an easy thing you can do. Spend quality time with that individual in a kind and cheerful manner.

Learn to do and be with things and people you don't like while continuing to live a wise, loving, and joyous life.

No matter how you currently define success, this short but mighty book will undoubtedly change the way you think about and define it. Here, in this chapter you might be finding a wide range of remarkable stories and examples. The message will strike a chord with you deeply and leave you feeling deeply responsible for how you decide to accomplish the success you want. These include initiative, enthusiasm, optimism, decision-making, using failure to your advantage, selecting heroes carefully, managing oneself, managing one's boss, managing others, and leading others.

The best thing we can do as we work to increase our effectiveness in a world that is getting more complicated and competitive is to constantly sharpen the saw. Reminding you that we are not supposed to be static but to constantly sharpen the saw is exactly what you seek to achieve.

In order to inspire and direct readers to want, pursue, and fulfil their earthly purposes—or to strive to yield abundant fruit and be a benefit to almighty, mankind, and all of creation—here I will discuss methodical ideas. It aims to instil a lifestyle of purpose in the reader so that, by almighty's grace , they may live by a plan, desire to be productive, and ultimately fulfil the almighty's purpose.

It might be challenging to overcome the obstacles that life presents. Situations like severe health issues or shattered relationships are handled differently by various people. In order to give readers a wide range of options, Inspirational stories compiles several new-age self-improvement techniques and complementary treatment modalities.

Here, I would assist you in addressing and finding solutions to all of life's most important concerns. What are you still holding out for? You can create and sustain it by using the resources you already have. Join me on this adventure to discover what true happiness is. You can create and sustain it by utilising the resources you already have. It's an expensive game that so many of us play to learn by making mistakes, often again.

You can only truly achieve success in life by developing self-mastery, which you may do by using the create your legacy tree paradigm. Then, rather than taking years, your own growth will direct you toward the accomplishment of empowering objectives. Your legacy has four primary legs—love, health, freedom, and purpose—can be strengthened and balanced, guiding you toward positive decisions, worthwhile experiences, and satisfying connections. I will presents the scientifically supported tactics mentioned inside in an interesting, easily comprehensible manner that will inform, amuse, and motivate you. You may have the foresight and self-assurance to build your own prosperous future.

It is not necessary to strive for excellence. You can still be a terrific human being even if you don't make your identity your primary issue in your life. If you look at certain people, their greatness came to them not because they sought it out but rather because their perspective on life went well beyond "what about me?"

You will be excellent in some ways if you can just let go of the thought, "What about me?" and work as hard as you can because you will inevitably be considering, "What can I do about all the life around me?" Consequently, you will inevitably improve your skills because there is so much to do! Success in life may be characterised as a constant increase in happiness brought on by the gradual accomplishment of important and constructive goals. Making money is only one aspect of success in life. Success should be viewed holistically, and one's approach to it should be more all-encompassing. It is the copious flow of all uplifting elements and forces.

Success is more a product of willpower than chance. Many birds perish in their cages because they mistakenly believe that the great expanse of the deep blue sky is the cage's roof. Those fearless explorers who are courageous enough to attempt new things are the ones who will rule the future. The height of your success may be gauged by how high you bounce back after failing. Success comes to those who are brave and take action, even when doing so seems extremely foolish. "Looking back... over the long and tortuous path that eventually led to the discovery of quantum theory, I am strongly reminded of Goethe's adage that mankind will always make errors as long as they strive for anything," Max Planck said in his Nobel Prize acceptance speech.

Develop a consistently positive attitude. Every action is preceded by a thought.

You must have heard this name Rosa Parks, who was a civil rights activist whose lone act of defiance sparked a movement to end racial segregation in America. She is famous for refusing to give up her seat to a white passenger on a bus in Montgomery.

Parks experienced racial segregation throughout her youth while attending segregated schools, and she was jailed after she refused to get up from her bus seat. Around 500 people came to support her in court during her trial, and afterwards, when African-American commuters opted to walk to work rather than use the bus, there was a city-wide boycott of buses. Parks emerged as one of the great figures who headed the biggest and most successful mass movements in American history and was among the leading campaigners to speak out against the practise of racial segregation on buses at the time. The National Association for the Advancement of Colored People later awarded her with the Martin Luther King Jr. Award.

Success cannot be felt until you are content with your work. Half the fight is won if you enjoy what you do.

Everyone has a distinct vision of what success for them should look like. Success must thus be determined on a particular, case-by-case basis. For instance, what does success mean to you in terms of money? emotional achievement? Physical achievement? How is your family doing? If you're seeking advice on how to succeed in life, you must first define success for yourself and determine what that means. Success may not mean the same thing to you as it does to your parents, coworkers, family, or friends. Your inspiration and enjoyment will both come from where your heart is. At the end of the day, we strive for accomplishment because we want to feel content and successful. To determine where you need to succeed in your life, consider what will make you feel content and successful.

"Success is not final; failure is not deadly," remarked Winston Churchill. What matters is having the fortitude to keep going. Very accurate. But it's so hard to follow since bravery may waver in the face of hardship. When you fail and feel your resistance fading, you reaffirm your bravery and conviction and decide to seek out favourable adversity. To accomplish this, pause for a moment and ask yourself three distinct questions. What's the benefit of what I'm going through, first of all? It might be difficult to notice right now, but if you're honest with yourself and have an open mind, it's there.

While hardship undoubtedly makes certain courses more challenging, it also most likely creates new chances. When COVID-19 hit, I had a client who was concerned about having to close their retail store because of the low customer traffic. They were struggling to find any silver lining in the difficult situation until they realised they had the chance to sell more products online, through door-to-door delivery, and in other inventive ways. They recognised the opportunity to forge closer ties with their neighbourhood and a stronger brand. They managed to succeed despite adversity. And you can. Therefore, how could things possibly be worse? And I mean this literally, not in a mocking way. Is there any way for things to get worse? This is about making the difficult circumstance less painful by placing it in context and looking at the bigger picture. You will quit self-pitying or catastrophizing about your situation sooner if you can make it seem less painful. By doing this, you cultivate thankfulness, which inspires you to keep going. And last, how would this promote personal development? This is deciding to take the necessary steps to make the unfavourable occurrence result in your own progress, not merely acknowledging that it may.

Adversity must be overcome via activity, which fosters development and achievement.

Here is an inspiring story of a winning attitude that changed the rules of success for you. Yes, I am referring to Karoly Takacs, one of my all-time favourite characters, who lost his primary shooting hand due to the explosion of a grenade at an army camp. Karoly Takacs served in the Hungarian armed forces. Around 1936, Karoly Takacs had already established himself as the world's top pistol shooter.

But Hungary refused to let him take part in the Olympics since he was only a sergeant and not a commissioned officer. Takacs was able to compete in the following Olympics as the management relaxed the restriction soon after the event. People backed Takacs as the favourite to win the gold medal at the Olympics in Tokyo in 1940. The marksman diligently practised while full of aspirations and desires. His ambitions and goals were dashed in 1938 when a malfunctioning grenade detonated while he was preparing for the army.

Although the explosion did not kill him, it severely wounded his right hand, his shooting hand, rendering it useless for the rest of his life. He was heartbroken by the loss of both his right hand and the chance to compete for a gold medal at the top level of the sport. After the grenade explosion, most people in Takacs' position would have expressed displeasure. Many would bemoan their bad luck, while others would criticise the government and a select few of the grenade makers.

To everyone's amazement, Takacs said he wasn't there to watch but rather to take part. Everyone anticipated Takacs would attempt to weakly pull the trigger with his right hand at the start of the event to slake his emotional craving for another shot. He spent more than a year in hospital by himself and kept a low profile for a month after he was discharged from the hospital. The Hungarian National Pistol Championship was held in the spring of 1939. When the other shooters noticed Karoly Takacs had come, they commiserated with him at his loss and expressed their pleasure in seeing him attend the event.

He reasoned, "Why should I be concerned about the right hand I don't have?" Let me try using my left hand to see what I can achieve. Takacs, on the other hand, grabbed the gun with his left hand when it was his time. The spectators stared in disbelief as he fired shot after shot with his non-dominant hand. And what was astonishing was that each shot found its target. Takacs was declared the event's victor.

There it was. After hard practise and perseverance over several months, he was able to play again. But his hopes of taking home Olympic gold were once more dashed. This time around, owing to the World War II-related cancellation of the 1940 Olympics by thc Olympic Committee. et it took him until 1948—only 12 years!—to capture the Olympic gold medal.

Only those with strong mental fortitude will be able to get past a traumatic experience, pick themselves up again, and resume performing at a world-class level. The majority of shooters would not have even bothered to attempt using their left hand. Takacs did not, however. He took no blame, returned to practise, and made a great recovery. Every person encounters problems. When they occur, you can choose to put the blame on external factors or look for ways to make improvements. If you want to, you can always come up with an explanation for why things went wrong.

Despite being disheartened, Takacs persisted. He waited for four long years in the hopes that 1944 would bring about his unfulfilled desire.Unfortunately, the ongoing war forced the cancellation of the 1944 Olympics as well. Takacs, however, was not the type of person to hang up his shoes. Takacs was 38 by 1948. He was no longer viewed as the favourite to win the competition in the London Summer Olympics that same year. The current world champion questioned Takacs before the competition as to his purpose. Takacs said he was there to pick up knowledge. To everyone's amazement, Takacs went on to win the gold medal and break the rapid-fire pistol world record in addition to winning the event.

When the 1940 Olympics were postponed, Takacs may have responded, "Four years is too long to wait." Most people would have given up if the 1944 Olympics had also been cancelled. But Takacs persisted in hoping for success until he finally did. He did not budge and maintained constant focus on his objective. Success stories abound, and many of them are the result of someone's unwavering will. Such individuals usually find the will to carry on because they like the adventure. Expecting outcomes to infuse the necessary motivation right now might backfire against you because results can take a while to manifest. Karoly Takacs would have been disappointed if he had started shooting with his left hand and immediately expected to win some kind of championship. He continued to train since he enjoyed the shooting process. He was unable to picture his existence without shooting, whether he used his right or left hand.

Here is his motivational path to the stage. What prevented the shooter from winning the coveted gold medal sooner? Takacs's climb to the top of the podium and his narrative are very inspirational.

Do not depend on others to assist you in achieving success in life. You are a power and your own master. Pay attention to what you have and work on yourself.

Being complacent will not help you. Those who are successful are successful because they went beyond their comfort zone to find new aspects of themselves that contributed to success. When you can reflect on the process you went through to complete a difficult task, that is when you will feel the most satisfaction. Keep your "why" in mind when things are tough. What rewards will achieving your objective bring? How will it affect your life or the lives of the people you care about?

You must force yourself to act differently if you want different outcomes from what you are now getting. The successful outcomes will make the work worthwhile. Be consistent. How many times have you begun something but failed to finish it? You must develop the ability to maintain consistency and keep turning up for yourself every day, even on difficult days, if you want to be successful.

Outlining your goal for the following day the night before is one of the finest strategies to maintain consistency. It is much simpler to stay on track when you have a list of tasks that are clearly defined and a schedule for when you will do them throughout the day. Keep in mind that sometimes being present for oneself requires taking a break. Or perhaps you need to speak with someone. It might also just mean waking up at the same time even though you don't want to leave your cosy bed. But no matter how reliable you are, life could have different ideas.

Always consider what could happen if things don't go as planned if you want to succeed in life. What would be your response, and what would you do? This will help you be prepared and in the correct frame of mind when that moment finally arrives, allowing you to face the issue head-on and succeed.

Failure is a part of your process of excellence.

Since we are open systems, external inputs have an effect on us. The likelihood of encountering negative inputs is higher than the likelihood of encountering good ones, and bad inputs often have a bigger and more immediate influence on us than positive ones do. The goal of the book is to push you to become a semi-open system. Why does this matter? It indicates that you would feel much more productive and content if we could just take in the required negative stimuli while retaining the positive inputs. You won't have to deal with the emotional load of negative inputs that affect your day in an unfavourable way.

Even if it is difficult to accomplish, it is now more crucial than ever. Due to technology and social media, the amount of information we receive each day has doubled over the previous several years. This has dramatically raised the likelihood of encountering negative inputs. To ensure that nothing or no one interferes with your productivity and enjoyment, you must learn to filter out these negative inputs. You must get to a point where you can either avoid or at least lessen the harm caused by negative inputs. Being unbeatable means having the ability to sustain damage yet not lose.

Excellence is a continuous process and not an accident.

What is an achievement? How does it appear? How can one accomplish that? I examine success in depth in this book. Life is setting you up for success, outlining what it is and isn't. To help you change your perspective and stop living a life of limitations, I will share the most inspiring stories of those who have faced defeat many times in their lives but have risen to make a difference on this planet.

"Many of life's failures are people who did not realize how close they were to success when they gave up." — Thomas Edison

Due to his inability to deliver language like a typical actor, people with speaking impairments are frequently passed over for roles in movies. But then came Rowan Atkinson, who, after facing several rejections, found success and cemented Mr. Bean's position in the audience's hearts with his own approach. One of his well-known quotations is: "I adore strolling in the rain because no one can see me cry."

Rowan Atkinson maintained his enthusiasm and put in significant effort to achieve his goals. His goal was to get people to chuckle. He has achieved this via consistent work throughout the years. He started writing unique comedic routines after receiving multiple rejections. If you enjoy the Mr. Bean television series, you will probably enjoy Rowan Atkinson, who portrayed Mr. Bean. He is an English comedian, actor, and writer with a $150 million fortune. He is also regarded as a master of physical comedy and has played a variety of roles that showcase his comic abilities. But did you know the tale of his triumph?

"I have to say that I've always believed perfectionism is more of a disease than a quality. I do try to go with the flow, but I can't let go. "- Rowan Atkinson

He had a great deal of rejection and failure in his life, but he overcame those setbacks by using his vulnerability to become one of the most well-known comedians in the world. He was devoted to creating his own comedic routines since he loved to make others laugh so much. He subsequently realised that he could communicate clearly anytime he portrayed a persona other than himself. He used this as an inspiration for his acting, and this changed Rowan's life.

Even so, he tried out for various TV shows and auditions, but he was turned down everywhere. His acting development is hampered by his appearance, physique, and stammering issues. He demonstrated that you can be one of the most respected and adored performers even without a heroic figure and Hollywood face, despite his appearance and impairments that caused him to be rejected for many jobs.

"People assume that since I can make them laugh on stage, I can also make people laugh in person. That is not all the case. I'm really just a quiet, uninterested person who happens to act. Nowadays, we are seldom ever startled by what we see thanks to the media. "- Rowan Atkinson

Through one of his television shows, he showed us how to create our own pleasure without relying on anybody else. Rowan's confidence in himself helped him to overcome criticism, views, and prejudice. He didn't give up; instead, he persisted, and later on, life rewarded him. People who are successful take actions that others don't, including how they handle rejection.

Throughout their working lives, the most successful people—whether they are corporate executives, politicians, artists, or entrepreneurs—run the danger of being rejected several times. They are aware that it is not personal when it occurs. The fact of life They thus reject the mistaken reading of someone else's subjective evaluation of them as implying anything about their own deserving.

Success depends on being consistent.

Those who seek shortcuts aren't interested in the knowledge, insights, and nuanced understandings successful individuals acquire through their pursuit of achievement in life. It takes time, patience, and persistence to succeed the old-fashioned way, so if you want to succeed, do it that way. The secret to success in life is being able to bring out the best in ourselves in practically any situation.

Your capacity to adjust and transform your life. You've done something that you believed would help you succeed, then. Next, what? Feelings of accomplishment, contentment, and enjoyment are all mutable through time. So, once you achieve success in one area, go for it elsewhere.

By overcoming obstacles and achieving one outstanding achievement in any field, you establish a pattern, a blueprint for personal achievement in your subconscious mind. Your natural inclination and ambition will be to replicate that achievement in subsequent endeavours you undertake. To attain a goal at work, school, or both, try to capitalise on your momentum from a personal success. You'll eventually produce a synergistic effect and discover that success is easier to come by in all areas. Examine the next area of your life where you'd like to succeed, and then start working toward that objective!

You are capable of success. You have the resources you need to achieve whatever objective you set out to accomplish by implementing these principles. Use my personal development plan to kickstart your journey toward success and achieving your objectives. In other words, success teaches you how to succeed. The more you accomplish, the more you are capable of. Success increases your self-assurance, self-control, and faith that you can succeed again in the future and ultimately realise personal success. You may use this free template to identify your areas of strength, form the habit of anticipating and assessing your objectives, and get a daily road map for successfully achieving your objectives.

Successful people not only don't mistake rejection for a sign of ongoing incompetence on their part, but they also use the information gained from a setback to increase their chances of success going forward. Ask for input when it is acceptable and practical, and consider what other people are doing that you aren't. Use the data to improve what you're delivering (a new product or service) or how you're delivering it (for example, rework your application letter, polish your presentation, and practise your interview skills). Just remember not to waste a rejection. It is too valuable to not use it effectively.

You may use your "rejections" as stepping stones to move closer to your objectives by resisting the need to compare yourself negatively to others, place blame, criticise yourself, or feel sorry for yourself.

What kind of rejection did you experience?

So you were turned down. When we've been let down, it's simple to start globalising. feeling abandoned by everyone and everything. to have the impression that the banner failure is pervasive. However, it is not the actual situation. So let's narrow our focus a bit. Giving precise details regarding the types of rejection you have encountered might be quite helpful. Localisation reduces globalisation. I get the awful sensation that nothing will ever work out for me. So tell me, was it a passive rejection of any sort, or maybe you were just passed up for a chance? They weren't necessarily rejecting you personally, then. Simply put, they missed you. Or perhaps you made an attempt but fell short of reaching the first spot. Early on throughout the procedure, you were sidetracked or confused. Maybe you made it halfway. Perhaps you made it almost all the way.

As I go through these, take note of which one appears to apply to you the most. Which ones do you think are better or worse? Was the rejection made in the dark? Did those who rejected you not know you, or was it a personal rejection? Did you experience blatant rejection? Sometimes, sorry, doors close, and folks simply, you know, don't make it onboard the aeroplane. Was it a massive, disastrous failure belly flop? Where have you publicly tried and failed? Was it kismat? Did you have any control over it? Was it a last-minute decision? Were you the victim of events? Was this a fresh urge or a long-held desire of yours? I'm not claiming that any of these will hurt more or less, but I do want you to correctly recount the events. If the truth be told, I never really got off the ground, and those individuals don't even know who I am. The specifics of your narrative may then provide some solace for you. So, do it now and put it in writing for yourself. what exactly took place. You'll really feel more in control of the situation and, ideally, the outcome if you have an honest knowledge of what actually happened and can properly pinpoint the type of rejection you experienced.

Sometimes, the ego will become more arrogant in response to rejection. Well, "it's their loss," as they are unaware of what they are losing. Sometimes the ego's response is to make it seem as though it didn't hurt. Well, I never wanted it in the first place. Some people use a practise known as "spiritual bypassing," in which they hold to an idealistic spiritual conviction in order to hopscotch over any uneasy emotions. Oh, everything is fantastic. And in doing so, you suppress or ignore your true emotions.

Although completely comprehensible, all of these processes will rob you of the depth of your actual feelings. And you get to learn one of the most crucial lessons of rejection, which is how to self-soothe, when you explore your genuine emotions. And you get to learn one of the most crucial lessons of rejection, which is how to self-soothe, when you explore your genuine emotions. Thus, I ask that you do two things. I want you to be very honest with yourself about how much you ache right now. Grief is a genuine emotion. Loss is a genuine experience. Rejection, disappointment, and failure all cause genuine anguish. And although it may be customary in some cultures to encourage people not to feel sorry for themselves, doing so just serves to make one feel sad and sorry for oneself.

What other person can you feel sorry for if not yourself? So feel free to write it down. What particular emotion are you experiencing? Do you experience pain? Do you feel devastated by grief? You say you're lonely. Possibly each of those emotions Go ahead and record them. The second point is that I want you to consider various methods for improving your own well-being. You may set a 15-minute timer and throw a fit. You might compose a love letter to yourself, perhaps one from your future self. Perhaps all you need is a little more rest and water. When asked for advice on how to deal with disappointment in an interview, Tony Robbins responded, "Drink more water," which is excellent advice. Going for a run or doing some housework are examples of physical activities that might occasionally be helpful. A key indicator of emotional maturity is being able to comfort oneself spontaneously. Admit your true emotions immediately, and then, like you would for a close friend, start taking efforts to start helping yourself feel better.

That's how life is. When things don't go as planned, the people who continuously show up and keep going will ultimately succeed and triumph in the broader game. And the same is true for you. You'll discover that taking a chance on rejection when life demands it will eventually pay off handsomely if you keep an open mind, take advice to heart, and resist the urge to wallow in your own little pity party.

Which raises the question: What would you undertake in the upcoming week that you may not do otherwise if you knew that rejection was nothing more than a stepping stone toward the success you want?

Doing something now that will make you proud of yourself tomorrow is a proven method for getting over being disappointed in yourself today and rejection. Starting a habit like this is simple and surprisingly productive. Start by listing three things you can accomplish each day that will make you proud of yourself tomorrow. Then come back the next day to thank me. "Oh, I see, I completed those three tasks. "I'm pleased with myself." I may have completed two of those three tasks, one of those tasks, or none of those three tasks, but I'm going to try again today. The actions that will lead to your success in life are those that make you feel good about yourself and proud of who you are.

I once worked with an arts group that was devastated when they didn't obtain a grant only to learn that it was because they weren't located in the correct area. They had never been eligible to get this award to begin with, but someway that fact had been overlooked. Re-read any instructions or correspondence, and attempt to see any early warning signs. Get more information next. Perhaps conduct some research online, phone some people, and speak with some important suspects, sorry, crucial actors. Ask around if you don't fully grasp the reasons you were turned down. Avoid being aggressive or accusing. Just state that you've become interested in the outcome and have questioned whether any further information would be accessible. Don't call anybody at whom you have unfinished resentment.

You could have some more knowledge and some more crucial information about what you can do differently the next time after you've started to piece together the image of what actually happened, not just from your viewpoint but from the perspective of others. Therefore, don't hesitate to jot down three potential actions, contacts, and study projects that you may carry out this afternoon. Please let me know what you discover.

When you are turned down, you must ask yourself specifically who or what turned you down. Is it someone you respect, like, and have faith in? Is it someone who is essentially neutral? Or perhaps someone whose opinion doesn't matter all that much? I'm not requesting that you look at this with your ego in mind; instead, resist the want to say to yourself, "Oh, well, that person doesn't even know what they're talking about therefore I don't have to feel awful about being rejected." Or, "Oh no, my hero has rejected me, and now I have to take it personally forever."

I want you to consider the person who rejected you so that you may dig a little deeper and uncover more of the truth. I distinctly recall being happy to receive a rejection letter from a college I had applied to since I had not intended to attend that institution. So it appeared as though we were rejecting one another. Those people's rejection made it so I didn't even have to think about attending a school I didn't really want to go in the first place. We were quite enthusiastic about it. Our script appeared to be a perfect fit for this contest. Then we received the rejection letter, which revealed that we had not only lost the competition but also failed to advance to the next stage.

However, after I read their comments on our play and dug a little deeper into the reasons we were turned down, it became obvious that the person who examined these scripts hadn't actually read our script. That information convinced me that, for us, staying out of the competition was the best possible outcome. Their expectations were vastly different from ours. They weren't a company with adequate professionalism. Once more, their rejection was a relief for us. So the next time you feel rejected, ask yourself if you truly wanted to be a part of that group.

"Far too many individuals fall short in life because they are too frightened to make the sacrifices required to fulfil their potential."- Richard Brandson

Some people show signs of anxiety as a defence against failure; others don't even attempt because they feel constrained; and too many others become mired in the status quo. Don't limit your mind to preconceived notions, and don't let fear stand in your way. People nowadays demand more than the usual; therefore, in order to stand out and establish lasting bonds with your target market, you must be remarkable. Delivering the best experience is essential, whether you are selling a good or a service.

Success on both a personal and professional level depends on confidence. People who lack confidence frequently pass up new possibilities, relationships, and challenges. The good news is that once you have confidence, you can use it to carry you from one circumstance to the next. I'll provide straightforward, doable strategies for boosting and sustaining self-assurance in this book. In the first chapter, I have shown you how to take responsibility for your actions, accept your flaws, and move forward, passing up new possibilities, relationships, and challenges. The good news is that once you have confidence, you can use it to carry you from one circumstance to the next. By the end of reading this chapter you will have straightforward, doable strategies for boosting and sustaining self-assurance. By connecting with the correct people, maintaining a positive viewpoint, and creating a strategy, you may learn how to retain your confidence after encounters by reading this book.

There is a link between our self-confidence and how we present ourselves on a daily basis.

All people are fundamentally flawed, although the majority of us spend a lot of time and effort trying to deny this. I comprehend. We don't want failure to define us or for people to focus on our flaws. True; however, for great self-confidence, making time to reflect on this fact and how to apply it is genuinely necessary. We are all human in a few specific ways. We all breathe, eat, and develop cognitively and physically, and sure, we all face difficult learning opportunities along the way. It's anticipated. Sure, when a mistake occurs, it stings for a while, but keep in mind that practically everyone in your immediate vicinity has also gone through this.

The first step is to be upfront about your flaws. I recognise how hard you've worked. I appreciate all of your accomplishments, including your degrees, promotions, and awards, but wasn't it difficult to get all of those things? Obviously not. You committed a few errors and encountered one or more failures along the way. That is typical. Next, you need to understand that mistakes are a powerful source of fuel for learning and development. If you pay attention, each error or failure is actually simply a sort of feedback guiding you toward a more fruitful course.

Success is realising that you are in charge of your own destiny. You alone are responsible for shaping your future. If you accept responsibility for your choices and the results, you'll discover that success comes more easily to you. The conclusion Success has many different definitions. You've already achieved success if you're now feeling joy, love, or adventure. Keep going. Success may be equated with many things by different people, including wealth, power, and having a positive impact on society. They're all accurate. Success may mean various things to different people. It would mean one thing to you, but a different thing to someone else. There are many books about success, yet each person's definition of success is different and personal. So, how might the same knowledge from each book be applied to all? As a result, following the advice of a single person is usually ineffective. With this in mind, getting advice from many people, who may or may not have different definitions of success than you do, can be a fantastic place to start.

You want to resume your pursuit of success, but you need a strategy that is effective for someone who is having difficulty with self-confidence. So let's begin modestly. Think about a typical little win first. A simple activity that needs to be finished and isn't expected to be exceptionally challenging is a little triumph. Getting back on your bike after falling off is analogous to doing this. It's a little step, but it puts you firmly back on the road to productivity and increased self-assurance. It may be as straightforward as deciding to always finish the weekly management meeting on time, or perhaps you only need to get in touch with someone in your network again.

Just keep in mind: defined, straightforward, and attainable. That is a good immediate victory. You'll be prepared for the smart objective after a few minor victories. That stands for specified, measurable, aligned, attainable, and time-bound, as the majority of you already know. The key here is that we're becoming larger, and you're working on them over the course of several months or maybe a year or more. If you're not familiar with the concept, you can spend only a few minutes on the internet to get a tonne of high-quality descriptions. We're not quite finished, though. After a few minor victories and one or two good, sensible goals, it's time to focus on the bigger picture.

When our confidence is shaken, we may become overly anxious and risk-averse. Those lofty long-term objectives can seem overwhelming and out of our grasp. However, they aren't. Dreams, therefore, stimulate our creativity and give us a sense of purpose. You can make changes to your feelings, regardless of the reason you find yourself doubting your confidence. begin straight away. Admit that you need a strategy. Take a modest victory, set a few sensible goals, and don't forget to sometimes take time to daydream. That's a proactive course of action that will probably increase self-assurance.

You must consider how you interact with your surroundings on a daily basis in order to comprehend self-confidence. Consider your most important professional social contacts. Although you try your best to bring a happy attitude to work, let's consider how others impact you during the day. Some individuals tend to make you feel better, while others, well, don't. What I want you to do is this: Make a list of the people you see the most frequently and consistently each week. Make a net positive and a net negative group to divide the group in half. While the other list is made up of individuals who put you under a lot of stress due to their toxic personalities or habits, the positive list is full of people who have a tendency to be kind and helpful.

Positive thinking is crucial. Positive feelings make everything else appear simpler and more controllable. Your self-confidence increases as you become more confident in your abilities. Your aim is to deliberately feed your positivity while being attentive to it. Visualising your success is a time-tested and very successful technique. Any professional should practise this habit for a little while each day. Find a quiet area, then list one or two goals that you have started but haven't finished.

Celebrate accomplishments that help you leave a bad place behind. Perhaps all you need is a small internal congratulations or a cup of coffee from your favourite café. Do it, but keep it modest. That next minor victory or that next significant accomplishment, each time you go beyond a mental block to achieve a healthy mentality, is cause for celebration. If you stick to these suggestions, you'll probably remain optimistic. You may begin right away. Can you think of a specific method you're going to use to increase your optimism during the next several days? Yes, you can, and you're already moving forward.

You must do three tasks for me. You need a tiny victory to start. What is one thing you can do right away to increase your self-confidence? It may be deciding whether or not to show up for a certain meeting at work. Or sometimes all it takes is a simple gesture to entice a wonderful person back into your life. To assist you in igniting that passion for progress, achieve one modest victory.

Many people will want to offer you advice and tell you how to alter your life when it comes to becoming successful in life. It's crucial that you focus on the issues that matter to you and refuse to allow anybody else to define success for you since these individuals may not necessarily understand what success means to you. Whatever your life objectives may be, there are certain tips for leading a successful life that we can share, regardless of whether you define success as being wealthy, powerful, or having made a meaningful contribution to the world. These insightful life lessons from some of the most successful people can assist you in taking the first step toward reaching your objectives. So, if you're prepared to improve your life, achieve your goals, and learn the keys to success in life, this post is for you.

We all want to succeed professionally, but you can't achieve it without having certain objectives and a strategy for achieving them.

Finally, you must begin to turn your objectives into habits so that they become routine and ingrained in your life if you want them to be truly sustainable. We frequently consider goal-setting once a year, generally around December 31. Instead, it turns out that we may do much more and reap disproportionate rewards if we only give the process a little bit more attention throughout the year.

You can achieve anything you can dream of!

CHAPTER TWO

Learning From Your Failure

"Life is a wonderful adventure that should be enjoyed to the fullest every day. The fact that life is a wonderful gift does not, however, imply that you always wake up ready to grasp the day."

We all struggle with failure, which is one of the few universal facts in life. It's a natural aspect of being human, just like breathing. In actuality, it is not only common but also necessary. How you perceive and respond to the challenges you encounter will greatly influence your personal and professional development. Unfortunately, failure has a very detrimental impact on far too many people. The term has a really bad reputation all by itself. People don't want to dwell on their mistakes or reveal anything about them to others. They really do hold the secret to your success; therefore, it's too bad.

Failure is rather simple to comprehend. We adore success and rejoice in it. We despise and avoid its opposite, failure, as a result. But it isn't actually sound reasoning. It all depends on how you define the terms. Stop seeing success and failure as chronic conditions, please. Viewing success as a feat in one specific area is a far more fruitful viewpoint.

What you do today, or what you did in the past, should not limit what you can accomplish moving forward.

Failure and blame are not always synonymous, yet many of us were brought up to think that if we fail, we must have committed a sin. In actuality, failure is an essential and common part of life. The author of this course discusses the psychology of failure, the distinction between good failure (considerate experimentation) and poor failure (careless neglect), and the idea that any failure is a chance to learn. He provides a number of methods for taking lessons from failure and explains how we may use them to develop qualities like perspective, humility, sincerity, and compassion.

Contrarily, failure is only a step in a learning process that helps raise the likelihood of success in the future. Currently, it appears to be quite helpful from that angle, but we are aware that most individuals find it really challenging to reach this conclusion. The fear of failing is the cause. In reality, we know that people consistently set poor professional goals while also failing to set personal goals. It's crucial to understand that this dread is not truly influenced by how confident we feel about ourselves. Because our fear of failure is socially constructed, it has an impact on everyone. To be honest, our educational systems are where it all starts.

The failure to recognise the inevitable nature of both pleasure and suffering is the problem. Recognising that change is inevitable will make it easier for you to be more prepared for when unforeseen difficulties arise in your life that, in some ways, may obstruct or undermine your happiness and that instinctive need for safety, security, and stability.

In each attempt, you have the capacity to increase your odds of achievement.

Failure is expected and required. I want you to consider that thought. You see, if you embrace and incorporate that concept into your everyday thought process, failure as a negative concept starts to diminish, and learning and improvement as a positive concept take centre stage.

Let's start with a strong concept: failure is a necessary component of learning. Everyone blunders. Keep in mind that you're in good company when you fail.

Your capacity to work will be greatly boosted if there is an atmosphere of trust. It's just that everyone will clear the way for you rather than put obstacles in your way. You must possess integrity to earn the trust of others around you, regardless of what you accomplish in your company, life, or work. One of the world's top investors, Warren Buffett, famously remarked, "When hiring individuals, seek for three qualities: honesty, intellect, and enthusiasm." And the other two will murder you if they don't have the first.

You're going to learn that happiness is truly a goal when I help you grasp what evolution has allowed to happen that sabotages our enjoyment. Our natural condition is one of tension and survival, which is what nature has favoured. We'll also learn about a fascinating aspect of brain science research.It is what we refer to as the "social brain." Everyone's brain—yours, mine, and everyone else's—basically developed as a social organ for connection, community, and a sense of greater belonging to something greater than oneself.

The pursuit of pleasure is an intriguing process through which evolution broadened your brain, in a similar way to how you learned that your brain developed to be focused on the negative and on stress. What makes that the case? The good news is that activities that help us survive—like reproduction, digestion, and sleep—are really enjoyable, according to research in the field of brain science.

"People who succeed have momentum. The more they succeed, the more they want to succeed, and the more they find a way to succeed. Similarly, when someone is failing, the tendency is to get on a downward spiral that can even become a self-fulfilling prophecy."-Tony Robbins

What would it be like to be unconstrained and to fly above your limitations? What can you do every day to find tranquilly and inner peace? These issues are addressed in this book in a straightforward yet deep manner. This book will alter the way you interact with both yourself and the outside world, regardless of whether this is your first foray into inner space or you have dedicated your whole life to the inward trip. You'll learn what you can do to stop the repetitive thoughts and feelings that are limiting your consciousness. I will demonstrate how the growth of awareness may help you all in the present and let go of upsetting memories and beliefs that prevent you from finding pleasure and self-realisation.

By altering your thoughts, you may attract wonderful chances into your life and achieve your objectives by using tried-and-true methods. Life is a wonderful adventure that should be enjoyed to the fullest every day. The fact that life is a wonderful gift, however, implies that you must wake up ready to grasp the day. So, overcome your fear and go with the flow of the universe; discover your higher purpose, and become a role model for others.

What would it be like to be unconstrained and to fly above your limitations? What can you do every day to find tranquilly and inner peace? These issues are addressed in this book in a straightforward yet deep manner. This book will alter the way you interact with both yourself and the outside world, regardless of whether this is your first foray into inner space or you have dedicated your whole life to the inward trip. You'll learn what you can do to stop the repetitive thoughts and feelings that are limiting your consciousness. I will demonstrate how the growth of awareness may help you all in the present and let go of upsetting memories and beliefs that prevent you from finding pleasure and self-realisation.

Failure is an illogical concept. Change the notion rather than attempting to alter the world. Simply changing it will make everything perfect. This would be the pinnacle of achievement if you were a street beggar today and could enter the restaurant and eat a dosa, don't you think?

Avoid being someone else's slave; achievement comes before anything else. The amount of money that comes into your life does not determine success or failure. The level of recognition you receive from the outside world has no bearing on whether you succeed or fail. If you can navigate hell with delight, you have succeeded in life. There are failures and successes for someone who sees the everyday activities of this life as the purpose of existence. There is no failure for someone who views this life as a stepping stone to a more promising future. Whatever the circumstance, whether you have a good deal or a terrible one, it's incredibly helpful since you use it for your welfare.

Every challenge you encounter has a single underlying question: how do you deal with yourself? An inability to manage what I refer to as the "You-Factor" is at the root of all of your stumbles, errors, and failures. &; The You-Factor is about managing yourself and your entire life properly, more so than self-worth or self-respect, even beyond character and sense of purpose.

The deepest form of achievement will then feel like it has been achieved once you have lived those ideals on any given day. That, along with the fact that living your values connects who you are with what you do, is what makes this practise so potent. You have a sense of authenticity and confidence in how you are allocating your time. It acts as an internal compass to direct your choices. something you can constantly turn to while you're feeling lost. And once more, success is closely correlated with living your values and having a sense of purpose that goes along with them. The power of purpose can help you feel accomplished and important.

No matter what your career, you must take challenges and come out of your comfort zone, and your humble background can't be an excuse if you fail. It is quite challenging to succeed in life if you don't respect others, whether they are your own or anybody else's. Let's imagine that when you enter any large building, you must treat everyone equally, from the first man you encounter to the managing director, for example. Go through the challenging time; struggle through it, but if you can do it with a grin, I am giving those great examples of people, perhaps five people, who set examples through their lives and can truly pull it off. Because we sometimes complain about life and the difficult times, it's vital to remember that it's going through the difficult moments that will really help you become a better person. I hope it is the start of something amazing and mind-blowing for you. This chapter illustrates how your thoughts may impact your mental, emotional, social, and physical health. It also covers the subject of how your willpower and visions might help you achieve inner tranquilly. A step-by-step examination of overcoming the internal obstacles to achievement may be found in from passion to peace.

You must restrict or eradicate unproductive behaviours while imposing new habits that boost productivity if you want to have the desire and motivation required to consistently put out the level of effort required for productivity. Oprah Winfrey's inspiring but painful success story Oprah had a difficult upbringing, growing up in poverty as the child of a single, underage mother. Because of the sexual assault she endured as a youngster, she had a difficult, rebellious adolescence. When she was thirteen, she fled her home. Oprah, despite having a challenging background, refused to let the past dictate her future. She served as proof that no matter what challenges we encounter, with passion, perseverance, and hard work, we can do anything.

A life filled with successes is wonderful, but one spent working tirelessly to get there is not as appealing. Decide to enjoy your victories instead.

Meet the "chaiwala," who quit his MBA programme to sell tea and developed a $4 million company. Prafull Billore founded MBA Chaiwala in 2017 in an effort to fulfil his ambition of being a "major businessman." He didn't much like drinking tea, yet he nonetheless managed to build a lucrative company with a 4 crore-rupee turnover.

"I aimed to grow into a large guy. Having experienced difficult circumstances since early infancy, my primary goal was to increase my income and lead a pleasant life. My parents believed that if I obtained an MBA, I would find a well-paying job and have a secure existence. But it didn't go like that. Despite my best efforts, I failed the CAT admission exam three times," says Prafull in an interview. Prafull, who comes from the Madhya Pradesh town of Dhar, had lost interest in his MBA programme at Ahmedabad University, which he had been attending since 2017.

However, reading books and absorbing the sayings of well-known business figures was what kept him inspired. Five years later, the 25-year-old has transformed MBA Chai Walla into a Rs 4 crore-turnover company with 50 stores all over India. He is now a multi-millionaire entrepreneur. In an interview , Prafull explains his motivation for drinking chai as well as how he overcomes challenges from both his family and his classmates. Prafull, then 21 years old, spent all of his savings on travel in 2016—by bus, rail, or rickshaw, depending on the cost. He thinks that conversing with and meeting new people has given him numerous insights.

However, his parents constantly put pressure on him to enrol in a full-time college so he could finish his studies and make a living. He therefore made the decision to take advantage of his layover in Ahmedabad by enrolling in college for the sake of his parents. "However, I also obtained a part-time job at McDonald's to experience working. How would I become a great man if even after an MBA I'd work like this?" he asks, referring to the low pay. "MBA ke baad bhi aise kaam karta rahunga," says the speaker. Prafull made the decision to discontinue his education midway and open a chai thela (tea cart) on Ahmedabad's SG Highway after realising that not everyone is fortunate enough to land well-paying employment.

However, Prafull was wise enough to ignore everyone and concentrate on growing his business despite the daily taunts from family members and angry parents. Many people were attracted by the tea cart that an English-speaking man was operating since it had begun to gain popularity. However, Prafull had no idea how to prepare tea and made a mistake by using too much sugar on the first day. But he eventually learned how to make tea. "I won't prepare chai today if someone asks me to. It bothers me." "I was having trouble while I was selling tea on the street, but now my attention is on growing my company," he chuckles.

In India, only chai is enjoyed as a meal or beverage. Despite not knowing how to create one, he was certain that everyone would drink. He didn't have the minimal investment required to establish another firm, which would have been Rs 1 lakh. He started selling chai on the side of the road with Rs 8,000 in his pocket," he recalls. However, Prafull didn't see anything wrong with launching MBA

Chaiwala, which stands for Mr. Billore Ahmedabad (MBA). You see, he continues, "Where there is a will, there is a way. "Where do the brightest minds in the world receive their inspiration?

Unfortunately, a lot of us spend our whole lives looking for our true calling and interests since they do not come to us naturally. Additionally, there are occasions when they are right in front of your eyes but you fail to see them. Humans are pleasure-seeking creatures, but if you let pleasure dictate how your life unfolds, you'll never discover your passion and purpose. Do you ever feel as though you don't belong where you are? If that occurs to you, you might want to reconsider your decision. By reading this book, you may change the way you think, uncover your passion and purpose, and locate the place where you belong. Your desire to live can be killed by trying to fit in; you may never find a setting where your abilities and skills are valued and embraced. Also, it feels like life is a never-ending battle to please other people. In this book, I will help you to overcome some of your fears; strengthen your mental fortitude; discover your passion and purpose; feel better about yourself; and reframe your life goals.

The majority of success books are filled with complex ideas that are challenging for most people to comprehend and use in their daily lives. You can do a miracle for yourself. From where you are right now, it will lead you to attain everything you desire in life. It is jam-packed with real-world examples and the essential success principles that you can quickly apply to change your life. The success of the book as a whole You only need your self-miracle and the desire to transform. This book is ideal for readers who are short on time or who want a thorough knowledge of the fundamentals and lessons of important business and life skills. In the context of success, I examine a range of subjects, including goal-setting, love, change, fear, and concern.

A multitude of ideas, counsel, and strategies are shared to assist you in overcoming unconscious restrictions and unlocking your full brilliance.Epic fail, rejection, and failure, those comments struck me like a blow. And what's this? They do hurt like a punch in reality. According to several studies, the part of the brain that activates when we experience rejection, passivity, or failure is the pain centre. Like any pain, it aches as though we are experiencing bodily discomfort, and it is meant to teach us something.

It takes work to succeed. Even when the way is right in front of you, getting there is difficult. The following five phrases will get you where you want to go. Happiness is a way of life, not just a sensation.

My keynote speaking career was impacted by COVID as well since live events had to be postponed or cancelled. Fortunately, I recognised an opportunity to expand my range of services at the time and built a home studio that I could use to stream keynotes to a distant audience. Along the way, I picked up a tonne of knowledge about technology and flexibility, and I'm better for it. Locate the agreeable adversity in order to succeed in the face of obstacles.

Unusual success is no longer reserved for a select few.

You must have faith. The only thing powerful enough to alter fate is belief. It will happen if you have faith that it can. A life without ambition is one without meaning. What will lead you to the top is your vision of all the things you could be. Give everything you do your all, as though it's everything you've ever wanted to do. Anything in the world is achievable if you have the motivation to make it happen.

As Joseph Campbell famously stated, "Passion will carry men beyond themselves, beyond their flaws, beyond their failings." Find the one thing that inspires and moves you. The highest motivation will lead you back home. If you make the decision, there is nothing you cannot do or be. Never allow anyone to convince you otherwise. You possess all the necessary qualities to lead and become the most prosperous man ever.

You can go far if you have confidence. Nobody will ever take pleasure in their own strengths if you do not. You should never compromise on your integrity. Although it can be simpler to succeed without ethics, they are what will set you apart from the competition. Take up saying yes. If you take advantage of every opportunity, the world will come into focus in front of your eyes. There are several potential outcomes of your efforts.

The Virgin Group is owned by English business magnate and philanthropist Richard Branson. The Virgin Group, which began with Virgin Records, currently includes more than 400 businesses. Branson, a serial entrepreneur, has had a remarkable life characterised by ups and downs. With his unwavering attitude, he has converted his setbacks into steppingstones for achievement. He has accepted his times of triumph and adversity. Branson's story will demonstrate that consistent labour, learning from mistakes, self-discovery, and tenacity lead to enormous success and progress for individuals and society whenever Virgin Galactic wants to launch non-astronauts into space. His way of thinking also shows how mistakes in the past just serve as more inspiration to go on and achieve new objectives. Richard Branson is unquestionably one of the world's most flamboyant and prosperous businessmen. Take advice from his stirring remarks.

"My interest in life comes from setting myself huge, apparently unachievable challenges and trying to rise above them."- Richard Branson

Three qualities are important to Sir Richard Branson when evaluating corporate success: leadership, connections, and enjoyment. Profits come when everything else is in place, and Branson certainly understands how to make things fall into place based on his tremendous financial profile. Richard Branson, a multibillionaire, has said that he finds it difficult to keep track of all the companies he owns. His net worth exceeds $5 billion, and the British government knighted him for his contributions to business. He has a well-deserved reputation for success.

"You don't learn to walk by following rules. You learn by doing, and by falling over." -Richard Branson

Branson founded Virgin Atlantic Airlines in 1984 to improve the flying experience for customers. His new business almost collapsed before it even got off the ground because he recognised a huge opportunity but lacked experience. A swarm of birds crashed into an engine during the first test flight of Virgin Atlantic's lone aircraft, a chartered Boeing 747, resulting in significant damage. Without a functioning plane, the airline was unable to obtain certification to begin transporting passengers, and it was also unable to secure funding for repairs. Branson maintained his optimism rather than succumbing to fear or quitting. He reorganised his businesses rapidly and borrowed funds from other projects to complete the repairs. His company received the necessary clearance, and Virgin's first flight from Gatwick to Newark was a success.

Branson is a real adventurer who pushes his boundaries in both business and life. We can all take a cue from his bravery. Every entrepreneur, from those just starting in their garages to the highest C-Suite executives, may benefit from his encouraging comments from economic interviews, social media postings, and leadership books.

"We deify willpower and self-control - and mock its absence. People who achieve through remarkable willpower are 'strong' and 'heroic.' People who need help or structure are 'weak.' This is crazy - because few of us can accurately gauge or predict our willpower."-Marshall Goldsmith

If you keep up with developmental psychology studies, you've undoubtedly heard that it's not a good idea to compliment children on their intelligence because if they make a mistake or fail, they'll assume that they are genuinely stupid and won't take any chances or leave their comfort zone.

However, there is an intriguing wrinkle since research has found that it is the exact reverse for character-related difficulties. It's good to thank children when they do something kind, but a study has shown that complimenting them on how much they shared actually has the most impact on how they perceive themselves and how they behave in the future. You are a supporter. In other words, that describes you as a person.

Once you've been given a favourable name, you begin to perceive yourself in that way and behave in ways that reinforce that identity. What does this have to do with you, with us, or with anybody else? I'd want to challenge you. Accepting responsibility and embracing it take dedication. It calls for discipline. And as we've spoken about, it's not always easy to keep up. But if you're an accountable person as opposed to simply keeping yourself accountable, it will be much easier. When you begin to embrace that identity rather than merely a certain set of behaviours, it starts to permeate everything you say and do. It shows up all through your life. I'll question you, "Do you want to be an accountable person?" if you truly want to take this in and maintain it. Someone who can be relied on by others, who does not require constant supervision or someone watching over them, and who not only accepts responsibility but also goes above and beyond to hold others accountable. Today, begin to see yourself as a person who is responsible.

Why are managers necessary in the business world? It's easy. because there are so many people to handle. They need someone else to hold them accountable since they aren't doing it themselves. But the sign of a true leader is when they hold themselves responsible. You don't require oversight or outside enforcement. You are able to concentrate and carry out your tasks like a genuine expert since you are aware of what has to be done. Because they set a good example for everyone, that is the sort of person who stands out and that leaders want to encourage. In this chapter, I will cover how to develop an accountability attitude and how to persuade yourself to do something.

It's simple to assume that successful individuals just have luck when you look at them. However, in my observation, successful individuals are far more tenacious than they are fortunate. I'll give you some advice on how to create your own luck in this class. First of all, I've seen that successful individuals don't just accept a refusal. If one course of action is not possible, another will be taken. They will receive 50% of what they desire if they cannot obtain 100% of what they desire. They will continue to inquire until they observe the desired movement. Certainty also plays a role in this.

The adage that the salesperson with the greatest assurance wins may have been mentioned to you. Therefore, you must put in the effort to persuade yourself that you can benefit someone or a project, that you have something significant to offer. And then focus on it, holding onto that assurance no matter what. Next, take a chance. Keep knocking even when it seems like the world is full of locked doors and individuals who won't allow you join their exclusive group or clique. And don't stop until you enter the space where it takes place. Attend the meeting when choices are made. Additionally, surround yourself with others who are already where you want to go. Find those in positions of authority if you desire greater leadership.

Be close by, observe them, and make notes. Be in the company of superior tennis players. If you are constantly the most intelligent person in the room, you need to move. Dare yourself to be even more persistent than you ever imagined possible by doing a double-dog dare. A business mentor once pushed me to make 100 sales calls in a month. You stop caring about who says yes and who says no when you're making that many sales calls. You simply move on to the next one, and the next one, and the next one, and so on. Keep talking to them on the phone until they buy or hang up, as my coach used to advise.

How can you then expose yourself and work even harder to achieve your goals? Where can you go today to try your luck? Look for chances to push yourself a little bit harder. One more question, please. Establish one additional link. Even if there is a chance of rejection, introduce yourself in a new setting. Growth produces opportunities, which are simply another word for luck.

Let's imagine you found out the launch failed because you didn't adequately test the messaging. What do you do then? Perhaps you offer to facilitate a number of consumer focus groups so you can discover firsthand what their concerns are and correct the first incorrect assumptions. If a technological fault caused the issue, you can decide to request or oversee a thorough examination of your department's tech procedures to ensure that you spot any possible issues immediately, before they have a chance to interfere with any upcoming launches. Take firm action to stay in the game and come back strong. It's a typical circumstance in weight reduction, to sum up. There is an error.

Let's assume they eat a doughnut they shouldn't have, which leads to depression and self-blame. How come they did that? Why didn't they exercise restraint? They consume the entire box of piza since they believe they have already failed. We've all experienced warped thinking like this when you feel like your mistake means everything is gone and destroyed. An additional 300 calories isn't fantastic, but an extra 3000 calories is definitely not beneficial. Don't cite a little error as justification for a major one. Don't quit attending staff meetings because you're uncomfortable around others. Don't let your depression prevent you from responding to emails from your boss. Don't insult your coworker just because you're feeling grumpy. These items are useless. Every time we fail, it's awful.

The most successful individuals aren't those that escape failure since, in this life, it isn't feasible. Instead, the most successful individuals are those who persevere in the face of setbacks by managing them gracefully, and you can too.

Maintaining accountability requires discipline. It might be challenging to maintain it day in and day out, much like going to the gym. Thus, it is crucial to recognise and appreciate your accomplishments. In fact, that may even serve as a motivating factor. I promise myself Y if I complete X. I often engage in this. In fact, when I was writing this piece, I promised myself a massage after I finished the last two. It was really lovely. Here are a few things to remember when it comes to acknowledging accomplishments.

As enjoyable as it may be, we can't reward ourselves constantly, so we must carefully consider when to do so. I like receiving rewards for accomplishments, so whether I've produced this course, written a thorough client proposal, or put the finishing touches on a presentation I'm making, I can do so and receive a reward. Even if my energy may be dwindling, the allure of the celebration frequently helps me cross the finish line.

It's crucial to consider the types of rewards you should use next. On the one hand, it's obviously about whatever drives you, so if ice cream sundaes are your favourite food and you have a chore that you dread doing, that can persuade you to do it. That's excellent, but you should only provide that type of prize sometimes. The ideal situation is to find something that, over time, is both enjoyable and healthy, so you can use it repeatedly. A nice example is the massage I described before. That's a fantastic reward if you like working out or going for a run. Perhaps it's social, like the prospect of meeting up with friends for dinner or a party later. If you can find a setting like this, it's great if it allows you to reward yourself while still advancing your task.

Finally, it's crucial to remember that while it's important to celebrate your successes, we aren't robots, and we can't always labour tirelessly until that moment. It's a fantastic idea to take a small break at that time, even if it's simply a 15-minute stroll or a fast stretch. This can help you stay focused and maintain your energy as you progress, rather than fighting fatigue and burnout caused by being constantly on.

How can one bounce back and become successful in life?

The number of individuals who can live better, more evolved lives as a result of what you developed is a stronger indicator of actual success than any of the aforementioned metrics. This is what success means. Not the medals others spend their lifetimes accumulating. You are frequently led to believe by the media and society that having a prosperous life entails having a lot of material possessions.

Success, however, is defined as leading a happy life and improving the quality of life for everyone on this planet. Is having a flashy sports vehicle the true mark of success? The meaning of failure is the reverse of success since it refers to failing when attempting to accomplish goals or objectives.

Never attempt to post a successful formula. When you use yourself to the fullest, you achieve real success. Success implies that you are enjoying your life to the fullest extent possible, regardless of whether you want to become a doctor, a politician, a yogi, or anything else. You require perception and active intellect if that needs to happen. You have the essential intellect to live life well if you can perceive it for what it is. Your intelligence will work against you if you are unable to accept life as it is. In our world, intelligent people tend to be the most unhappy individuals. They just do not see life, although they have an active mind.

In addition to the conventional understanding of failure, it is also true that even affluent and successful people experience failure in their lives. Just consider all the scandals, addictions, and suicides involving the affluent and famous. All of them were amazing people, but many of them were also profoundly dissatisfied with their lives and unable to comprehend what success really meant. The qualities in your life that make you a happy person, such as friendship, connections, and your family, rather than money, are what define wealth.

People who are afraid to try and those who are concerned that you will succeed are the two groups of people who will tell you that you cannot change the world. Successful individuals are prepared to take risks that failed people are not. Instead of wishing it were simpler, strive to improve. Keep in mind that success often seems to be linked to action. Successful individuals never stand still.

They make errors, but they keep going.

One of the things I frequently tell people when I deal with clients or students is that whatever you desire is just one degree away. Everything you desire is one degree away from you. I really like the idea that anything you want is just one degree away. It's a simple shift to start with. We're not suggesting that you alter every aspect of who you are, including how you appear, behave, and interact with the outside world. We're talking about a very small adjustment of only one tick. What would it look like for you if you were only one degree bolder, one degree kinder, or one degree more prepared? What one-degree change would you make today to go closer to your goals if that were the case for you? Simply thinking in terms of steps that can be taken is the same as thinking in terms of a straightforward one-degree change.

A rocket would land in a completely different location if its trajectory was changed by only one degree during launch. So you don't necessarily have to make major changes to see a major change. So, let me ask you something right now. What one-degree change could you make right now that would have a significant impact on your final destination? Could you be a little more confident? Your expectations are a tiny bit more clear now? Could you exert only 1% more effort? Could you just make one more call on the phone? Just one more question, please? Just 1% more totally present, 1% more authentically you right now? These small adjustments might alter not just where you are headed but also where you are right now.

Your future may be altered by your attitude.

Do you know Dwayne "The Rock" Johnson's origins? You undoubtedly already know how accomplished an actor he is. It's reasonable to say that he has a unique origin story that deserves to be the subject of a film or television series all on its own. Let's examine the "rags to riches" story of Johnson's rise to fame in more detail. For him, success might have appeared inevitable, but it wasn't. He tried his hand in the Canadian Football League before getting cut after sustaining injuries in college. He discovered that he was out of money and football. It wasn't until Johnson took on a very different persona that people began to take notice of him. In what is known as a "heel turn," he changed from being a hero to a villain, or in wrestling terms, from being a babyface to a heel, in what is known as a "heel turn," and after that, he was simply referred to as "The Rock."

"What's the key to success? The key is that there is no key. Be humble, hungry, and the hardest worker in any room. With drive and a bit of talent, you can move mountains. "- Dwayne Johnson

His persona changed into one who was haughty, used a lot of catchphrases, and spoke in third person. Johnson continued to sporadically appear for WWE, but by the early 2000s, his career as a professional wrestler was all but over. He thereafter started appearing in several Hollywood films. He first began with straightforward yet lucrative action movies like The Rundown and a Walking Tall remake. He then moved on to projects with higher budgets. Because we are basic beings, we always fall in love with compelling narratives. Every person that lives on Earth has a story to tell, and those stories might be upsetting, terrible, happy, or a combination of all those feelings.

Everyone loves tales of rags to riches. People enjoy hearing tales of valiant guys who battle against all difficulties to become among the richest people in the world. We are never tired of being amazed by butterflies. Everything and anything makes it genuinely majestic, including its enduring beauty and its mobile wings. But is that really the cause of our affection for butterflies? Is it only because it is beautiful? Never. The stories of butterflies—their struggle, their attempt to hide from the world, their quest for freedom, and their triumph—are what captivate us.

The last category is the one that consistently triggers our "inspirational nerves." A butterfly's life tale and Dwayne "The Rock" Johnson's life story both fit into this category. The man we see on tabloid and magazine covers now only spreads the wings of success and welcomes the sun, but he too had hardship in the past.

"The wall! Your success is on the other side. You can't jump over it or go around it. You know what to do. When life throws you a curve ball, don't say "Why me?" instead say "Try me."- Dwayne Johnson

Johnson is without a doubt one of the biggest stars of the present, and his star doesn't appear to be going out any time soon. He will play Black Adam in a feature film adaptation of the DC Comics superhero. After his poor origins, it appears like Johnson is in the best possible situation right now. Johnson, a former professional wrestler, has managed to become one of Hollywood's top box office draws. Furthermore, he was compensated handsomely for it; according to Celebrity Net Worth, his net worth is estimated to be around $400 million (and growing).

"Success isn't always about 'greatness'; it's about consistency. Consistent, hard work gains success. Success at anything will always come down to two things: focus and effort. And we control both. "-Dwayne Johnson

When you think positively, you will inherently feel more inspired to take action on your goals, which will help you advance and succeed. Positive thinking has the potential to change your life. Even scientific research demonstrates that being upbeat and actively attempting to decrease negative thoughts may be beneficial to your health. Even among those who have a family history of cardiac issues, positive thinkers are 13% less likely than negative thinkers to experience a heart attack. Being upbeat reduces stress, guards against discouragement, and improves coping mechanisms for when things get tough.

Consider smiling more frequently, using comedy in your life, engaging in positive self-talk, and making a list of the positive parts of a difficult circumstance as ways to help you maintain your positive perspective. Make an effort to surround oneself at home and at work with positive people, pictures, music, books, podcasts, and settings.

There are frequently just self-imposed restrictions on what you may accomplish, own, or be. True success is so much simpler and more likely to happen once you make the firm, unambiguous choice to alter your life by letting go of all mental constraints and devoting your entire being to the attainment of some lofty objective.

Personal objectives are a necessary component of living a successful life. But frequently, after making some first strides in that direction, our ambitions remain unfulfilled. That can be a result of the way we create objectives. The greatest and most feasible objectives are smart objectives. Because they are reasonable, well-considered, and include a timetable, SMART objectives are attainable. Make smart objectives by doing the following:

- Create a precise, succinct statement that spells out exactly what you hope to accomplish.
- Specify a figure or another means to assess your objective, such as "create 250 business leads" rather than "get more leads."
- In order to succeed and maintain your motivation, make sure your objective is difficult yet doable.
- Align your objectives with the things that will make you feel successful and content in life.
- Establish a deadline for when you will accomplish your objective and establish manageable checkpoints along the route.

The most difficult and sometimes least pleasant duty you have to complete each day is your "frog." The remainder of your day, week, and life may become more exciting if you swallow that frog and tackle challenges right now. Procrastination is less likely to occur as a result, giving you more time to work toward the objectives you actually want to accomplish. Make it a habit to start with the most challenging and crucial activity. Ask yourself, "What would make the most difference in my success overall if I only completed one item today?" Use the same logic to achieve the objectives you have set for yourself. Which are more crucial for long-term contentment and happiness? Prioritise them first.

Put your physical health first. It is easy to become engrossed in the never-ending list of duties we have to complete each day and the act of crossing things off our to-do list. But if you want to succeed, it's crucial to put your physical well-being first. Being physically healthy and fit improves self-esteem, which in turn helps you think more positively. You genuinely feel physically energetic and more capable of doing more tasks as a result. Being health conscious has been cited as one of the secrets to success in life by some of the most successful people.High achievers place importance on both their physical and mental well-being.

Make sure you consume a lot of nutritious foods and a few harmful ones. Create a daily fitness schedule that involves movement. Get enough sleep to revitalise your body and mind so that you can function more effectively when you return to your job.

Have faith in your abilities and yourself. If it's difficult for you to believe in yourself, compile a list of all your strengths. Do you maintain order? a capable listener? Do you bake delicious pumpkin pies, lead effective team meetings, or inspire confidence in others? Do you excel at coming up with ideas, or do you excel at using those ideas to create a strategy? Gaining self-confidence and learning to believe in yourself is one of the finest strategies for achieving success. A higher level of self-assurance inspires you and gives you the strength to act on your ambitions.

When you're feeling down, remember your successes and the time, skills, talents, and strengths you have that will enable you to achieve more. You have the strength to continue until you reach your objectives when you have confidence in your capacity to do so.

The chaos of life may easily overwhelm us, and we can become stressed out over tasks that need to be completed.

Find a little pleasure every day on purpose. To relieve tension, find the humour in a stressful circumstance and laugh about it. In stressful situations, studies have shown that even a simple grin may decrease blood pressure and pulse rate. Being content is necessary for success in life. Fun is also among the finest ways to achieve happiness. Play outside, spend time on a pastime you enjoy, view a humorous video, and cultivate a sense of humour.

It may be quite beneficial while building yourself up to be successful to have someone to bounce ideas off of, chat with, and get feedback from about how you're expressing yourself to others. Seek advice from people you respect and trust, such as close friends and relatives. Everyone will have an opinion on how you live your life, but only those with your best interests in mind should be heard. Initially, it could be challenging to accept constructive criticism. But instead of letting it bring you down, let it inspire you. A gift that has a long-lasting effect on your present and future satisfaction is the chance to improve.

You need to keep developing if you want to succeed in life. Your development may be greatly influenced by sharing your improvement strategies with people you can trust. If you keep working toward your objectives without taking a break, burnout can strike quickly. Your progress toward your goals will be aided by taking regular pauses. It's really helpful to take time off from your ambitions in order to reset, recharge, and discover success in life. Even after taking a day or even a week off for your mental health, your ambitions will still be there.

You could approach a challenge with a lot of excitement, but should you keep going if no progress is being made? Most individuals give up because they perceive it to be too difficult.

Do you know that the first book in the "Harry Potter" series was rejected 12 times before Bloomsbury accepted it and J. K. Rowling made Harry Potter well-known, and she was advised not to quit her day job. All of these are fascinating, but this one is my favorite.

"It is impossible to live without failing at something unless you live so cautiously that you might as well not have lived at all, in which case you have failed by default." — J.K. Rowling

You can't just admit that you made a dangerous choice at some point. To achieve what you want, you must be prepared for the sort of ability that is actually required. You must, nevertheless, take chances in order to succeed in life. Being honest in life is crucial to you. The well-known British novelist, who has a tenacious mind and a generous heart, is unquestionably the deserved recipient of all the accolades received worldwide. She carved her way into the reader's heart with the first book in the Harry Potter series and has been living there ever since, pledging never to leave. She emotionally collapsed as a result of her terrible marriage, experiencing domestic abuse, and falling into a deep despair. She was on the edge of being classified as "poverty-stricken" since she was a single mother working in a coffee shop for a small wage.

However, neither she nor true heroes wear capes. A positive outlook has a significant role in how fate plays out. Her writing was the only thing that kept her company during this protracted period of hopelessness and sadness. something she clung to tightly. By writing on paper napkins while working as a server, she demonstrated her desire to unwaveringly trust in her ideas and the likelihood that they will be wonderfully realized. Rowling always anticipated becoming a writer. Her website states that she knew she wanted to be a writer as soon as she learned what they were. But it didn't only take wishful thinking. While on a delayed train from Manchester to London, she began writing the Harry Potter books. As Rowling imagined each character, the plot began to take shape. She jotted down the names and magical abilities of every single character and spent the following five years scripting the stories for each book. The stories are so fantastic because of this meticulous attention to detail.

The "J.K. Rowling" story was one of many that I got the chance to read. The abrupt loss of her mother left her in shock when she first had the inspiration to write Harry Potter. And at that point, she had to stop working on the book of her dreams. She was totally upset by her mother's unexpected death and was unable to continue working. Why do we presume that women are weak and unable to manage their lives on their own if they like their exits? After reading several successful accounts of women who had to battle on their own without any support, I found the assertion to be utterly incorrect.

The key to realising a dream is to focus not on success but on significance and then even the small steps and little victories along your path will take on greater meaning.

Don't just relax. Take the initiative to make your aspirations a reality. You'll soon feel inspired and perceive new possibilities. You will be able to overcome obstacles and cultivate your own abilities. Learn how to calculate "Estimation of Effort" to make sure you surpass your goals. Learn about the fallacy of time management. Discover the precise causes of failure and success. You own the precise formula for problem-solving. By definition, extreme success is outside the bounds of customary behaviour. Take Tremendous action with your efforts , remove luck , and lock in massive success rather than acting like everyone else and accepting ordinary outcomes.

Similar to a muscle, willpower requires continual nurturing.

Determining the true cost of rejection is a necessary step in evaluating its lessons. Here are three instances of rejection and their actual or lack thereof effects. I first received a refusal for a promotion. You haven't lost anything in this situation; all you've lost is your idea of what could have been. Even if it was a pleasant dream, you are still still in the same position as before. You haven't actually paid anything for it. Actually, not much has changed. What can we learn from that type of rejection, then? The power of that imagination is where it is. Your ability to see a better future for yourself is clearly demonstrated by the dream you have of it.

So, try to advance on that by using the energy from your dream. Then there is the opportunity cost caused by doing all that labour without receiving any compensation. You invested time, resources, and perhaps even relationship capital to position yourself for an opportunity. Perhaps you spent a lot of time or effort putting together an offer or making a presentation. It might be painful when they seem to be in vain. The lesson here is to make sure that the work you are doing is worthwhile, regardless of what you are doing. Try to find a new use for some of those resources, or at the very least, make sure the lessons you picked up along the road are valuable.

Can you figure out who I'm referring to? He attempted business again in '33 and failed once again after failing in '31, losing his bid for the state assembly in '32. He lost his true love in 1935. In 1936, he had a mental breakdown. In 1936, he had a mental breakdown. He lost his bid for Congress in 1943, lost his bid for Congress again in 1948, lost his bid for the Senate in 1955, lost his bid for the vice presidency of the United States in 1956, and lost his bid for the Senate again in 1958, but he never gave up. Abraham Lincoln was elected as the 16th president of the United States in 1860. The question is not whether you will fail; therefore, keep this group in mind the next time you fail. That is a certainty; everyone does, including the greats. The key to success is learning something new and persevering; therefore, the only decision you have to make is whether or not to do so.

Develop ties despite failure - People like those they believe to be human beings rather than merely professionals. They like to see that you are competent, but they also like to see that you are flawed because, well, they are flawed too. Additionally, you become more relatable since you are aware that you must overcome obstacles and disappointments.

Unfortunately, far too many people do not believe that it is acceptable to openly acknowledge the fundamental truth that we are all flawed. They therefore conceal errors and refrain from discussing setbacks. I'd want to push you to think otherwise. People who are healthy, effective, joyful, and successful deal with reality head-on, which involves owning up to mistakes and taking failures to heart. The gains are substantial.

As a result, people will find you to be more approachable and trustworthy. When you do, people start to respond to you with greater sincerity and honesty. These things foster stronger relationships that result in more creative and higher-quality work, whether at work or elsewhere in life. First off, being honest about your failures from time to time helps you seem more genuine and real. On the other hand, too many people engage in straightforward boasting in an effort to appear strong. The only thing that is stronger, though, is to reflect sincere compassion. People like to deal with genuine people.

People like to deal with genuine people. Just being aware of particular instances when you failed, made a poor choice, or otherwise saw a project go awry may be really helpful in getting others to see past your successes and see a more nuanced version of you. Trustworthiness therefore follows genuineness. Being vulnerable to someone means you trust them. to have faith that they will treat you fairly and in your best interests. What comes next is magic after more sincerity and greater trustworthiness? People become more frank and open around you as you become more approachable. The finest kind of communication is always two-way, regardless of who you are communicating with—a friend, parent, or boss. You cooperate rather than direct. People will feel more eager to share with you and even confide in you if you are willing to reveal a whole human version of yourself.

People become more inclined to take the chance of being vulnerable and offering their honest opinions. This openness and familiarity reciprocate over time. They develop into a natural component of the reciprocity of beneficial partnerships. Your relationships may also be affected by this, but you must genuinely want it to be so. You may think about wonderful partnerships in that way.

"Change is the nature of life, but challenge is the aim of life. So always challenge the changes not change the challenges" – Amitabh Bachchan

However, rejection might occasionally cost you a lot of money. When a launch fails and you are rejected publicly, you are either physically or symbolically abandoned at the altar. Then, it involves more than just your time and money. It's also someone else's. You could not be the only one affected; your entire workplace, neighbourhood, and family might as well. Stop wasting time blaming others. The lesson from these larger, more expensive setbacks is that things happen in life. Furthermore, even the best-laid schemes of mice and men frequently fail. Therefore, take a moment right now to make a brief inventory. What exactly has this rejection cost you? And from that, what lesson do you hope to draw? Take the lesson to heart and get moving.

Amitabh Bachchan had several physical and financial hardships before he rose to fame as the millennium's biggest celebrity. These difficulties may tear someone to pieces. The rise of Amitabh Bachchan from obscurity to prominence in Bollywood serves as a terrific example for everyone who is battling obstacles and wants to do great things in life, not only those who wish to try their luck in the movie industry.

Amitabh Bachchan, who is renowned for his tall stature and deep voice, has been rejected several times as a result of these two attributes. Because tall performers were not commonly used at the time in movies, he was turned down by producers, and he was also turned down by All India Radio because of his heavy voice when he auditioned for a radio jockey. He gave up because he was broke and received his first break in Bollywood with the film Saat Hindustani, for which he also won a national award, shortly after. Following the success of this film, he battled for two years to land a part in Anand and Zanjeer, which radically transformed his life.

Nobody promised that life would be simple. Big B was slowly moving up the ladders of success when he had an accident on the Coolie set, which caused everyone to fear that Amitabh Bachchan would not survive. But he is a natural survivor since he bounced back fast and resumed his acting career. Unfortunately, this accident caused him to get an illness that makes a person feel depressed and weak, and he is still battling it. Since then, he has developed into the Shahenshah of Bollywood and is one of India's wealthiest actors. After losing everything, he visited his buddy Yash Chopra's home and requested a part in the upcoming film "Mohabbatein." After that, he received a call to host "Kaun Banega Crorepati," but his wife Jaya Bachchan objected, saying it wouldn't be appropriate for a famous actor like Amitabh Bachchan to anchor a TV show. Beggars can't be choosers, Amitabh Bachchan said in response.

According to a statement made by Amitabh Bachchan, "Bad luck may either ruin you or expose the person you are." He was able to rise above all the rejections and succeed greatly because of his perseverance and devotion to his objective. He acknowledged his shortcomings, which enabled him to keep becoming better. In one of his interviews, he advised everyone that "accepting and learning from your errors can help you become a better person." The life of Amitabh Bachchan teaches us that in order to attain great success, we should never linger on the past. Instead, we should always learn from it.

The mere mention of Amitabh Bachchan is enough to send chills down your spine and inspire deep admiration in your heart. This living great has delivered not just outstanding performances but also undeniably unmatched depictions throughout the course of a career spanning more than four decades. He is one of those performers who immerses himself so fully in the role that viewers frequently lose sight of the fact that they are watching a movie. Big B has demonstrated extreme variety, playing roles as an "Angry Young Man" in "Shehenshah" and an "Annoyingly Cute Constipated Father" in "Piku."

According to a statement made by Amitabh Bachchan, "Bad luck may either ruin you or reveal the person you are." He was able to rise above all the rejections and succeed greatly because of his perseverance and devotion to his objective. He acknowledged his shortcomings, which enabled him to keep becoming better. Taking motivation to advance in life from none other than Amitabh Bachchan, who is regarded as a household synonym for the term "role model." We begin to make decisions about our future while we are in the prime of adolescence. We choose our courses based on those taken by successful people in order to emulate them while making decisions about our own lives. Depending on the career path we choose, what constitutes a successful person for each of us will vary, yet we believe that everyone of you has looked up to this particular individual.

It can put us in the best possible position for our own big success. Maybe some of this wisdom will help you during those difficult moments.

The notion that sometimes it's not the fact that rejection occurred but the manner in which it occurred provides a key explanation as to why rejection can hurt so deeply. Not what she said, but how she said it, is the problem. It's how they told me, and it's how they actually did that. If that's the true issue, you're probably going through a values conflict. Then there's the issue of sex. So, here's a straightforward method for naming your values. Start by listing five things that have happened to you in your life, along with three instances where things appeared especially positive or enjoyable.

Like you, I recently experienced a fairly recent rejection and an extremely difficult split. Right. So, list five things that, for whatever reason, seem to be important to you, and then try to determine what the underlying meaning of each of those things is. I purchased a home. For me, that embodies the values of family and community. Perhaps those things that weren't so good came next. Whichever of your principles was broken. This most recent rejection damaged my values of being nice and giving everyone a chance to be heard. an awful breakup, you know. My value of community and having someone on my side was undercut by that. Obviously, your responses will differ from mine, and that's the fun thing. So feel free to play about with these. As you work, you'll probably come up with some more values. Make it a practise to ask yourself, "Oh, and what value of mine does it represent?" when you begin to notice things in the environment that either pleasure or annoy you. Why am I experiencing that? Clarifying your values can help you do the same for your life.

"Your work is going to fill a large part of your life, and the only way to be truly satisfied is to do what you believe is great work. And the only way to do great work is to love what you do. If you haven't found it yet, keep looking. Don't settle. As with all matters of the heart, you'll know when you find it."- Steve Jobs

Epic fail, rejection, and failure, those comments struck me like a blow. And what's this? They do hurt like a punch in reality. According to several studies, the part of the brain that activates when we experience rejection, passivity, or failure is the pain centre. Like any pain, it aches as though we are experiencing bodily discomfort, and it is meant to teach us something. Let's examine this from the standpoint of evolutionary biology. Why do we detest rejection so much? We are tribal creatures, so keep that in mind. Even if there are moments when we wish everyone would simply go away, we are built to live in communities and are aware that we cannot thrive on our own. We thus pay close attention to what the group thinks is positive.

We want affirmation from others. Instead of someone you would want to leave on an ice floe, we want to be perceived as valuable and helpful. Therefore, your response to rejection is not a sign that you lack self-worth. You're not taking it personally or taking it too seriously. It's a strategy for surviving. When you are rejected, your inner self feels as though your literal survival is in danger. Additionally, the brain has a tiny negative program, thanks in part to our parents, is that right? How do you raise your kids? Don't touch that, please! Don't say that, please! "No, please don't make that face."

You'll recall your mistakes and shortfalls excessively. It's also possible that errors were treated with criticism or even punishment in the family or community where you were raised. But now that we're adults, we can accept our faults with grace. Accept your flaws, rejections, and failures with grace. I sincerely apologise for your rejection, passing over, colossal failure, public humiliation, and failure. I'm so sorry again. But I'm optimistic that realising that you're naturally and culturally programmed to feel awful when you're rejected may help to lessen the hurt. Would you like to continue? Take note of this phrase right away. I graciously accept my rejection. I gracefully accept my errors. I make myself feel welcome.

Life is full of surprises.

I've experienced what it's like to rise beyond rejection. I've had a lot of opportunities and doors shut in my face. But I refused to let that deter me. I do not wish for it to deter you. I'll show you how to deal with rejection and move on in this course. I'll show you how to search for the truth while facing rejection. The facts surrounding the situation and, most crucially, your honesty You'll discover effective techniques for self-care and emotional intelligence; learn how to do a cost-benefit analysis of rejection; and I'll share with you my methods for seeing chances when it seems like they've all dried up—because they haven't, by the way. A person's capacity for growth is closely correlated with how much truth they can accept about themselves without resisting it. So where can you go to learn and develop now that you've been turned down?

The 10,000-hour rule or the proverb "success is 1 percent inspiration, 99 percent perspiration" may be known to you.

Your brain developed over thousands of years to understand the value of banding together into tribes for your security, stability, and enjoyment. When we experience a sensation of detachment, loneliness, or isolation, a problem arises once more. In the activity that follows, I'd like to highlight some of the ways we might reconnect. So, in the exercise that follows, I'd like to share with you some of the ways we might re-engage with what nature has already given us the ability to master: the need for socialising, the need for connection, the need for trust, and the need for belonging. All of this together enables you to invest in both your pleasure and a wiser and more successful business.

In the early 2000s, a study was conducted to better understand what happens in your brain when you experience social rejection, when you lose a loved one, when someone you really trusted or cared about betrays you, or even when you consider being rejected by someone you care about a lot or when you're in a relationship. And this is what we're referring to here: a condition known as social pain.

The purpose of the study was to determine which part of your brain lights up when you feel social distress. The researchers were astounded to discover that the same area of your brain that processes social pain also handles physical pain, such as pain from a broken bone or hitting your skull against a wall. What does all of this mean? Why does this matter so much? In your brain, all pain is the same. This understanding of how your brain evolved into a social organ is, therefore, critical. What we're discovering now is that the absence of real-time connection is enabling more of us to feel the grief, anger, alienation, and sadness we discuss. Additionally, this sickness of hopelessness is on the rise. the notion that there is greater hostility, anxiety, and addiction in the world as well.

Managing other people's lack of efficiency some people are fortunate enough to be what I refer to as concentration masters. These are people who have never had any kind of time management difficulty. The chaos that surrounds them presents these folks with their greatest obstacle. I want to give you concentration masters some advice so you may learn how to be a bit more understanding and helpful while dealing with the difficulties of others. First, show people some courtesy. The majority of individuals have trouble managing their time.

All of us desire greater success in one or more areas of our lives. Maybe you'd want to have a more fulfilling profession, a closer and more passionate love life, to purchase the home of your dreams, or to have a bigger good effect on the world. Whatever success means to you, it is attainable with the winning attitude.

The precise thing you wish to prevent becoming your consciousness.

It has some psychological and social importance but no existential relevance, so you can just disregard it and assume everything will be well. It will only provide comfort. Because you think you can't bear reality, you try to find consolation in travelling from reality to unreality. And since it's unlikely that you can, you give in to optimism. Negative thoughts should be avoided in favour of optimistic ones. To put it another way, you work to avoid the negative. The thing that makes you strongest about yourself will never be what you attempt to avoid. Anyone who attempts to compromise between two aspects of life will only experience self-loathing.

Why do you like to view things in this manner? Why not consider each circumstance as it is, accept it as it is, and then determine what you can do to make it better? Situations can be neither good nor bad. Avoid attempting to form opinions and ideas. Why are you unable to simply be present, without any sort of attitude? lacking in philosophy? Just mindful. simply conscious.

Because of the way the mind works, if you tell it, "I don't want this," just that will take place in your mind. You will only experience it if you state, "I do not desire the bad." Why do you even bring up good or bad things? Different responses are required for different circumstances. If you adopt an optimistic outlook, it could be effective in one circumstance.

However, in another sort of circumstance, you'll act foolishly because you have a preconceived notion that you must act a specific way. You could experience the worst outcomes if you continue to think positively in the wrong situation. It's unnecessary to be upbeat. Also, there's no need to be pessimistic. Just be mindful. Being conscious allows you to see things exactly as they are. You can respond to a situation to the best of your skill and intellect when you see it for what it is. That is all there is to it.

Simple actions you can take to win people over!To succeed, you will almost certainly need the assistance of others, and this chapter will show you how to do it with ease. Relationships in both your personal and professional lives will get better. This step-by-step approach is everything you need to transform your outlook and your life! The divided cultures of the twenty-first century do nothing to aid individuals in the development of their emotional and behavioural selves. Instead of fostering unity, they frequently create conflict, segregation, and ruthless rivalry in place of help and support. In terms of emotions, our culture just tosses individuals into the water and lets them try to swim or sink.

You don't receive a lot of assistance or support while trying to understand who we are or discover a profound feeling of inner peace, pleasure, or purpose in life. Many people feel they have what it takes to make great changes in their lives but are hindered by issues with poor self-esteem, unfavourable feelings, and unsatisfactory behaviours. It can be difficult to go over them. The greatest of all challenges is the secret of imagination, whose solution everyone should strive for since it holds the key to supreme power, knowledge, and joy. Where do brilliant ideas originate?

Those who have read about Steve Jobs know that while he was still an outstanding leader, his success may not have always been attributed to his capacity for leading others. Everyone will tell you that networking and putting on a good show are key components of doing business, but Steve

Jobs was able to think creatively and motivate others around him to work toward a shared objective.

Even if some of his contemporaries thought Steve was crazy, Apple wouldn't have developed the items that have now become standards if it weren't for his remarkable vision. The lesson of life? Steve Jobs kept coming up with fresh concepts, which gave him a competitive edge. Steve Jobs is without a doubt the greatest commercial innovator in contemporary history, and for good reason. He was a technological pioneer and the creator of Apple, one of the greatest businesses in the world and a testament to Steve's unrivalled intelligence.

Sometimes you come up with a brilliant concept right away that you can develop and run with. Everything seems to be going great until you have a setback. You get punched in the gut by failure, leaving you with aching wounds and no choice but to whine about what might have been. Nevertheless, have hope since failure isn't the end until you let it be. Failure indicates you are travelling the same path countless others have taken to success. You don't trust me? The person who gave us the delicious milk chocolate delicacy we all enjoy wasn't popular at first. He had previously worked at a nearby candy manufacturer before starting his own candy company. But when he made the decision to go out on his own, he utterly failed. Despite suffering two more setbacks, he went back to the family farm and mastered the technique of producing beautiful milk chocolate candies, which we now enjoy in the form of Hershey chocolate.

Over the course of 27 attempts, this author tried to produce a book that publishing houses would not dismiss as "absolute garbage." But the dude simply wouldn't give up. He met an old buddy who had just started working as an editor of children's books one fateful evening. The buddy consented to release Giesel's writing. Giesel, who is now better known as Dr. Seuss, was never again labelled a failure following the success of his first book.

Franklin was a founding father, the creator of the lightning rod and bifocals, and a dropout from elementary school. It seems absurd, yet this is a true statement. After he turned 10, his family could no longer afford to pay for his schooling, but that did not deter him. He devoured literature and pursued education at every available moment. Ironically, Franklin may now be found in the history textbooks that 10-year-old students study on a daily basis all throughout the world.

Everybody encounters unanticipated challenges. It was an uncommon cancer for Carr. Carr adopted a new dietary lifestyle to combat her illness head-on, launching a thriving writing and health coaching profession in the process. Despite having to deal with difficult conditions from the beginning, she is now regarded as one of the most informed authorities on healthy living available online. In the end, you and the individuals on the list above are the same. At some point or another, we will all fall short. Learning how to bounce back from setbacks and continuing to work toward your goals are crucial.

You should anticipate making errors and perhaps even failing while beginning a business. Most successful people's journeys usually include failure. We get stronger as a result of learning how to deal with these situations and developing from them, which positions us better for success in the future. Just consider Walt Disney, Richard Branson, and Bill Gates. Gates co-founded the unsuccessful Traf-O-Data traffic monitoring website before quitting Harvard and founding Microsoft.

Branson has struggled even within Virgin, having tried to launch a soda company, a wedding firm, and a digital download agency, all of which failed. You'll make errors if you live long enough. You will, however, grow as a person if you apply the lessons they teach you. It's not how hardship affects you; it's how you respond to it. "The most important thing is to never give up," was Bill Clinton's remark, which served as the inspiration for this article. Many Indian company owners and entrepreneurs have experienced great hardship and upheaval over the past several years as a result of the country's economic stagnation and political gridlock. Branson has suffered with dyslexia his whole life. When he was 16 years old, he quit school, yet he later founded Virgin. Entrepreneurs must thus understand that perseverance is the key to success and that sometimes overcoming obstacles in life is important to achieve success. Now let's have a look at a list of 10 Indians who defied all obstacles to achieve extraordinary achievements in their lives. A spectacular Indian "rags to riches" tale was written by some of the most well-known celebrities, businessmen, and athletes that we all know and like.

The man known as the "father of the Indian IT Sector" and one of Fortune Magazine's list of the top 12 businessmen of all time, Narayana Murthy, hasn't always had tremendous success with his businesses. Softronics, Narayana Murthy's first business endeavour, collapsed around 1.5 years after it began. Narayana Murthy joined Patni Computer Systems after his first business failed, where he spent around five years. In 1981, he established Infosys with the help of six software specialists and a little funding from his wife, Sudha Murthy. Today, Infosys is the third-largest Indian-based provider of IT services and the fifth-largest publicly listed firm in India.

Kiran Mazumdar-Shaw founded Biocon in a leased garage with a capital of Rs 10,000 in 1978, when she was only 25 years old. Early on, Kiran Mazumdar-Shaw had a lot of difficulties and hurdles starting a business in a young sector. She struggled with getting a bank loan, finding the necessary skills, and other issues. Over the years, Mazumdar-Shaw surmounted these obstacles and expanded Biocon to become one of the top Indian biopharmaceutical companies, with sales exceeding Rs. 15.55 billion.

Sushil Kumar is a well-known Indian wrestler who has won three Olympic medals: a bronze in the 2008 Beijing Games, a silver in the 2012 London Games, and a gold in the 2010 FILA World Wrestling Championships. The well-known Indian wrestler is from a lower-middle-class household; his mother is a homemaker, and his father worked as a bus driver for the DTC. Sandeep, Sushil Kumar's cousin, who finally gave up wrestling because their family could only support one wrestler, served as Sushil Kumar's inspiration to take up the sport. Sushil Kumar has worked tirelessly and with unwavering resolve to become a recognised wrestling champion despite the limited resources, subpar training facilities, and absence of nutritional supplements. Sushil Kumar works as an assistant commercial manager with the Indian Railways at the moment.

The son of a truck worker who struggled to make ends meet, Schultz grew up in poverty. He came from a low-income household, but because of his athletic ability, he was given a football scholarship at the University of Northern Michigan. Schultz worked for Xerox after earning a degree in communications. But when he happened onto a little Starbucks, everything was different. After quitting

Xerox in 1987, he became the company's top executive because he enjoyed the coffee so much. Starbucks quickly expanded with Schultz's assistance, going from a tiny coffee company with 60 stores to a profitable behemoth with more than 16,000 locations worldwide. The current value of Howard Schultz's assets is $4.1 billion.

Lakshmi Mittal, a titan of the steel business, wasn't always rich. Instead, he was raised in a low-income Indian household close to Rajasthan. By doing a large portion of his business in the steel industry's equivalent of a discount warehouse, Mittal "built the foundations of his fortune over the course of two decades," according to BBC News. He purchased low-cost pieces of other steel companies and turned them into profitable enterprises. With a current net worth of $11.8 billion, Mittal has more than five times led the UK's Rich List.

"Champions aren't made in the gyms. Champions are made from something they have deep inside them-a desire, a dream, a vision."- Muhammad Ali

When you begin to think positively, your mind gets free of any negative ideas, and you begin to perceive the world in a new way. You will no longer blame yourself or other people. You will have complete emotional control and make an effort to learn something from every setback you encounter. It is well known that happiness and a good outlook go hand in hand. Happiness is a mental state that originates from the inside and is not reliant on outside circumstances. Positive thinking will bring harmony and happiness into your life. Simply said, no matter what circumstances you are in, you may be happy right now if you have a positive mindset.

The above mentioned short stories of those people who failed before becoming well-known figures around the world just because of their positive thinking in life.

You develop, mature, change, and gain experience via failing. You are aware of what doesn't work, potential trouble spots, and downward spirals. With a clear picture of everything in your head, you can better prepare yourself and feel more confident and self-assured. Your vision of the difficulties and hurdles changes as a result of your faith. Every "no" indicates you need to find another route, and every "barrier" means you need to find a different route. Failure in no way entails packing it up and walking away. This optimistic perspective completely transforms your life and raises you to the rank of a champion. When you have a winning attitude, you become unstoppable and motivated to pursue goals that other people would consider unachievable."

Positive affirmations are a powerful tool for teaching your mind to think positively. Repeating them will help your mind build a positive attitude. Reading motivational and inspiring quotations every day can help you combat negative thoughts and cultivate optimism in yourself. Any negative incident should be approached with optimism, and you should strive to draw a good conclusion from it.

Keep in mind that your ideas influence your moods and behaviour. You should, therefore, instantly replace any negative thoughts that enter your head with positive ones. Even if things are bad, having an optimistic outlook will help you get through the challenging period without too much difficulty. Whatever the circumstances, make a commitment to be upbeat. Instead of worrying if things aren't going your way, keep working toward your objectives with an optimistic outlook, and you'll soon start to see wonderful results!

Why are life changes and personal development so challenging? Does the creator want us to fail? Obviously not! The grand plan of the universe is to make us successful. The obstacle is caused by our ignorance of the universal rules. Spiritual rules control the trip, just as physical events are governed by laws.Understanding them allows us to understand why some people succeed so easily while others struggle; why some people are still putting on their shoes while others have finished the race.The heavenly rules guiding fulfilment and happiness in life are beautiful in that they have the same everlasting validity as the laws of physical nature.

You can either use different circumstances in your life to make yourself stronger and better or you can sit and cry, just as the maize crop used the winds to strengthen itself. You have the option of doing this. No matter what occurs, even the most terrible incident in your life may be used for your development and well-being. Your business, your marriage, and your children are merely stepping stones in the big picture of your life. You are not unfamiliar with this because people have been ingrained with it for centuries in Indian culture. "Your life is about mukti," they remarked. All of these—your marriage, business, and social life—are only means to an end. Your sole objective, whether you are a sanyasi or in samsara, is mukti; therefore, you may either proceed with it or without it.

Losers give up at the drop of a hat, whereas winners spend time persevering through difficulties.

Everyone aspires to have a more successful life, but sadly, very few people know how to take the necessary measures to get there. The good news is that, regardless of your exact objectives, if you use everything you're going to learn in this book, you will succeed in every aspect of your life. No matter what happens, never lose your motivation, appetite, or optimism.I appreciate you taking the time to read my LinkedIn article and thank you for doing so. To help people, I used to write articles about self-empowerment, life, career, and personal development (yeah, that is my love). If you share my belief that we live in a society where people support one another, let's connect and discover how we can do so!

Life is a game, so play it; life is a challenge, so face it; and life is an opportunity, so seize it.

Recognise your innate potential for success. You'll have your chance. Make the decision to keep going towards your dream despite the adverse results you are experiencing. Make the decision to keep pounding on the door of the prosperous life you've imagined. No matter how long you've been trying to start your ideal company without success, rest confident that it will be your turn soon! Although you've been showing off your ability for a while now without much to show for it, the notion of giving it up regularly crosses your mind. Don't give in. You'll have your chance.

"It's fine to celebrate success, but it is more important to heed the lessons of failure." -Bill Gates

Failure is okay because only then can you learn to get up and try again. As a result, without failure, success becomes boring. Neither success nor defeat are ever lasting. The more times you fail, the more methods you learn to avoid failing in a certain way. Anything you obtain without making an effort loses its worth. Everything you accomplish through a lot of effort and struggle is more valuable and precious. If coal is so accessible, what about diamonds? Instead, success is a deliberate decision to do things that you may not particularly enjoy doing when all the odds are against you, when it seems like nothing is working and there isn't a shred of hope: And you still cling to your fundamentals. Take immediate action!

Small doses of willpower and determination are needed in our everyday lives at every step. there is always a choice that looks simpler and that will lead us away from our objective for every decision we make.

CHAPTER THREE

Recharge Your Energy

"The simplest way to ignore your own faults or stay in your comfort zones is to blame other factors."

Humans contribute to some aspect of this universe with every action they take. Whatever you may be doing, it could help someone. Knowing what you can contribute will help you. Integrity is crucial since it affects how simple or difficult your everyday efforts will be based on how much trust you build with the individuals you engage with. Simply put, if there is a culture of trust, everyone will clear the way for you rather than put up barriers, which will considerably improve your capacity to work.

It's been stated that the average individual thinks between 60 and 90,000 times every day, and that the majority of those thoughts are negative and repeat those from the day before. A significant portion of those thoughts are self-critical, and it's especially easy to listen to the voice in your brain that tells you why you tried that and that was so foolish after you've just been rejected or had some other type of failure or setback. You were far too loud and overbearing. You erred in your execution. to allow such voices to rule. The amazing thing about your mind right now is that you have virtually complete control over it. You might as well think positively if you're going to be thinking, which it appears that you are.

Positive thinking has a beneficial impact on your health as well, reducing stress and enhancing your general welfare. Even when you are sick, your body heals more quickly. By adopting a positive outlook, you can establish emotional equilibrium, which really aids the brain's healthy operation. You develop the ability to maintain attention, which enables you to make wise choices in difficult circumstances. You'll start to feel better about yourself after you adopt an optimistic outlook. Your confidence and inner strength will increase as a result of treating yourself with more love and respect. You'll overcome your self-limiting beliefs and take on fresh tasks.

Prowess of the intellect and body are what you essentially need to succeed in the world. Equanimity is one of the most crucial traits if you wish to master the mind. You can enter several mental realms while you are centered. You have far less mental capacity if there is no serenity. Another crucial characteristic is your degree of energy; you must be vigorous on the inside as much as on the outside. You can only overcome challenges in daily life and progress toward achievement when your energies are vivacious. Success will come to you much more readily if you bring serenity and joy into your mind and body.

"Ability is what you're capable of doing. Motivation determines what you do. Attitude determines how well you do it."

The ability to perceive things that most others are unable to see indicates that you are paying attention to the world around you. Without understanding, there is nothing to work for or pursue. Only when there is a profound understanding of something can ordinary action be converted into remarkable activity. Being motivated all the time is a crucial component. Consider the bigger picture of your motivations and the impact you are making on the world with each and every action you take.

Avoid waiting until you are really exhausted before taking a break. The brief breaks you take throughout the day and week to maintain your life's balance are crucial to recharging. Step away from an activity or circumstance for a while if it is making you frustrated. By doing or thinking about something entirely else, you may distract yourself from it. You'll be able to do it more quickly and effectively if you return to it with fresh eyes and a new perspective.

When morning arrives, dreams aren't what you leave behind. They are what fills each and every minute of your life. The only thing standing between you and your dream's fulfilment are your willingness to try and your conviction that it is truly achievable.

Never stop learning. In your personal or professional life, try to learn something new every day. Learning is the foundation of growth; therefore, if you want to achieve, make it a daily priority to learn as much as you can. Your quality of life will increase, and you will be exposed to more chances that might provide you contentment and happiness if you are always learning new things.

Begin the day with an inspirational quote about overcoming obstacles. Put an end to comparing yourself to others. Everybody has a distinct set of goals. Even if someone else is pursuing your goals, your lives are very different from theirs. It is therefore unfair to you and your future success to make a direct comparison. Additionally, comparing your unique life circumstances to someone else's doesn't exactly inspire you to feel happy about your life and your decisions.

"Dreams are not what you see in sleep, it is the thing which doesn't let you sleep." – A.P.J Abdul Kalam

To succeed, concentrate on you, your surroundings, conditions, and objectives. You will succeed in life if you commit your time to constantly learning new things. A lifelong learner makes the effort to advance their own growth and pursue new knowledge. While recognising others' successes, keep your attention on the next SMART goal-related action. You will be satisfied as long as you remain committed to your own unique personal growth.

The amount of rejection you experience is typically inversely correlated with your level of success. The enemy of success is rejection anxiety. If you postpone making difficult calls out of concern that others may reject you (such as clients, workers, coworkers, or colleagues), your effectiveness will suffer.

Your attitude sets the tone for a better, more prosperous life, and you have power over it.

With a net worth of 420 crore, Kanika Tekriwal, 33, emphasises the advantages of starting early and the vast opportunities available to young businesspeople today. The Kotak Private Banking Hurun Leading Wealthy Women list for 2021 has the youngest lady ever. Kanika Tekriwal, a Marwari woman born in Bhopal, founded India's first marketplace for private aircraft and helicopter charters after overcoming cancer. Her aviation company, JetSetGo, has grown to 10 private aircraft in the last few years. In order to offer services as a private jet and helicopter operator and aggregator, Kanika founded JetSetGo in 2012. JetSetGo is now India's first online private aviation charter marketplace.

Kanika Tekriwal, founder and CEO of JetSetGo, demonstrated that nothing is impossible if you believe in yourself, despite her declining health and dominance of the airline sector. She was diagnosed with cancer a few years ago, but she battled through it and beat it, and today she is the CEO of a business that has been compared to the Uber of the aviation sector. She is bringing good change to the heavily male-dominated aviation industry. She is a remarkable individual who made it onto the Forbes 30 under 30 Asia List for 2016.

Making excuses is part of being human.

Even the most successful people occasionally veer off course, but they are able to recognise their justifications early on and get back on course. It's crucial to always consider whether an objection or problem is something you can keep an eye on and go beyond in the future. Or is it a justification, a story you tell yourself? To begin with, writing things down can frequently assist you in beginning to overcome obstacles or voices that keep appearing in your mind while attempting to do anything. If you'd like, you may really stop this and finish it right now.

List all the reasons you're having trouble or think you're going to have trouble. You could say, "I don't have a big enough budget," "I've never done this before and don't know how to do it," or "I don't know whether my work is good enough." Whatever it is, make a note of it. Got it?

Our capacity for productivity and performance at work is not determined by how much time we devote to each activity, but rather by the vigour with which we do them. Learn how to better manage your energy in this chapter to increase your productivity.

In fact, it's been estimated that a whopping 95% of people are unsure about their life goals. I was inspired when I realised how successful I had been. After seeing the incredible results for myself and realising how it could help others, I was inspired to compile everything into a single, concise book. You are living your life on purpose when you are enthusiastic about it. If you've ever had trouble figuring out your life's passion or purpose, you may have found that it's really challenging to find answers to these questions by merely pondering them. This book is organised using a special approach based on simple habit adjustments that make you face your fears, set practical objectives, and start succeeding in every aspect of your life. Don't settle; begin acting now to lead the life you choose.

Your legacy has four primary legs—love, health, freedom, and purpose—can be strengthened and balanced, guiding you toward positive decisions, worthwhile experiences, and satisfying connections. This is not just a book; rather, it presents the scientifically supported tactics mentioned inside in an interesting, easily comprehensible manner that will inform, amuse, and motivate you. You may have the foresight and self-assurance to build your own prosperous future. Let's start by claiming your very own happiness tree right away!

In every sense, we are the most comfortable generation ever, yet we are not the happiest generation. We are grumbling more than ever before about everything. This is due to our outside environment. However, our wellness has not been improved by comfort and convenience. So instead of altering the outside environment, learn to change yourself. If you don't learn how to work on your inner self, no matter how wealthy you are or how luxurious your home is, you will continue to feel empty and unhappy on the inside.

Give up trying to find shortcuts.

You could be angry with the government for the weak economy, with society for having dirty streets, and with your job for giving you a low-quality raise. Yet you fail to make greater use of what you already have. Put an end to your concern about what the rest of the world does or does not do for you.

If we enjoy cooking, we always consider fresh flavours to add and inventive methods to prepare foods so that everyone will enjoy them more. It will compel us to read periodicals, hunt for cooking-related videos, and much more. Moving toward idea generation is motivated by passion. This will assist you in applying creativity and innovation to your job. Since I launched my consulting business four years ago, my business service has had numerous ups and downs. I don't want to give up though. Analyze every issue and solve them one at a time. This is regarded as my loyalty to my job. The motivation is the same. Whatever the issue, it will occur.

"You are well aware that no matter how quickly or persistently you run, you will never arrive at your destination if you are running in the wrong direction. While diligence is essential, success requires a combination of intellect and diligence."- Dr. Amit Das

We have a lot of things to do, but we don't enjoy them. Everything is based on an individual's needs. When we enter, we are delighted. When we take a tour with our friends and family, we are excited. With our loved one, we are content. When we do something very intriguing, we get excited. But have you ever considered how you feel when working? Do you actually feel content, ecstatic, or happy? Ideas are created out of passion. Being enthusiastic about something encourages the creation of fresh ideas. Because when we love someone, we always work to keep them shining, and this encourages us to think of new and inventive methods to improve the quality. These will spark the development of fresh concepts for solving that problem.

Having a good attitude involves more than simply having a grin on your face. It involves keeping a positive outlook and attitude even while everything around you is in complete disarray. Positive and negative ideas are considered to have a similar effect on your mind as a healthy or unhealthy diet has on your physical health. Positive ideas will help you witness great improvements in the world around you.

Life is always equal parts positive and negative if you look at it as it is. When you see things for what they are, neither the good nor the bad can overwhelm you. Everything is happening the way it is because they are equal. Both must be controlled so that you may create what you can. Because electricity has both positive and negative charges, a light turns on. We are getting a good outcome, therefore we don't mind the bad. If there is a man and a woman, we don't mind who they are as long as they are happy.

All that ever occurred to you—darkness and light; agony and pleasure; joy and despair—happened within you.

Every aspect of existence is a struggle between two dualities. Male and female, light and darkness, day and night, are what you mean by positive and negative. Without it, how can life exist? It would be like declaring that you just desire life and do not want death. Life exists only because death does. There is light only because there is darkness. Just don't let the bad beat you down. Let them both be present and consider ways to make them both productive. It is crucial that we tell the truth about where we are right now if we care about this life. If they were to start producing a lot of undesirable effects, we might start to view them as a concern. The issue is with the outcome you generate, not with the good and bad.

You only need to use it to your advantage to produce a favourable outcome; resisting either the positive or the negative is not necessary. It is crucial that we tell the truth about where we are right now if we care about this life. Then, and only then, can we go. Many opportunities for people have been destroyed by positive thinking. There is a poem composed by a thinker who is optimistic:

There is no way to change life if you are unable to accept it as it is. There is nothing you can do about it. You can only perform amusing mental feats, which may amuse you briefly but won't get you anywhere. There is a lot of information available regarding how positive thinking may change your life. Can you avoid accumulating more karma by using positive thinking, or can it even help you get rid of it?

Change your negative self-talk to a positive one.

Whatever you observe in this world is something you are witnessing within. You are able to see a pen on the table because light strikes it, reflects off of it, travels through your eyes, and then passes through your mind, where it is recognised as a pen. Actually, what happens is that you are perceiving internal events with your eyes and intellect. And you alone are the solution. If you control what's occurring within you, you alone will define your whole experience of life. Even if the incident in your life may not have been planned by you, how you perceive it, how you feel about it, and how you respond to it are all up to you. Therefore, if you want to succeed and have a better life today, you must learn to be self-reliant. According to best-selling author Jack Canfield of the Chicken Soup for the Soul series, your outcome is influenced by the incident and your response.

How much time are you willing to devote to honing your abilities in order to raise your worth per hour and advance in your career?

How much time, specifically, besides your regular working hours People frequently believe that they should only work during the hours for which they are getting paid. While performing your duties and receiving a fair salary are undoubtedly crucial, you should also invest in your career by frequently enhancing your abilities outside of your usual work duties. Spending time in this way can help you develop your strengths, which will increase your worth per hour and work stability. By following a straightforward four-step procedure, you may make this investment in yourself. Identifying the time commitment you're willing to make is the first step.

I advise budgeting at least an hour each week and blocking out time slots on your schedule. Give it a name that is specific, such as "your strength investment." It will be simpler for you to keep your promise if you schedule time in advance on your calendar. Gathering your resources for the short course you are designing for yourself comes next. You must now locate your own classes, books, and other resources in order to improve the most important strength you choose to concentrate on.

Practicing gratitude increases your likelihood of achieving happiness and contentment in life. True happiness can only be attained by being grateful for what you have.

I may take online classes regarding my favourite apps if I want to strengthen my computer skills. Books, periodicals, websites, blogs, and community classes are other sources of information. Decide to deliver something that plays to your strengths as the following phase. Inform your supervisor, a peer mentor, or a colleague about this strong investment you are making. Inform them that you'll be giving them an assignment to show them what you've learned. If I'm a writer, for instance, I may promise them that I'll finish the first draught of one chapter in a month. To ensure that you are held accountable, request that they mark that day on their calendar. This will make you more devoted to your goal and enable the other person to be your supporter. They will want to help you and provide you with any resources they can since they have been actively involved from the beginning. Finally, adhere to the schedule you made.

Consider the positives, no matter how minor.

Remain true to your word to yourself. Stop doing whatever you're doing at the appointed time and concentrate on building your strength. Your use of information is considerably more useful than just knowing it. Your strengths will develop as you stick to your training plan and complete the assignments assigned to you by your accountability partner. This will allow you to advance consistently in your profession.

Eliminate and overcome the inability to plan well due to a lack of drive and willpower.

The founder of Air Deccan, Captain Gopinath, who revolutionised air travel in India, comes from a modest background. The second of eight children, Captain

Gopinath's father was a schoolteacher. Gopinath joined the Indian Army after completing his education and was given a commission for an eight-year term. He started a sustainable farm, developed an Enfield dealership, and operated an Udipi hotel after leaving the military. Captain Gopinath started Deccan Aviation, a helicopter charter service, only after several attempts, failures, and hardships; this business subsequently served as the foundation for Air Deccan.

I will explain practical techniques that will show you precisely how to make excellent plans that are effective with habits, break poor plans, throw out ineffective plans, and master the small actions that produce amazing outcomes. It's not you; it's your regular plans that need to change, not you. Your system architecture is the issue. The reason why terrible plans, sluggish plans, dispersed plans, and bad habits keep happening isn't that you don't want to change; it's that your change management strategy is flawed. You fall short of reaching your objectives.

Your plans may be used to design your environment and make success simpler. They can also be used to get back on track when you get off track and make up lost time. The complete guide to planning your everyday in 30 days, whether you are a team trying to win a championship, an organisation hoping to redefine an industry, or simply a person who wants to stop smoking, lose weight, reduce stress, or achieve any other goal or anything at all that envisions long-term and successful outcomes, will reshape the way you think and work about your very own progress and success, and give you the tools and strategies you need to transform your habitual plans. The key to transforming your life is in realising how important imagination is in shaping your awareness.

Discover how to use the law of attraction and the power of positive thinking in your life to start attracting more money, a new profession, improved health, or meaningful relationships. How I found the key to unleashing the full force of the law of attraction: wealth from the inside out; the soul of language; prosperity and the body, mind, and spirit connection; the gifted heart; overcoming adversity; you were created to be healthy; the prosperity factor is your road map to completely embracing the life you wish to live.

The reasons why most people struggle to change for the better and how to avoid making the same mistakes. How to incorporate a new routine into an existing one? How to make changing your behaviour easier. What do you anticipate? ? Are you prepared to change?

Can you train your brain to become faster, stronger, wiser?

During the past few decades, we've discovered some straightforward yet effective guidelines for how the brain regulates energy from the top down and bottom up. The brain is the supreme controller of the human system from the top down, and whatever we focus on absorbs our energy. For instance, even though your big right toe is likely receiving blood and oxygen right now, if you were to pay attention to it right now, you'd likely begin to notice how it feels.

Our awareness delivers new feelings or sensations when we pay attention to anything, and it can alter both the quantity and quality of our energy. You could notice a change in how you are now feeling physically and emotionally if you think of someone in your life for whom you are thankful and focus on the area surrounding your heart. Top-down processing occurs when you deliberately think about something, focus on it, and then notice a change in how you feel.

In addition, a very potent bottom-up process is at work, much like when your body takes control when your brain perceives a potential threat in your environment. Your brain may detect a possible threat in your environment when you begin to feel worried and breathe shallowly and quickly. Most of the time, we try to stop these bottom-up processes by telling ourselves things like, "You shouldn't be stressed," "Others have it worse than you," or "I'll take care of it tomorrow." But consider this: Everything changes when our bottom-up feelings indicate a threat to our survival. Because this sensory information is given priority by the brain initially, this is why you've felt that your thoughts are diverting your attention. The brain's mission is to keep you safe at all costs, even if doing so prevents you from achieving your objectives. So consider what can undermine your sense of security during the day.

Maybe eating the incorrect meals or going too long without eating. Going too long without breathing or moving in a stressed-out manner. concentrating excessively on analytical and logical work without pausing to be contemplative or creative. Being truly present is impossible when we begin to feel overextended. We can only direct the energy we require to the upper area of the brain, where we enable these more logical, reasonable, and deliberate actions, when we feel comfortable and have the capacity to handle all of the demands in our lives. You can rely on your brain to feed you more efficiently and assist you in achieving your most significant goals when you learn how to be in control of it and provide it the things it actually needs to feel safe.

Every living organism, including the human system, has some type of rhythm or pattern. Everything, including your heartbeat, brain waves, and blood sugar levels, should fluctuate. Your energy is no different. You want a rhythm or pattern to the way your energy rises and falls throughout the day. The fluctuation of energy will support your peak performance and make you feel less stressed. Before I give you some helpful advice on how to do that, I want you to take a moment to consider your own day. Or do you wake up and go and go and go and then be astonished when you can't unwind at night?

Do you expend energy and then invest it back in yourself to recharge? an energy flatline, in my opinion. Now, while it might sound a little excessive, my argument is just that. You're effectively taking over your own system and wearing yourself thin if you don't follow the normal course of stress and recuperation.

How do you ensure that your energy fluctuates in a normal pattern each day?

Here are a few straightforward tactics you may use. First, if you drink coffee in the morning, take your time drinking it and read a few pages of a motivational book or listen to some motivating music to make it a conscious and perhaps even inspirational experience. In this way, your energy comes from more than simply coffee. Taking regular breaks during the day is definitely something I'd advise, especially if you find yourself spending a lot of time sitting down. Setting a timer to remind you every hour is the best course of action. Then stand up and go outside for five minutes. Your body receives an immediate boost from the activity and fresh air, and your mood may also be lifted.

Additionally, it will unquestionably sharpen your focus and attention for when you go back. You should also make an effort to obtain a full night's sleep each night. Although you've probably heard of it before, it's really important to refresh your body and mind. Good sleep helps you wake up feeling more awake and decreases stress and inflammation. Sleep offers the brain the time and energy to evaluate your day and draw crucial connections between the significant events that occurred, which can help your memory. Nature follows these predictable rhythms, much like day and night, to keep us alert enough to be productive while maintaining a healthy balance with adequate rest, relaxation, and restoration.

Furthermore, as we strengthen our ability to handle whatever life throws at us, the more we can really use the stress and problems in life to drive achievement. Consider how a baby uses their time and energy if you've ever been around one. Babies focus entirely on the events that are important to them. They will let you know if they need something. You are aware if they are referring to you. Now consider your day. How frequently do you give your all to the things that are most important to you at the time? Are you easily distracted when you receive a new email, message from a friend, or text from a coworker? When you're driving, do you ever check your texts? Our mental and emotional well-being may be completely destroyed by these distractions, especially if they start to form thinking and behaviour habits.

Because the brain isn't made to continuously multitask, be stimulated continuously, or do anything continuously at all. In the same way that eating only vegetables is equally harmful as eating only pizza, continual stimulation can cause our energies to flatline, which is always negative.

At least, that's what I tell myself. But in all seriousness, the plague of distractions is dangerous, whether it's the accelerated ageing process that causes illness and disorder to develop more quickly in our bodies or the fact that individuals cause automobile accidents when they multitask while driving or even just crossing the street. This trend must be broken.

You may do this by establishing guidelines and limitations for your behaviour in each situation. Here are a few things I recommend you do. First and foremost, always strive to prioritise energy over time. To do this, pay attention to your body, monitor your energy levels, and take breaks throughout the day to rest and recharge. Keep in mind that the important thing is to ensure you have the energy necessary to complete the necessary tasks in the proper manner, not how quickly you complete them. Use those frustrating small pauses, such as traffic lights and long lines, to genuinely breathe and be grateful rather than feeling upset or agitated, is a specific guideline I've started to follow that has been extremely helpful.

While you wait, you might want to check your phone or send one more email, but by seeing downtime as an investment in yourself, you'll be able to recharge more frequently. You may begin to teach your brain to stop multitasking over time to make it less alluring to try to pass the time whenever you get a minute to yourself. You could forcibly restrain yourself from reading your email while speaking to a friend or a member of your family. You could even come to the realisation that you don't have to act on every notion you have because it is only a thought. These methods will assist you in revitalising your energy so that you are prepared and able to take action once more.

There are easy things we can do at work and at home to revitalise others around us in addition to replenishing our own batteries. Making rules and setting boundaries for our time is one of the most effective methods to do this. and truly combine energy management with time management, putting more of an emphasis on the value we derive from the time we have available and not promoting the unhelpful notion that we must constantly be running and stressed. There are numerous other approaches you may take, but I'll only mention the two that I believe would be most beneficial. More meaning-making and less multitasking. We manage our energy considerably better when we stop attempting to accomplish too many things at once. This keeps the brain's more primitive, sensitive regions calm, adaptive, and flexible. And it spreads easily. Consider this.

When someone's phone rings when they are near you, their mood and focus are affected. However, it can also cause you to think about things you might or ought to be doing in the present rather than concentrating on the discussion or work at hand. On the other side, when we provide more possibilities for meaning-making, we activate the pre-frontal logical cortex, which supports higher-order abilities like creativity, curiosity, and teamwork. This improves our ability to think effectively and allows us to do a great deal more in less time.

Simple actions like asking others to share something for which they are glad or anything amusing that occurred to them today might serve as meaningful-making chances. Alternatively, it might be more extensive and continuous, such as assisting individuals in making connections between their own missions and values and those of the business so that everyone is aware of how the work they are doing contributes to the overall success of the whole team.

If you're like most people, you've had nights when you were so exhausted that you couldn't get your brain to shut off and really let you sleep, leaving you wired and exhausted at the same time. You'll be able to work at your best and genuinely switch off your energy when you need to relax and recharge if you develop better habits throughout the day. Following what I refer to as a "High Five" is a fantastic approach to going through these new rhythms. The five key periods during the day to refuel your body and mind for maximum performance are as follows: The first two—first thing in the morning and then just before you go to bed—are the day's bookends. When you refuel at the start and end of the day, you actually prepare your brain to enter the state required for the desired result, whether it's being intensely focused on work tasks, being loving, patient, and kind with your family at home, or feeling relaxed enough to let go of the worries from the day so that you can sleep well and wake up feeling rested.

If you're unsure of where to begin, think about including a few seconds of appreciation in your daily stroll or cup of coffee. Consider an amusing event that happened to you during the day when it's time to go to bed. Both of them are quite quick and easy to accomplish, yet they help you channel your energy in a more useful way. The following three tactics are focused on how you eat, move, and take breaks, and we're going to pay extra attention to how you do these things even more than what you do after you have routines to start and finish your day appropriately.

Everyone is aware that what and how much they eat affects their energy levels, for instance, but you might be shocked to learn that how you eat matters just as much. Everyone knows we need to exercise during the day, but what may surprise you is that how often you move may be more important than how much time you spend at the gym.

When you take a moment to really appreciate your food, you put your brain in a more positive state that actually enables you to digest food more effectively. Regular movement is a crucial component of energy management.

Finally, it actually matters when and how you take breaks. This is the hardest habit to form for most people since we have a tendency to feel as though we must always be creating. However, we all know that producing poorly when we are always working makes it crucial that we take frequent breaks to recharge.

Now, if you feel that self-care is selfish or if you're concerned that if you slow down, you might not pick up speed again, it might be difficult to prioritise it. Remember that everything is normal. With just a few easy steps, you can begin to rewire these thought and behaviour patterns, making it easier for you to incorporate them into your daily routine. As you begin to feel better and receive encouraging comments from those around you, you'll be even more inspired to continue on your current path.

How much energy do you now have?

We actually don't notice the majority of the time since we are so preoccupied with getting things done. Gaining more awareness of our energy levels during the day gives us insightful information that enables us to decide what needs to be changed in order to recharge most efficiently. Then I'll lead you through a brief energy audit after we discuss the five main forms of energy we have and how they are related. First, the body's supply of nutrients like glucose and oxygen determines how much physical energy we have at any one time.

Our emotional energy therefore determines the type of energy we have and whether we are concentrating on possibilities or possible threats in our environment or on good or negative things. We focus thanks to the power of our minds. It's our capacity to focus attention on the things we decide to pay attention to. Then, our morals and beliefs serve as the source of our spiritual vitality. It is what propels us towards the people and things that are most important to us.

Finally, the kinship we experience with others is what we refer to as our social energy. When we feel connected and protected, both our bodies and minds flourish. Let's consider the degree of connectivity between these energy systems now. Like when you skip meals for an extended period of time, it affects more than just your physical vitality.

Like most people, you can start to feel angry or lose your temper more frequently than you'd like. Then, because your emotions are diverting your attention, you probably won't be able to concentrate properly or think in a creative or flexible way. There really is a mind-body link. The brain processes information and energy in a two-way process to calculate how much energy you have to use in the time that is available.

Understanding your capabilities in each of these areas will thus enable you to develop more focused and planned recharge strategies. Now is the time to print the energy audit guide from your workout files. Right now, we're going to assess your energy. An easy approach to achieving this is to rank each energy domain from zero to ten, with zero representing complete emptiness and ten representing full fuel.

What are your current feelings like?

Write down your results for each of the five categories on your handout. Add up your numbers after you're done, then multiply the result by two. This will provide you with a total number out of 100, which will also show what proportion of your overall energy you have charged at this time. For instance, if you sum up the five domains and receive a score of 40, you'll be charged 80% of that amount after multiplying it by two. You are at 50% if you tally up your points and obtain a total of 25. As a result, if you're not feeling as energised as you'd like, consider doing something right away to recharge in one of those energy regions, such as going for a short walk. Consider something or someone for which you are thankful, or read something motivational. Focusing on the energy domain where you need it most will yield a substantial return, even if it doesn't take much time.

Let's not go too personal here, I think. I'm simply curious to see what goes through your head when you first realise it's time to begin the day. Do you feel motivated, eager, or inspired? Or do you feel worn out, overextended, or exhausted? If you're like most people, your alarm jolts you out of sleep and makes you anxious enough to get you out of bed quickly. This implies that what you do immediately after you get up is a crucial step in determining whether your day will be good or bad.

Your brain's task is to assess whether you need to remain in this high-stress state or whether you can switch into a more peaceful, focused, and productive mode.It's crucial to attempt to delay reading your email, social media, or any other type of media, when you first get up. Although it may be tempting to check in straight soon, please resist the urge and wait until you have given your mind something uplifting, motivating, or invigorating. Bad news and additional tasks to add to your list before you've refilled your own tank just don't sit well with your sensitive brain.

You can do this by reading a few pages of an uplifting book or listening to a guided meditation. You may play a brief podcast or a few upbeat tunes while working towards your daily objectives. Depending on how I feel when I wake up and how I want to feel, I have a few different playlists that I listen to. I put on some soothing music when I'm feeling pressured or anxious. But if I'm more down or discouraged, I turn to music that inspires me or makes me feel like I'm part of something greater than just trying to serve another day. Another fantastic technique to boost your energy is through physical activity. You may take a stroll, practise some mild yoga, or resolve to work out for for five minutes.

You could discover that once you get going and feel the energy flowing, you wind up accomplishing more than you anticipated and even like it. You could also want to inject some healthy humour into your morning by finding a hilarious movie to watch or telling a funny tale to a friend or relative. Instead of laughing at what's wrong, you should train your brain to see the lighter side of things more frequently. This will strengthen your resilience and improve your problem-solving skills. What will it be for you then? Take a moment right now to jot down two or three morning routine ideas that you think you'd want to try, and you may as well attempt one of them right away to get yourself ready for the rest of the day.

We can exercise our brains to help us manage energy more efficiently, just as we can train our physical muscles at the gym to help us move through life more successfully.

I like to see this as being similar to brain exercise. Our capacity to use our brains to help us be the best versions of ourselves in the situations that are most important to us Similar to physical fitness, there are three distinct sorts of capabilities you might consider: your strength, flexibility, and endurance. And just as we need a solid plan to ensure that our workouts at the gym are effective, it's crucial to bear in mind certain analogous ideas when considering how we exercise our minds.

Anything that is going to generate a big change must first be difficult enough to require the brain to adjust.

It is obvious that just repeating the same actions day after day won't make something different occur just because we want it to. The difficulty of forming new habits should be just severe enough to make us strive for them without being too stressful. We may increase the level of difficulty as we gain strength and find it easier to keep up the habit in order to get better over time. Second, repetition of the new habit must be made frequently enough for adaptations to begin to accumulate if anything is to result in long-lasting change. Consider visiting a gym. Even if going once a year can seem amazing at first, it won't be enough to prevent your fitness level from rising. Or if you started taking vitamins, it would be excellent if you did so every day for a week, but that wouldn't be enough to strengthen your immune system for a whole year.

So keep in mind that if you want to teach your brain to help you manage your energy more successfully, you must challenge it by doing something new that just barely pushes you outside of your comfort zone. Don't try to run a marathon on your first visit to the gym, but do ensure that your exercise is at least somewhat painful. Then, practise the new habit consistently and often until it begins to naturally drive you in that direction. One new habit can be added at a time as you develop momentum to ensure that you can maintain your drive.

When you wake up, what is the first thing that comes to mind?

We work better both individually and in groups when we focus on the things that are most important to us rather than attempting to achieve too much at once. This is because the energy we bring to the task at hand is so much more useful. Because our surrounds and feelings of safety occupy a significant portion of the brain's attention, it is crucial to consider how our environment affects our energy. This is something to consider both in your own space and the spaces of those around you, both at home and at work.

Even though it may not seem rational, between 95% and 99% of your brain's energy is really directed towards subconscious environmental cues that make you feel comfortable or endangered. For instance, even while we are aware that common city sounds like traffic, sirens, or construction are not always signs of danger, the brain still needs to filter these sounds and form opinions about them, which may be extremely taxing on a brain that is already overworked.

Even while hearing natural sounds like birds tweeting or waves crashing doesn't always put you near the beach or a dense forest, research has shown that these rhythmic sounds can make individuals feel more at ease.They even boost immunological response while lowering blood pressure and inflammation. Therefore, it could be worthwhile to consider how you might enhance natural patterns in your surroundings while minimising those that are disruptive, such as doing your best to replace harsh lighting with more natural light. or turning on a sound machine to block out commotion.

The brain and body can be relaxed by just altering the sort of artwork or paint colour in a space.

According to studies, being around nature—whether it's genuine plants and water features or just photographs of nature on the walls—makes individuals feel more at ease. You might even use aromatherapy or a candle, depending on the environment, to assist you change your mood.You might feel more at ease and grounded by inhaling earthy aromas like clove and lavender. While energising scents like citrus or vanilla might support the improvement of motivation and vitality.

Last but not least, although it may seem trivial, having pictures of your loved ones around gives your mind something uplifting to think about while switching between jobs. Inspirational sayings, upbeat colours, and even upbeat music may all be deliberately employed to refuel and shared with others for special occasions that are mutually beneficial. As they collect during the day, these seemingly little changes to your surroundings might result in considerable energy benefits.

In addition to assisting us in keeping our promises, social support is an essential component of boosting energy capacity as a strategy in and of itself. According to a recent study, feeling lonely is really worse for one's general health than being inactive, eating poorly, or even smoking. Being alone in the world is a terrifying concept that puts a lot of stress on our bodies since the brain's largest dread is running out of resources.

Unfortunately, one of the first things we often do when we start to feel worn out or overcommitted is to put off social responsibilities. The last thing we want to do when we're feeling bad is ask for help because we don't want to put anyone else through it. However, when we do ask for help from others, the brain releases Oxytocin, a highly useful molecule that actually increases both the body's and brain's resistance to stress.

When we face stress with individuals we care about, the brain actually becomes even stronger rather than tearing us down. Thus, something that ordinarily harms us suddenly turns to benefit us just because we are with someone we care about. I could list several studies that show the significant benefits of social connections, but I'd like to nudge you to consider how you might make fostering and forming relationships with others a top priority both at work and at home. To actually feel comfortable, it's first necessary to take your time and give each other your whole attention. We refer to this as psychological safety, which calls for a sense of being seen and heard. Rushing about and juggling many tasks all the time sends the message to others that they aren't as essential as anything else, which not only renders the time we spend with them useless but also dangerous. The good news is that connecting and being completely present in the moment don't need a lot of time or effort.

However, it does require some work to educate your brain to be able to do this more frequently. Turning off your phone at the door or leaving it in the car can help you focus on the here and now. You can also try deliberately listening to music while sitting in the driveway to help you change your vibe and leave work at work when you enter the house. As you practise these small adjustments over time, you might start to wonder how you ever allowed yourself to live your life without putting all of your energy into the time that you have. These small adjustments help to prime your brain to be able to show up fully in the moments that matter most to you.

Why are you unable to simply be present, without any sort of attitude?

Just mindful. simply conscious. It is critical that you accept the situation as it is. You don't make any denials. Grief will come if it does. Sadness is inevitable. Joy is what comes. Ecstasy appears immediately. You are not trying to deny or halt anything when you do this. Everything is occurring all at once, but you are not a part of it.

Individuals have become frivolous by concentrating all of their attention on what is easy for them, which they refer to as positive, which is why their lives have lost substance. They want rapid response times for everything. There isn't any commitment to anything. Imagine if someone had to train to be a scientist. He has to spend years studying. He forgets everything and gives himself, so perhaps he will forget his wife and kids. Only after that does he experience something, even in the physical realm. Because of the overabundance of instruction that says, "Do not worry, be joyful," this type of continuous attention is mostly lacking in our society. The situation is fine. Enjoy yourselves, please!" This type of bliss will unavoidably end, and people will experience mental illness. Be cheerful and live in the now is a particularly well-liked adage I hear in the West, and it's starting to catch on in India as well. Please show me how to live somewhere else. Where else could you be right now, wherever you may be? Everyone mentions this because books have been written and programmes have been run by people who lack knowledge or experience.

The people who are constantly telling you to "be joyful" eventually get depression. Because your energies are allocated for various possibilities based on your karmic framework, they will always hit you extremely hard. There is something available to ease your suffering, sadness, pleasure, and love. The term for this is prarabdha karma. Not just in your head, either. Data is karma. According to this information, your energy is working. Prarabdha resembles a wounded spring. It must discover a way to let go. If you suppress and deny those feelings, they will take root in unexpected places.

Who do you believe should decide what is occurring around you if everything that happened to you happened inside of you? Even though you may occasionally experience negative things, how you choose to respond to them will influence how things turn out for you. You have a choice in how you respond to company failure or financial challenges. And the crucial factor that will determine your outcome and, eventually, your life is your response.

Never forget this saying: "I can't control the wind's direction, but I can modify my sails to always get there."

Focusing on the positive aspects of life and expecting good things to happen is known as positive thinking. A positive attitude is a way of thinking that resists giving in easily and is not deterred by challenges, problems, or delays. True optimism involves anticipating challenges and thinking about failure in addition to just asserting that everything will be fine. A positive attitude has to become your daily default mental attitude if you want to make good adjustments and improvements in your life. It needs to develop into a habit and a way of life. Although it can seem difficult, doing this is a slow and fun process.

What you do, not what occurred to you, is what counts most. And exactly like my advises, in order to achieve more success and have a happy life, you must learn to take command of your life.

True optimism involves being realistic about potential setbacks while still maintaining the belief that things will work out for the best. A positive attitude has to become your daily default mental attitude if you want to make good adjustments and improvements in your life. It needs to develop into a habit and a way of life. Although it can seem difficult, doing this is a slow and fun process.

This chapter discusses a few techniques for cultivating a positive outlook in order to achieve a healthy physical and mental condition. True optimism involves anticipating challenges and thinking about failure in addition to just asserting that everything will be fine. The tone of the day is determined by how we begin each morning. Even if you think it's stupid, say things to yourself in the mirror like, "Today will be a fantastic day" or "I'm going to be amazing today." These encouraging words will get ingrained in your subconscious mind, guiding, inspiring, and motivating you to think more positively and productively.

There's never going to be a flawless day; you're going to face challenges almost all day long. When faced with a difficulty like this, keep your attention on the advantages, no matter how minor or insignificant they may seem. Find humour in difficult circumstances: Give yourself permission to find humour even in the grimmest or most stressful circumstances. Try to get a laugh out of this scenario by reminding yourself that it will likely make for a wonderful tale later.

Learn from your mistakes.

No one is flawless, and we frequently make errors and fail in various situations, at various occupations, and with other people. Turn your failure into a lesson by considering what you'll do differently next time rather than dwelling on how you failed.

Be careful to replace any unfavourable ideas with positive and joyful ones. Start paying attention to your ideas, and as soon as you notice any negative ones, calmly and naturally replace them with helpful, joyful, and optimistic ones. Always work to keep your mind's door closed and prevent any bad thoughts from entering. We can stop our negative thoughts from arising and having an impact on us by keeping our attention in the here and now. The majority of sources of negativity are based on memories of recent events or overly optimistic predictions about prospective future events. Therefore, it's crucial to remain in the present.

You'll hear positive perspectives, nice anecdotes, and positive affirmations when you're surrounded by positive individuals. Their encouraging comments will stick with you and influence your own way of thinking, which spreads to others. Avoid being among folks who could make you feel inferior or discouraged.

Read success-related tales that will inspire and motivate you.

You will be motivated and inspired by this, and you will learn what they actually accomplished so you may copy them. Use the power of vision to see yourself performing and reacting favourably in various scenarios. One of the most effective ways to change your attitude and your life is to visualise the results you want to attain or the way you want to act or behave. Be proactive by taking initiative on both little and major issues. If you keep yourself busy, you will be more likely to be optimistic and less likely to become negative.

Before becoming one of the wealthiest people in the world, Kenny Troutt supported himself while attending Southern Illinois University by doing a side job selling insurance. Troutt, a bartender's son, was raised in a low-income household. He would go on to create Excel Communications, a long-distance phone firm, nevertheless, after earning his undergraduate degree. Twelve years after the company's founding, in 1996, he decided to go public. In a $3.5 billion agreement, Kenny Troutt sold Excel Communications to Teleglobe in 1998. He used the gains from the transaction to buy more stocks, bonds, and racehorses. Currently, he is the owner of WinStar Farm in Versailles, Kentucky, which produced a Kentucky Derby victor. Troutt's current net worth is $1.4 billion.

"He who is not courageous enough to take risks will accomplish nothing in life"- Muhammad Ali.

There is no way to do this wrong. If you desire happiness for one hour, the Dalai Lama says to take a nap. Go on a trek if you want to be happy for the day. Win the lottery if you want happiness for a year. But if you want lasting satisfaction, do good deeds. By assisting others in their success, you will also be assisting yourself in their success.

Creating opportunities out of obstacles people who are successful must consume a lot of lemonade. We've all heard the proverb, "When life gives you lemons, make lemonade." They are masters at transforming challenges into chances. In fact, it could be one of their most admirable character attributes. When the Dalai Lama was still a child, he was banished from his homeland. He said that his exile had given him the chance to travel the world and make every place he went his home when asked how difficult it must have been to never have a home. He credits that with enabling him to broaden his horizons and develop into the well-known leader he is today.

How networking works for those who are successful (and what success entails!) A short-term transaction is not what networking achieves. Creating relationships that benefit both parties is key to networking success. Similar to learning a language, it is a continual give-it-first process that demands an ongoing time commitment. As a result, it is not a series of acts you perform only when you need something; rather, it is a continuous process since you never know when someone could need you. Disseminate knowledge, provide pertinent information, and assist others in achieving success in life. Do it since you enjoy it.

Authenticity is essential.

Helping others achieve success and happiness will make you happier and more successful.

Nelson Mandela spent a large portion of his life in jail, which he describes as an "extended vacation for 27 years." He made the most of it by reading and writing, which helped him develop into the powerful leader that he was. "I am inherently an optimist," he said. Keeping one's feet going ahead and one's head pointing toward the sun is a necessary component of optimism. Successful, productive individuals have a lot of similar tendencies.

Can you tolerate pain, pressure, stress, interaction with nasty people, and unfavourable conditions while being joyful, committed to your purpose, successful, and persistent? What it means to be unbeatable is this. Mindset, skills, and habits that must be developed if you want to become invincible. These part was chosen based on the author's research over the previous ten years and his work with a variety of people, including students, senior professionals, and celebrities. Find the temperament is the amount of activity that ensures that businesses and individuals achieve their objectives and fulfil their desires. "Your Action," which enables you to break beyond business clichés and risk aversion while taking actual action to achieve your goals. Additionally, it shows how to proceed through the first three steps and establish the rule as a discipline. To get massive action outcomes, learn exactly where to start, what to do, and how to follow up on each action you take with additional action. How to overcome illogical fear and grow very self-assured! You're shown in this chapter and how to become incredibly confident quickly! What self-discipline and time management have in common, and why having both is essential to achieving your goals.

An underprivileged family gave birth to Rajinikanth, a cultural icon and hugely popular movie actor, as Shivaji Rao Gaikwad. His father was a police officer, and he grew up with four siblings after losing his mother when he was five years old. Following the completion of his formal education, Rajinikanth continued to work as a coolie, carpenter, and bus conductor in the cities of Bangalore and Madras. He saw an ad for acting classes while working as a bus driver and decided to sign up for them with the help of his friends. He was seen by Tamil film director K. Balachander when he was taking an acting class, and the rest is history. All these stories talk about one common thing in life is "positive thiniking."

Recently, NDTV named Super Star Rajinikanth one of the 25 Greatest Living Indian Legends. His acceptance speech is heartfelt and a testimonial to his life, which has been nothing short of amazing. Speaking at the NDTV Award, Rajinikanth said, "Most people don't believe in miracles, yet they do happen." A miracle occurs when a regular bus driver shares the dais with the greatest living legends. Yes, miracles do occur. Without their love and support, I would not be where I am today. I dedicate this honour to my brother Sathyanarayana Rao Gaikwad, who is like my father and mother, to my teacher Balachander, and to the people of Tamil Nadu.

A positive attitude may produce bad results just as easily as a negative mindset can provide good results. In addition, Henry Ford is credited with saying, "Whether you think you can or you think you can't, you're correct." Assisting others in achieving success seems to be a regular behaviour among successful people, and this habit promotes their success. Some could refer to it as karma. Some people can completely miss the link. But in actuality, relationships are the foundation of success. We create the world around us.

Always give yourself the benefit of the doubt. Don't give in easily or give up.

It has been demonstrated scientifically that smiling and laughing may elevate one's attitude and outlook on life. The best medicine is humor. Join a yoga laughter group for assistance in practising laughter and meditation to relax your body, mind, and spirit.

Write down your daily objectives and prioritise your list of tasks. Setting goals will provide you with the energy and inspiration you need to be content and successful in your life. Eating well and exercising will keep you in a fantastic mood and help keep your mind sharp. Run, go for a lengthy walk, or visit the gym. Include pranayam, yoga, and meditation in your everyday practise as well. These lessons may be used by almost anybody in any circumstance to improve their outlook on life. Positive thinking produces compound returns, so the more frequently you use it, the more advantages you'll experience.

Although the measures indicated above can help you manage your stress levels, certain people might additionally need psychological therapies. In many multispecialty hospitals medical team provides patients with individual counselling services to explain how to think positively.

Positive thinking can be harmful? Since it might make you oblivious to the situation's reality. I will tell you how, despite your best efforts, negativity may persist despite your efforts to dismiss it. There are far too many individuals in the world who constantly discuss "positive thinking." In a sense, you are attempting to run away from reality when you say, "Positive thinking." You don't want to consider things from only one perspective while ignoring the other. You have the option of ignoring the other, but you cannot ignore the other.You will live in a fool's paradise and suffer the consequences if you don't consider the bad things in the world. Imagine there are dark clouds in the sky right now. Imagine there are dark clouds in the sky right now. They won't ignore you, even if you want to ignore them. Rain falls when it wants to. You always get wet when you get wet.

Do any religious theories, practises, prayers, pilgrimages, or other religious rituals actually advance your cause? Do they aid you in developing your spiritual self and beginning a journey? Can you truly affect anything in the environment around you if you don't strive to alter who you are within? Genuine spirituality is more concerned with truth and eternal realities than with serenity and enjoyment. Finding the truth about oneself, flaws and all, is the most important aspect of any serious journey. But how many of you are willing to look yourselves in the eye and accept who you really are?

Productive people have productive habits.

As it happens, excellent leaders have a lot of the same behaviours. Developing good habits involves both doing and avoiding the appropriate things. The most productive habits practised by the most successful and productive people in the world are listed below. This list is intended to inspire you to create your own habits that will improve your effectiveness and productivity in daily life.

The fastest approach to meeting people and finding opportunities is through networking. The secret to success is relationships. At 12 years old, Steve Jobs utilised the Yellow Pages to locate and get in touch with Bill Hewlett, the co-founder of Hewlett-Packard. Jobs called the firm to request computer components but ended up getting a job there. When he was 22, Bill Clinton made and sent individual contact cards to every prominent person he met. This was advantageous when he campaigned for governor of Arkansas since he had over 10,000 connections in his personal network that he could readily call. It often comes down to who you know rather than what you know.

Successful people have a reputation for eschewing the conventional in favour of radical innovation. The largest change-makers and individuals who have contributed the most to developing society have always been those who refused to accept the status quo. Henry Ford, who established the Ford Motor Company, dramatically altered transportation when he unveiled the Model T, the first widely available car. If I had asked them what they wanted, they would have responded with faster horses, according to a famous quotation from him. And as Elon Musk works hard to achieve his objective of populating Mars, he imparts this wise counsel to anyone who might be thinking of taking a different path in life. "I'd advise people not to follow trends heedlessly.

Arriving early many successful people enjoy the early morning hours and maintain a routine that enables them to start the day off well. Tim Cook, the CEO of Apple, awakens at 3:45 AM and begins checking his emails. By 4:30 a.m., Michelle Obama is in the gym. Jack Dorsey, the CEO of Twitter and Square, gets up early to run 6 miles. "Not losing focus," Franklin once said.

Your attitude is the first step on the path to a happy life, and you have influence over your perspective.

Have you ever noticed how rushed everyone seems to be these days? So it feels somewhat unexpected but amazing when someone gives you their whole focus and attention. Getting this kind of energy boost might significantly impact your work. I prefer to refer to it as a "neurological nudge." We can really do more in less time because it truly wakes up the brain and gets you ready to perform at your best without causing all the stress-related wear and tear. Given everything you have to do during your busy day, or if you're in a meeting with an extremely full schedule, I understand that it may seem like a waste of time at first. However, this power is what allows us to operate. And our time management reveals where we put our efforts in order of importance.

We can't always offer our best if we aren't deliberate about how we show up in our time. So let's discuss how to receive that easy energy boost or neurological nudge throughout the day. Three options are available. Any encounter or conversation should begin with an honest energy exchange. Like expressing your gratitude, sharing a humorous anecdote, or developing relationships via enjoyable events that have absolutely nothing to do with business. People will remember it if you promptly make the most of your available time. Another technique is to never multitask and to be fully engaged in the discussion. Make genuine eye contact with the person you are conversing with, and turn off your phone. For instance, when I worked with my mentor, I most vividly recall the times when we engaged in conversation about a topic unrelated to work at all, and I could see he was really engaged. He would ask me a question and then genuinely appear engaged in the response, which at first struck me as odd. However, I always felt inspired and uplifted after such meetings.

Take some time to contemplate and ponder as well. Everyone benefits because you can respond to situations rather than merely reacting. We have improved health, are happier, and do considerably better at work. Please understand that I'm not discounting the value of your time. We are all aware of how valuable time is. We truly worry about it and are preoccupied with the idea that we don't have enough. I'm advocating that we put energy first so that we may use our time more effectively and feel better and happier while doing so.

Every living organism, including the human system, has some type of rhythm or pattern. Everything, including your heartbeat, brain waves, and blood sugar levels, should fluctuate. Your energy is no different. You want a rhythm or pattern to the way your energy rises and falls throughout the day. The fluctuation of energy will support your peak performance and make you feel less stressed. Before I give you some helpful advice on how to do that, I want you to take a moment to consider your own day. Or do you wake up and go and go and go and then be astonished when you can't unwind at night? Do you expend energy and then invest energy back in yourself to recharge? an energy flatline, in my opinion. Now, while it might sound a little excessive, my argument is just that. You're effectively taking over your own system and wearing yourself thin if you don't follow the normal course of stress and recuperation. How do you ensure that your energy fluctuates in a normal pattern each day?

Here are a few straightforward tactics you may use. First, if you drink coffee in the morning, take your time drinking it and read a few pages of a motivational book or listen to some motivating music to make it a conscious and perhaps even inspirational experience. In this way, your energy comes from more than simply coffee. Taking regular breaks during the day is definitely something I'd advise, especially if you find yourself spending a lot of time sitting down. Setting a timer to remind you every hour is the best course of action. Then stand up and go outside for five minutes. Your body receives an immediate boost from the activity and fresh air, and your mood may also be lifted.

Additionally, it will unquestionably sharpen your focus and attention for when you go back. You should also make an effort to obtain a full night's sleep each night. Although you've probably heard of it before, it's really important to refresh both your body and mind. Good sleep helps you wake up feeling more awake and decreases stress and inflammation. Sleep offers the brain the time and energy to evaluate your day and draw crucial connections between the significant events that occurred, which can help your memory. Nature follows these predictable rhythms, much like day and night, to keep us alert enough to be productive while maintaining a healthy balance with adequate rest, relaxation, and restoration. Furthermore, as we strengthen our ability to handle whatever life throws at us, the more we can really use the stress and problems in life to drive achievement.

"Your most unhappy customers are your greatest source of learning." –Bill Gates.

We must develop a love for the pursuit of goals and the sacrifices required in order to differentiate ourselves from the competition. Success comes to those who are willing to travel the difficult road and work toward difficult goals.

Without the so-called "work smart," I don't believe in luck or hard effort. It's not only about working hard; it's also about managing your time, resources, and thinking to get greater results."When it comes to things like team selection or job promotion, we will end up blending in with the herd if we choose the basic and straightforward routes in life.

There is no quick route to success; only steadfast labour may make one's life's goals and aspirations a reality. We frequently hear people's justifications for giving up. "It wasn't meant to be," "It wasn't enjoyable anymore," or "Life is all about having fun" are typical lines of speech that are used in response. It's important to note that our minds are capable of creating whatever mental state we give them. Instead, we should impose a commitment state that will enable everyone to realise their own goals.

Man needs his difficulties because they are necessary to enjoy success. Climbing to the top demands strength, whether it is to the top of Mount Everest or to the top of your career. Great dreams of great dreamers are always transcended.

The trip through life is not an easy one, and it gets even more difficult if you are working toward success in your endeavours. When things are difficult, your aspirations appear unattainable, and the circumstances are adverse, it is your conviction in yourself and your capacity to achieve your goals that keeps you going. When you have confidence in yourself, you work more diligently, passionately, and enthusiastically. You go into turbo mode because of the mental conditioning that says your efforts will pay off and you'll succeed; nothing can stop you from accomplishing your objectives. Your confidence will increase in direct proportion to how much you believe in yourself. You'll feel inspired to act, move beyond your comfort zone, seize new possibilities, take risks, and explore the unknown. Your confidence increases your self-assurance.

Self-belief is what motivates you to take action and won't let you give up until you achieve your goals.

Self-belief is the first step toward success. You start on a good note and give yourself a head start when you have a strong sense of self-belief. Self-belief believes that you will succeed even before you start. You carry out all the actions of a champion because you behave and think like a successful person.As a result of your victory, your success has started to materialise.

"Every morning in Africa, a gazelle wakes up. It knows it must move faster than the lion or it will not survive. Every morning, a lion wakes up knowing it must move faster than the slowest gazelle or it will starve. It doesn't matter if you are the lion or the gazelle, when the sun comes up, you better be moving." -Roger Bannister

Identity, significance, and perspective are the three dynamics that I name as being crucial to winning the war of the You-Factor. Knowing who you are and having a solid understanding of who you are establishes your identity. When you recognise your importance, you may realise the value and brilliance for which you were made. And if you grasp the concept of perspective, you may see your difficulties not as obstacles to success but as steppingstones to greatness. If you fully comprehend these three dynamics, you can control your You-Factor.

Healthy self-belief is neither arrogance, boasting, nor narcissism. Instead, it is a realistic yet upbeat assessment of who you are and what you are capable of. You are inspired to undertake things that you previously believed were impossible for you when you believe in yourself. You can take the first step, the next one, and then another step because of your faith. Before you know it, you're walking briskly along the road that once gave you anxiety.

The sensation of zeal you have from someone or something that provides you with fresh, imaginative things to accomplish is referred to as inspiration.

Successful individuals maintain concentration (obsessing over their goals). Maintaining concentration does not entail charging headlong towards your objectives while wearing blinders. Instead, it entails continually assessing your choices to make sure they are in line with your objectives. It involves keeping your objectives top of mind and making decisions based on whether they will likely move you closer to accomplishing them. Keep your focus on the goal and try not to be sidetracked or distracted, as the saying goes.

"The difference between average people and achieving people is their perception of and response to failure." — John C. Maxwell

I'm as proud of many of the things we haven't accomplished as of the ones we have, as Steve Jobs famously stated. Innovation is a thousand no's at once. According to best-selling author Jim Collins, a great enterprise is more likely to perish from the indigestion of too many opportunities than from a famine of too few. Your outcomes will be more amazing the more narrowly you focus. Be a 20-year expert on one subject rather than a 1-year expert on 20 other things. "A man becomes wealthy, intelligent, and healthy by rising early."

"You can't connect the dots looking forward; you can only connect them looking backwards." So you have to trust that the dots will somehow connect in your future. You have to trust in something—your gut, destiny, life, karma, whatever. This approach has never let me down, and it has made all the difference in my life. " -Steve Jobs

When we are young, we create goals and aspirations that we want to achieve. In order to do that, we need to have the necessary information, abilities, and, most importantly, confidence to make all of these things stronger. For the same reason, we make an effort to follow anybody who can provide us with the support we need to accomplish all or any of these things, as doing so motivates us to pursue our aspirations. You get self-assurance that you can achieve something when you see that person or hear their remarks. Our parents are the first people who inspire us all because they help us develop the confidence we need to begin thinking rationally.

Our culture is more preoccupied with justice than the business world is. If you look at the newspaper marriage ads, it says that the girl or the guy should be fair, in addition to other things. The Indian market has a large consumer base for fairness creams. I want customers to understand that they are not required to become fair. I think it's important that those who advertise these goods shoulder some of the blame as well, since they might not be aware of how they're not just promoting their goods but also developing an inferiority mentality. That's not right!

You may encounter many defeats, but you must not be defeated. In fact, it may be necessary to encounter the defeats, so you can know who you are, what you can rise from, how you can still come out of it.

How to make sure you remain on path and finish what you started when the unexpected occurs! You will discover a highly useful approach in this chapter that is not present in any other chapter. There are a lot of suggestions to help you determine what you want in life in general! You won't ever run out of life-altering thoughts again. The most important step you must take to guarantee your success! Fortunately, this topic demonstrates how simple this is. Your systems determine how high you can fall. Here, you'll find a tried-and-true strategy that can help you succeed.

Working towards your goals and dreams can be challenging because the path to success is always a bumpy one.

Because people like to reward those who are willing to put up the effort necessary to complete all duties in order to succeed in life, hard work is something that has to be recognised. A person with discipline, devotion, and resolve to succeed in life is someone who works hard enough. You can achieve anything with effort. We have heard this piece of advice so frequently that its original meaning has been obscured. The issue is that despite our seeming laborious efforts, nothing seems to be happening. Many worthwhile goals in life need a lot of hard work to be accomplished. It's possible that working hard isn't always enjoyable or desirable. When you put off a difficult job, issues may develop in a variety of ways later. Laziness, which has a variety of negative effects on our lives, can be encouraged by avoiding hard labour.

Although your goals won't be attained right away, you will gain a competitive edge. Having a strong sense of attraction to something might help develop new values. You'll be able to view events from an insider's vantage point. If this helps you develop a better grasp of how to provide that value, it will be a significant benefit for you.

"Your success would be defined by your own confidence and fortitudes"-Michelle Obama

We frequently find ourselves in circumstances where we can instantly tell if something is correct or wrong. Perhaps you witnessed a coworker being treated unfairly and believe the situation to be wholly unjust. Alternatively, perhaps you were asked to do a project at work and knew right away what the appropriate course of action was. We've all experienced the sensation at some point that, despite not having all the information, we just knew something to be true. This conviction that you are doing something correctly is built on beliefs. Your beliefs are the people or things in whom you have trust, faith, or confidence. They are cognizant of something's veracity. Because of how strongly you feel about some things, you frequently respond to circumstances in an instant, almost reflexively. It's remarkable that we frequently struggle to recognise our beliefs and that we rarely take the time to delve deeper and learn the truth.

What makes it so crucial that we comprehend our beliefs? Enhancing your self-awareness will allow you to make correct self-assessments, control your emotions, and understand how you come across to others while improving your self-confidence. This is because the first stage in developing self-awareness is knowing and recognising your beliefs. How you act and engage with other people will be influenced by your views. Your emotions are also governed by your beliefs. You will experience emotions depending on whether you think something is right or wrong. Making an effort to recognise and comprehend your core beliefs is essential if you want to improve your self-awareness.

Self-awareness requires dedication and concentration. As a result, you may strengthen your connections, which will enable you to respond positively to adversity, transform setbacks into opportunities, build confidence, and generally make you happy. As with mastering any new ability, you will undoubtedly go through ups and downs. This is very normal, and if you need more help, I advise you to persist with it and revisit the techniques from this book. You can achieve the outcomes you desire and make the influence you desire in your life if you make a commitment to exercising control and increasing your self-awareness. Wishing you luck as you go. Please feel free to contact me or find out more by going to my website. Remain devoted and focused, and keep in mind that even if it's difficult, I have every confidence you can figure out how to make the most of the circumstance and continue growing as a person.

Your thinking sets all of the boundaries. You have put yourself on the definite route to success the moment you decide to pick yourself up, depend on yourself, and have faith in your capacity to become an expert in your field. It doesn't matter if you start off with skill, knowledge, or competence.

People that are successful never give up on what they really believe in. Though you've done your homework and know that your beliefs are the right ones for you, even if many others disagree with them, you shouldn't give up on them without a struggle. Perseverance leads to success. Perseverance breeds grit, and success is the result of grit. Persistence is essential if you want to succeed, even if it takes years to complete a task. Remind yourself of your goals whenever you feel like giving up. You will be able to persevere as long as your "why" is compelling.

In today's world, successful individuals are easy to come by. Every time we turn on the television, we see pictures of sportsmen being celebrated for their victories. We read articles in newspapers and publications about successful businesspeople scheming for their next lucrative investment idea. Our favourite actors and actresses may be found in movies as well, and they frequently amass more wealth through their labour in a single year than some of us will ever see. The media is prepared to show us the outcomes of these people, but they omit to reveal the processes involved. All of these folks put forth a lot of effort and commitment to get where they are. People compete for top honours and grades in school and college, for better positions at work, and to launch their own businesses in our world of continual competition. I have shared the most inspiring stories of those who used their indomitable perseverence to accomplish their goals on this planet.

Dream while you sleep, and when you wake up, you'll be determined to reach your goals.

CHAPTER FOUR

Finding Your Greatest Strengths

"Motivating others to take action towards a clear, immediate objective is the purpose of motivation. People need to be offered something they desire in return when you're trying to persuade them to do something they might not necessarily want to do."

When you have self-belief, no setback or failure can make you lose confidence or cast doubt on your abilities. You won't always succeed despite your best efforts; you'll make errors like everyone else and make blunders, miss opportunities, and perform poorly. But there is a distinction. Your confidence gives you power.

You have to do it, and Roger Bannister is an example of this. He achieved the unthinkable and broke the "Four minute" barrier because he was absolutely positive that he would succeed, not simply because he thought he could. Many thousands of attempts ended in failure. Both physicians and scientists concurred that it couldn't be done. Not only was it risky, but it was also impossible. "Anyone who tried to run a mile in under four minutes would perish in an idiotic endeavour." He had an incorrect bone structure, too much wind resistance, insufficient lung capacity, and a heart that could not withstand the effort.

"However ordinary each of us may seem, we are all in some way special, and can do things that are extraordinary, perhaps until then...even thought impossible." — Sir Roger Bannister

In order to be as effective as you can be, it is crucial to be enthusiastic about the task you are doing. Steve lived this out every day. Never content with less than the best, he worked tirelessly to achieve excellence in all facets of his profession with the goal of building a company he could be proud of. To sum up, Steve Jobs was a role model and will be missed. He accomplished a great amount of work each day he lived on this planet, mostly as a result of his outstanding work ethic and desire to make the world a better place. He was, in our opinion, among the best motivational speakers of all time, and his modest teachings will endure for all time.

Whatever angle you choose, they all agree that hard work is the secret to real success.

People have been attempting to break the 4-minute barrier for years and years. Some came very, very close, but the record remained at 4:01.30 for about nine years as runners began to believe that perhaps, just perhaps, the experts were correct. Perhaps the human body had reached its limit, making it impossible. Then, on May 6, 1954, a chilly and rainy day in Oxford, England, a man by the name of Roger Bannister appeared to alter everything when, at the age of 25, he accomplished the unimaginable and ran the distance in 3:59.4. Everything that had previously been thought to be impossible became suddenly possible, and all preconceived notions that it couldn't be done were disproved.

In reality, he often imagined achieving the goal as part of his training to instil confidence in his mind and body. Before actually breaking the record, he had experienced what it was like to do so. Without seeing any tangible evidence that it was possible, he was the only one who could generate assurance inside himself.

Even more astounding than Bannister's inconceivable, world-record-breaking run is the fact that another runner achieved the same feat just 46 days later. And this time, he sprinted the distance in only 3.57.9 seconds, a whole 1.5 seconds quicker. Yes, another runner achieved the impossible not much longer than six weeks after Bannister.

"With each encounter, when we truly pause to confront fear, we acquire strength, bravery, and confidence." We need to take action on what we believe we cannot. " -Eleanor Roosevelt

However, as more and more athletes came to believe that it was feasible, more and more of them smashed the mark. By the end of 1957, almost three years after Bannister's unbelievable, record-breaking run, 16 athletes had also done the unthinkable and broken the four-minute barrier. How on earth is it even possible? How is it possible that other runners started to break the four-minute barrier so soon after Bannister did? Has human evolution had a rapid upswing? Did every runner suddenly start to improve? Did everyone alter their exercise and nutrition at the same time? Or was there another factor at play—something deeper?

You see, all it took was one man with a notion so deeply embedded in his head to challenge experts in his field and accomplish the seemingly impossible. You must act when you have such a strong belief in something and such a clear picture of it in your mind that it becomes your reality. Whatever it is, I don't care.

Roger Bannister is such a light and an example of mankind because of this. Not just because he was a fast runner or ran a mile in under four minutes, but also because he demonstrated to us that the only limitations we face are those that we place on ourselves. He accomplished the inconceivable, the unthinkable, and what both science and medical professionals believed could not be done.

It doesn't matter if you start off with skill, knowledge, or competence. Self-belief is the first step toward success. You start on a good note and give yourself a head start when you have a strong sense of self-belief.

Never let anyone tell you what you can or cannot do. Don't allow other people's limitations to restrict your vision. You will find a way if you don't give up on something you genuinely believe in.

Self-belief believes that you will succeed even before you start. You carry out all the actions of a champion because you behave and think like a successful person. As a result, your success starts to materialise because success becomes a skill that feeds itself.

You can do things you never imagined possible if you can get rid of your self-doubt and have faith in yourself. What is the relationship between accomplishment and self-belief? Self-belief is the foundation upon which you can build the life of your dreams. Your protection against the what-if scenario that occasionally enters your mind is self-belief. Self-belief keeps you going when you are aware that the deck is stacked against you, your opponent is stronger than you, and everyone believes that you can't compete with him.

The inner voice encourages you to follow your gut, rise to the occasion, and take measured risks. By doing so, you may expand your horizons and empower yourself to achieve greater things. High self-esteem and a feeling of self are characteristics of those who believe in themselves. They have unconditional love and acceptance for themselves and don't care what people think or say about them. Their own opinions are the only ones that matter to them.

All of your self-doubts, anxieties, and apprehensions are dispelled by self-belief. People with conviction are motivated from the inside out and exert great effort to achieve their objectives. Only when you have a strong belief from the inside out can you overcome obstacles and give every task you take on your best effort. When you decide to seek achievement, you will frequently face hardships and challenges. However, having confidence in yourself will give you the strength to act with unwavering dedication to your objective.

No one is born with all the skills, abilities, or information; everyone learns in their areas of passion.

When you have confidence, you understand that you alone are accountable for your achievements and that, with enough willpower, you can accomplish everything you set your mind to. There is an abundance of information available, and there are no restrictions on the knowledge or skills you may pick up. The convenience of having everything at our fingertips in the digital era is a gift. All you need is an eagerness to learn and an open mind. When you have self-belief, no setback or failure can make you lose confidence or cast doubt on your abilities. You won't always succeed despite your best efforts; you'll make errors like everyone else and make blunders, miss opportunities, and perform poorly. But there is a distinction. Your confidence gives you power.

Whether you are aware of it or not, you engage in negotiations on a daily basis. A highly useful talent that isn't frequently taught is how to bargain without undervaluing yourself or deceiving the other side. Making a win-win outcome of a negotiation produces a positive image in the opposing party's mind, which enhances the likelihood of receiving more favours. Naturally, Jobs left college to follow his creativity. We are all aware of the outcome. His curiosity and intuition then, and throughout his life, allowed him to "stumble across" several sources of inspiration that would have a significant impact on his subsequent works.

Your self-belief factor reveals easy actions you can start using right away if you're ready for a significant change in your energy, perspective, and financial wellness. It delivers fresh tales, explains new processes, and offers new ideas. You always lean forward to the task at hand. No one can stop you from performing the work if you are motivated enough. Nobody can stop you from disclosing the truth. This will make it easier for all of you to confront the reality of life.

Once the beloved donkey of a guy plunges into a narrow chasm. It doesn't matter how hard he tries; he can't get it out. As a result, he decides to bury it alive.

From above, soil is being poured onto the donkey. The donkey feels the weight, stomps on it, and shakes it off. They dump in more dirt.

It shrugs it off and advances. The burden got higher as more was dumped on it. The donkey was munching on lush meadows by lunchtime.

After much shaking off of issues and moving forward, one will graze in green pastures.

"Believe in yourself! Have faith in your abilities! Without a humble but reasonable confidence in your own powers you cannot be successful or happy."-Norman Vincent Peale

It takes a lot of confidence to maintain and accomplish your goals, and negative thinking about yourself is useless. It will just make you feel worse. Make the decision to maintain your good attitude; it will benefit you, especially through your most trying times. According to Will Smith, "You simply decide, and the universe is going to get out of your way." Will Smith went from being divorced and on the verge of bankruptcy to being a megastar.

Self-belief and hard work will always earn you success.

On Extreme Makeover, a celebrity trainer assists those who are extremely overweight in losing weight. The characters in the programme occasionally have poor attitudes, but other times, they absolutely amaze you, like Sara. Sara is a small person, standing about 4‘5" tall. At the beginning of her trip, she spoke about nutrition on local television programmes, but she was ashamed of herself. She had not only struggled with her diminutive height her entire life but also with her sister's cruel treatment of her. She started overeating and gained 200 pounds by the time she was 37 years old.

By altering your thoughts, you may attract wonderful chances into your life and achieve your objectives by using tried-and-true methods.

Her first task on Extreme Makeover was to ascend the stairs of an amphitheatre while carrying an 80-pound weight. The stairway rose over her knees. Yet she never voiced a complaint. She continued on. Everyone in the theatre gradually began to pay attention to her. The people were clapping for her by the time she got to the last step.

Six months after beginning her diet and training regimen, her trainer set the goal for her to complete a half marathon. Sara answered no. She refused to complete the half. She would rather do a full marathon. That would be particularly difficult for her physique, and thus her trainer recommended against it. Due to her small stature, she would need to walk many more steps.

Sara was unconcerned. She finished the entire marathon. She achieved her goals of losing more than half of her body weight and taking up running.

Life is a wonderful adventure that should be enjoyed to the fullest every day. The fact that life is a wonderful gift, however, implies that you must wake up ready to grasp the day. So, overcome your fear and go with the flow of the universe; discover your higher purpose, and become a role model for others.

Vadilal Gandhi is creating a 650-crore-rupee ice cream business by selling soda pop. Vadilal, an ice cream company that Vadilal Gandhi began in Gujarat in 1907 and is still well-known in India and 45 other countries. The ice cream Vadilal has humble origins in Gujarat, even before India became independent in 1907. It is currently a well-known brand across the whole country.

The company began making ice cream using the traditional Kothi process, which involved churning milk, ice, and salt in a hand-operated machine. The firm now provides its customers with over 200 unique ice cream flavours made at its state-of-the-art production facilities. The Better India discovered more about Vadilal's rich heritage via an interview with Kalpit Gandhi, a fifth-generation family company owner. After Ranchod Lal Gandhi assumed control of the business, Vadilal started to focus more on ice creams.

Vadilal established its first ice cream parlour in 1926. The same year saw the introduction of an ice cream machine from Germany. By the time India attained independence, the company had four sites dispersed around the city. By the time Ranchod Lal Gandhi's sons, Ramchandra and Laxman Gandhi, joined the business in the early 1970s, Vadilal had expanded to twelve locations in Ahmedabad. Vadilal constantly establishes a warm and unique connection with its customers. One of its selling points was that all of its ice creams were entirely vegetarian and were advertised as being appropriate for consumption even during times of religious fasting. This company has always had its finger on the pulse of the consumer.

The company allegedly "entered the processed food sector in the early 1990s and developed Vadilal Quick Treat," according to the allegation. In 1995, Vadilal was the first Indian company to sell frozen vegetables in the United States. He further notes that each of their sites has a green cover of close to 60% and that all of the wastewater is transferred to a treatment plant and used for the lawns and gardens within the buildings.

After earning a reputation for itself in Gujarat, the company started looking for ways to develop and started its expansion in 1985. By the 1990s, the fourth generation of the Gandhi family had joined the business. This comprises Virendra, Rajesh, and Shailesh Gandhi, the three sons of Ramchandra Gandhi, and Devanshu Gandhi, a son of Laxman Gandhi.

The company's trade name when it was listed on the Bombay Stock Exchange (BSE) in 1990 was Vadilal Industries Ltd. Two names from the family were added to the BSE due to a family split in the same year. After posting revenue of Rs 650 crore in the fiscal year 2019–20, the organisation is still confident about increasing revenue this year. Kalpit claims that Vadilal, which is sold in 45 other countries, is presently the most popular Indian ice cream brand in the US. With pride, Kalpit says that while doing business ethically is essential to the reputation of the company, they also greatly value and work to protect the environment.

Roadblocks and failures become speed bumps in your way when you have an unquenchable appetite combined with dedication and effort to accomplish a goal.

You will get various experiences via hard labour, which will strengthen and improve you as a person. Simply be patient and believe in yourself. We want to be respected by those around us and have our thoughts valued. This is exactly what hard work and self-esteem boosting bring us. People always value those that put in the effort and are aware of their potential, regardless of how successful they are currently or will be. Working hard will help you improve every day and every moment. We frequently reflect on our past and ask ourselves, "What have we learned?" Working hard makes us better in every way; it turns a novice into an expert. Growth is not possible without effort.

Bill Gates reads more than 50 books annually, while Warren Buffett spends 80% of his day reading. Sam Walton picked the name Wal-Mart over Walton-Mart to save money on signs, while Shark Tank's Kevin O'Leary would rather save $2.50 than spend it on a Starbucks. Although adopting the behaviours of these role models won't put you on the fast track to landing rockets on Mars, it can set you up for great success.

Following in the footsteps of others, especially successful ones, makes learning life lessons much simpler. And after viewing the biographical film "Jobs," which is based on the life of Apple co-founder Steve Jobs, I discovered that there are many lessons to be learned just from the way his persona is portrayed. Making goods that straddled the lines between art and technology, intuitiveness and design, was central to Jobs' ideology. He was able to live his philosophy and, in turn, inspire others because he was open to being inspired.

It's crucial to believe that people are fundamentally decent and intelligent and that, with the right tools, they can do great things. "Tools are simply that—tools." They either function properly or they don't. To put it another way, Jobs felt that the finest ideas come from the confluence of technology and the humanities. Thus, in order to succeed greatly and bring about revolutionary changes in the world, we must learn to prioritise this area.

We're talking about B. Ravi Pillai, a businessman from Kollam, a seaside town in Kerala, who now resides in Dubai. As the farmer's son, 68-year-old B. Ravi Pillai had hardships growing up. Although he suffered from poverty, he made a lot of effort to get out of it. Ravi Pillai is the first Indian to possess a $100 billion Airbus helicopter. Because they don't have the chance to make their dreams come true, many people are compelled to give up on their goals. But this person put a lot of effort into getting what he desired, and he was finally successful in achieving it.

Ravi Pillai has always aspired to be an entrepreneur. Along with his studies at Kochi University, he started it. At this point, he started his own chit-fund company by borrowing Rs 1 lakh from a local moneylender. After his company began to generate profits and he paid off his debt, he did so. Then he started his own building company. Ravi Pillai experienced several highs and lows during his life. He experienced a major setback when he was given the contract by Vellore Hindustan Newsprint Factory. He had to shut down his company as a result of a strike by workers. But Pillai wasn't one to give up quickly. He travelled to Saudi Arabia in 1978 after departing from India.

He rapidly founded his own construction company, Nasser S. Al Hajri Corporation, with 150 workers (NSH). His construction company expanded as NSH began landing big contracts, such as one to build a hangar for a French aviation company. In addition to this, his company was building the Royal Terminal, a $50 million project. B Ravi Pillai, who was raised in an agricultural family, today employs around 70,000 people across several enterprises. Forbes estimates Pillai's net worth to be $2.5 billion. His wealth may be extrapolated from the 30,000 guests from 42 countries that came to his daughter's wedding, including CEOs of significant online businesses and members of Middle Eastern royal families. According to Forbes magazine, Ravi Pillai is one of the top 1000 richest people in the world. He is also recognised as Kerala's richest person.

Ravi Pillai received the Pravasi Bhartiya Samman in 2008 and the Padma Shri from the Indian government in 2010. He graduated with a degree in philosophy from New York's Excelsior College. B. Ravi Pillai's leadership and tenacity may serve as an example for many young people, since he can tolerate and accept any form of setback merely because he is confident in their ability to succeed.

How do you turn rejection into success?

The amount of rejection you experience is typically inversely correlated with your level of success. The enemy of success is rejection anxiety. If you postpone making difficult calls out of concern that others may reject you (such as clients, workers, coworkers, or colleagues), your effectiveness will suffer.

There is likely a reason this didn't work out the way you expected, and I like to believe it is because you deserve something even better!

When you challenge the ideas and presumptions that led to your experience of rejection, you can lessen its negative effects. Examine the expectations of other individuals who are doing what you are doing if you feel like you are receiving too many rejections. For instance, before identifying a prospect, salespeople may make 100 calls; similarly, before receiving financing, entrepreneurs may give presentations to dozens of investors. Disassociate yourself from the result of the scenario if you are emotionally invested in the other person. If you believe the other person to be extremely significant, balance your appreciation with a healthy dose of realism. Even well-known business moguls are often below-average performers who luck into success. Even if not, they are still just regular individuals like you and me and not gods on earth.

But overcoming that fear is just the beginning. If you truly want to succeed, you must figure out how to use rejection as a tool to propel you closer to your long-term objectives. Imagine you get the opportunity to present your elevator pitch to a significant investor. Despite your best efforts, the investor just tells you to "go away" or, worse yet, "your concept stinks; we'll contact you." If you were hoping to get any investment capital, it is undoubtedly a dismal result. But why would you feel "rejected" as opposed to, say, annoyed, irate, or sad?

The reason is that, rather than focusing on the problem itself, you took the investor's remarks personally and allowed them to make you feel horrible about yourself.

There are three main reasons why people feel rejected:

It happens frequently. Let's say you've approached 100 investors, all of whom have responded negatively. Since you are very certain that your concept is brilliant, you draw the inference that there must be a problem with you based on "public opinion." While you're feeling invested emotionally. Anyone who has ever been married can relate to the fact that when you've invested a lot of time and energy into a relationship, it hurts far more when the other person disagrees with you on a matter that is important to you. When the "rejector" is respected. The "rejection" seems to have more force and weight when you have a strong and enduring regard for the person who isn't acting the way you'd like. It's crucial to be aware of these elements because, in order to take advantage of the circumstance, you must first reduce the "sting" of the rejection.

The most successful people will tell you that they would not be who they are today if they had not faced rejection head on!

After gaining some perspective on your feelings, it's important to use some practical reasoning to distinguish between legitimate and unjustified complaints. When a person refuses to do what you ask them to because of anything within your control, this is a justified refusal. When your "failure" occurred as a result of an arbitrary event outside of your control, that rejection is illegitimate. You meet with a client and say something stupid, such as the wrong client's name. The customer's departure is a legitimate rejection because you were to blame for the triggering event.

In comparison, let's say you contact a potential customer on the phone, and they shout a profanity before hanging up. Despite the fact that this is how "sales rejection" is typically defined, the prospect's response has nothing to do with you. You were unaware that the potential customer you were calling was both preoccupied and irritable. Anyone who had contacted that potential would have undoubtedly received the same response. It is not an appropriate denial. The fact is, there are much more invalid rejections in business than legitimate ones. The correct approach is to dismiss the invalid ones because there is nothing you can do about them. Honestly, they aren't about you, so don't take them personally.

It applies to everyone equally. Anyone who is successful in any field will all exhibit the same traits. They don't feel bad about their job since they're at the beginning of a new learning curve and it's decent but not outstanding. Instead, they are eager to learn and go up the curve more quickly. The proverb "You have to break a few eggs, to create a perfect omelette" is one that they genuinely live by. Let me put something in a different way. Cooking itself can start to become as delightful as the finished product.

You may train yourself to value learning and attempting just as much as success. When you sincerely adopt this straightforward approach, the advantages may be significant.You can develop your resilience to failure's drawbacks, for instance. Meaning that as time goes on, you become less afraid of failing and less ashamed of failing. Additionally, you develop greater tenacity in the face of difficulty. You become a better risk-taker and acquire skills more quickly. Your chances of success are increased by a combination of all of these factors. It all depends on how you approach the matter in your head. The primary objective is to create the conditions and mindset that increase the likelihood of success, not to actually accomplish success. Get going straight away. Find a place that is calm and a writing tool. When was the last time you undertook a truly difficult or novel task?

The well-known fashion brand Chanel was founded by Gabrielle Bonheur "Coco" Chanel, a French fashion designer and entrepreneur. The contributions Coco Chanel has made to the world of fashion and design, including their characteristic smell, little black dresses, tweed jackets, bell-bottomed trousers, and gold-chained purses, make her one of the great personalities.

As a result of Coco's strong conviction that fashion cannot be limited to couture garments, accessories and perfumes have become integral components of the industry. She sang on stage and worked as a seamstress to save money for her first business. Coco was able to open her first business in Paris in 1913 before opening a second one in Deauville.

Today, if you're a leader of any kind, you can't just yell orders at people and expect them to comply. If you are looking, they might comply with your instructions, but if you leave them alone, they will resume doing what they perceive to be essential.

More than ever before, today's leaders must gain the support of their followers. There are two basic strategies for accomplishing this: inspiration and motivation. Although the two words are frequently used interchangeably, depending on what you want to accomplish, they actually signify rather different things.

Motivation is used by coaches when they motivate their teams at halftime. Even if they might be too exhausted or discouraged to try, they want their players to sprint back onto the field or court with newfound vigour and determination. Their merit? Victory. Don't be ambiguous, since the goal of motivation is to compel others to act. Be careful not to say something like, "I want everyone to achieve their best." Instead, say, "I need you to come in over the weekend so we can finish this job before the deadline."

Unstoppable individuals resemble warriors. They are always prepared to face the world. They are driven by an inner light, possess limitless energy, and are unshakable in their objectives. They now know how to use their innate talents and acquire the abilities needed to succeed in anything they set out to do.

Those who are unstoppable are in their own world. They don't compete with anyone but themselves. You never know what they will do — only that you will be forced to respond. Even though they don't compete with you, they make you compete with them.

Unstoppable individuals take enormous risks without waiting till they feel "comfortable." They plunge in and proceed! Action is key to success, from the initial push to get things started to those pivotal times when you must change your direction. It may be both dreadful and thrilling to make significant decisions and leaps of faith. This is your moment to be fearless and think big. Inaction can occasionally be masked by other problems, such as ineffective time management or a lack of discipline. Stop procrastinating and stop putting it off. Put your energies into action right now if you want to be persistent. If you don't, your goal will remain unrealized and gather dust on a shelf.

- **How do they achieve this?**
- **Where do they get the strength and endurance to carry on?**

Unstoppable people maintain their inner flames by cultivating the traits required for success.

The real secret to success is to form new behaviours and break old patterns. You can do this by learning how to:

- Identify the secret to better health, more energy, and a better mood.
- Optimise your mental performance and feel more alert with six nootropics.
- Interrupt your stress response by breathing.
- Align your biochemistry with your soul's purpose in simple steps.
- Increase your cognitive load gradually to become a better version of yourself.
- Gain access to the unstoppable assessment as well to identify your identity type, gauge your energy, and develop a strategy for going beyond your own limitations to become unstoppable.
- Disrupt your stress reaction via breathing.

"The difference between outstanding and unstoppable is the determination to narrow the gap between near-perfect and perfect," said Albert Einstein.

You may develop certain qualities can help you advance from being a solid achiever to a person who is absolutely unstoppable.

- You don't even care about the end result. The goal of the climb is to test your personal limits. Do you feel resentful as a result? without a doubt. You are completely appreciative and humbled by everything in your life. As a result, you will never become complacent or lazy. The easiest way to enjoy life is to finish one objective and get immediately into the next one. The only way to enjoy another meal is to become hungry, so don't stay too long at the table of prosperity.
- Use any label you like—gutsy, brazen, badass—but the fact is that confidence is essential if you want to be unstoppable. To begin with, you must have the courage to put yourself out there. You must have confidence in your abilities. The largest barriers you'll face are going to be mental ones—the sort that make you doubt who you are and what you're doing. When you should be looking for a solution to overcome failure, you'll be inclined to accept defeat if you don't have a healthy dose of self-confidence.
- Avoid rivalry with others. Make them struggle against you. The majority of people compete with other people. They frequently check in to see what their "competition"—those in their immediate vicinity—is up to. They imitate and reproduce what is "working" as a result. In contrast, you've abandoned any rivalry. To you, competing with others makes no sense at all. You are dragged away from your genuine self. As a result, you tune out all the outside noise and focus on the internal pressure to create.

- You have control over what you put in your body, how you spend your time, and how long you stay in the zone, in contrast to most individuals who are dependent on narcotics or other outside stimuli. Act on instinct rather than impulse. You don't necessarily have to, since you could. And if you do, it will be out of choice, not obligation.
- You need to form the habit of persistence to get through difficult circumstances and prevent procrastination from winning. Long-term goals need a lot of work. You must be there every day, rebuffing discouragement and keeping your attention on your goal. Understanding who we are as individuals, outside of the roles we perform with friends and family or in society, comes from developing self-awareness. Understanding who you really are—your behavioural patterns, strengths, and weaknesses—means being self-aware.
- Don't be concerned about failure's repercussions. Where it is safe, most people stay close to the earth. They won't be wounded too badly if they fall. However, if you decide to fly high, the fall may be fatal. and you accept that. You perceive neither a ceiling nor a floor. All of it is in your brain. If anything goes wrong, you make an adjustment and carry on. The weak-hearted waste time hopping from one opportunity to the next in search of the right one.
- Accept full responsibility for your mistakes. Extreme ownership demands working with a high level of humility and putting your ego in check. Any successful team must recognise its faults, accept responsibility for them, and create a strategy to deal with obstacles. Just the unvarnished facts you are solely responsible for your own mistakes. And if your team fails, you take

responsibility as the leader. You can only have total freedom and control with extreme ownership.

- Keep learning new things. The average person seeks amusement. People who are extraordinary pursue study and knowledge. You never stop learning if you want to excel at what you do. Your abilities and expertise are things you constantly hone and develop. Your strength comes from your unmatched preparation. Nobody else is prepared to pay what you did.
- Success doesn't suffice; it just adds to the burden. Most individuals consider being "successful" to be sufficient. Success, on the other hand, only increases the pressure to work harder if you're persistent. When a goal is accomplished, your attention immediately turns to the next task.
- Continue to develop your mental toughness. "Mental toughness is probably the most important quality in a world-class player, and it should be consistently cultivated." If left to my own devices, I am always thinking of new strategies to strengthen my psychological defences. My natural inclination when feeling uncomfortable is to become at peace with it. My natural tendency is to seek out challenges rather than avoid them.
- Stay loyal to who you are. Despite the fact that just one in three Americans say they are happy and that 70% of US workers despise their jobs, obstinate and irrepressible people remove everything from their lives that they despise. Possess the self-respect and self-assurance to conduct your life as you see fit. Change it when anything in your life isn't right. Immediately.
- You can establish a distinct vision. Every successful route begins with a vision because it gives you focus.

It is the motivation behind your arduous efforts. When you have a clear picture of how you want your future to turn out, you need to create a number of objectives to help you get there. Your mission is your vision, which you should have outlined in detail and documented. It's an opportunity to put your beliefs, principles, and ideals into action. Additionally, you may use it as a benchmark to track your development, gauge your success, and serve as a reminder of your goals.

- Your biggest asset is your confidence. It's been said before: A marathon requires considerably more mental than physical strength. The ability of a person to complete a marathon or any other difficult task is more a function of their level of confidence than of actual skill. Your level of confidence affects how big your objectives or goals are, how likely you are to succeed in achieving them, and how quickly you recover from setbacks. If you lack confidence, you won't even attempt to put yourself out there. No matter how many times you fail, you'll succeed if you're confident. It also doesn't matter how overwhelming the odds appear to be against you.
- Even if you are the most gifted, wisest, and most creative person in the world, you will achieve mediocrity at best if you lack perseverance. People who are successful and unstoppable are aware that in order to succeed, they must grit their teeth and dig deep. They overcome challenges to continue going forward, rather than letting them hold them back.
- Unstoppable people spend time getting to know themselves better. You'll get the ability to build on your strengths and identify areas in which self-improvement is required by doing this. Setting goals requires self-

awareness, which is essential for anyone who is unstoppable.

- Surround yourself with those that inspire you to think about the future rather than the past. You'll find it difficult to advance if you surround yourself with people from your past. This is why we find ourselves unable to escape from certain positions (e.g., the fat kid or shy girl). You can start over by surrounding yourself with people who inspire you. Your history no longer defines you; your only definition now is the future you are building. The Pygmalion Effect states that how well you do is greatly influenced by the expectations of others around you.
- Sometimes taking a step backward is necessary in order to advance. You're probably treading water if you're worn out, unwell, dissatisfied, and unable to retain your energy. Being relentless requires taking care of one's body, mind, and soul in order to maintain a balanced state.
- You must maintain your physical and mental well-being in order to do everything else on this list. Maintaining a healthy work-life balance is essential for preventing burnout, relieving chronic stress, and avoiding other mental health problems like depression and anxiety.
- Let things go, but remember them always. The research is clear: Forgiving others improves both physical and mental health. We should all think about forgiving others, but don't forget to forgive yourself as well. Having no extra mental or emotional baggage is a must for being unstoppable. As a result, you'll need to totally and instantly forgive everyone who has done you wrong. But accepting forgiveness does not entail forgetting. Additionally, it does not obligate you to continue doing

business with individuals who have harmed you.

- Set definite goals. Short-term objectives may be helpful developmental tools if they are balanced within a supportive long-term perspective, even though a concentration on outcomes is undoubtedly detrimental. Several psychological studies have shown that objectives with a clear definition and a deadline are the most motivating. Your objectives may be behavior-based (for example, "I'm going to write 500 words every day") or outcome-based (for example, "I'm going to get published on The Times by Jan 1, 2024").
- Every industry will see upheaval and radical transformation. Relentless people don't allow change to stop them from achieving their goals. They are aware that if they are not adaptable and robust, they run the danger of losing their usefulness and relevance. Either you learn to flex and bend, or you will be broken and thrown away.
- People who are unstoppable remain calm in the face of change. They recognise the value of adaptability and the need to welcome new ideas and advancements. Being adaptive entails having a flexible mentality and changing as your surroundings change.
- Refrain from being driven by money or other outside factors. It is good to have lovely stuff. However, for you, it has never been about the cash, the fame, or anything else external. If you don't have these things, nothing will change for you. You'll continue to exert yourself and give it everything you've got. If I give you these items, they will not kill you, as they do for the majority of people.
- People who are unstoppable possess an inner drive that drives them to achievement. They are intrinsically

driven, which means they have a strong internal urge or desire to achieve their objectives. You feel motivated to keep going even if there is no external reward when inspiration originates from inside; it tends to be more significant.

- Prefer simplicity to complexity. You don't understand anything well enough if you can't describe it clearly. Einstein, Albert It's simple to be complex. In academia and industry, most research and language are overly complex. Being straightforward and striking the truth square in the face is difficult. "Simplicity is the greatest sophistication," remarked Leonardo da Vinci. Very few individuals will be honest with you. Asking them a question causes things to get extremely difficult.
- Be ready at all times so you can respond spontaneously. Creative leaps are rooted in a technological basis, much like the yin-yang symbol has a kernel of light in the dark and of darkness in the light. So that your right brain can have unrestricted freedom to invent and disobey the rules, learn the left brain's rules inside and out. Your experience of time will slow down as your consciousness grows. You will see things in more frames than others. While they are attempting to respond, you will be able to modify the situation to your liking.
- Behaviorally-oriented objectives are more effective and inspiring for the majority of individuals. However, if you are so focused on the results that the job loses meaning, your goal should be to achieve those results. However, short-term objectives that are based on your long-term vision and philosophy are preferable to results-focused objectives. The how will be taken care of once your why is strong enough. Make a list of your own "WHY."

- Develop the ability to act right away when you believe you ought to. Quit analysing yourself. Don't think about it. Never doubt whether it exists. Don't doubt if it originated with God or with you. Just do it. Once you start acting, you'll know what to do. The situation will remain hypothetical unless you take action. But once you do anything, it becomes useful.
- In order to acquire the wisdom and understanding required to seek even greater aspirations and objectives, they acknowledge both and learn from them. Accepting responsibility is realising that you are the only one in control of your life. Nobody else can decide how your future will turn out since you are in control. Because we frequently emulate the attitudes and actions of the people we spend time with, relationships are an essential element of life. You could develop a gloomy outlook if you spend too much time with negative individuals.
- Individuals that are successful and unstoppable surround themselves with positive people. They are drawn to other ambitious people. Seek out people who can inspire you and whose perspectives can help you see new possibilities.
- Know what to do; don't think. Stop thinking. You are already aware of what has to be done and how to go about doing it. What's holding you back? Every wise choice I've ever made has come from my gut, as Oprah Winfrey has stated. I've made a lot of bad decisions because I didn't pay attention to my inner voice. You've already lost when you start to think. Do what seems right to you, in sync with your senses, and with total confidence in yourself. Quick thinking takes you out of the moment.

- Pick up knowledge by learning it. Never be jealous or envious of another person's success. Being unstoppable entails having the best interests of everyone in mind, including those you would view as rivals. Envy and jealousy are manifestations of the ego, which is driven by fear. You celebrate other people's successes since it has nothing to do with you, which makes you pleased for them. You have control over yourself. and you are unique from everyone else who has ever stepped foot on this planet up to this point and throughout all of time. No one else is capable of doing what you are. You possess a special talent and a special capacity to contribute. And you're going to carry out that plan.
- Avoid becoming distracted by your successes' outcomes. Keep your attention on the labour that produced those outcomes. When you start accomplishing things of consequence, there are advantages that may become distractions. To "surf the wave" of your prior labour might seem simple. Continue to train. Make your craft better. Never lose sight of how you got here. Think and do 10 times more. When you use 10X as your benchmark, it's easy to see how you can go around what everyone else is doing. 10X thinking naturally gets you 'beyond the box' of your existing hurdles and restrictions," according to Dan Sullivan. It frees you from the issues that the majority of people are facing and exposes you to an altogether new range of opportunities.
- Schedule time for rest and renewal. Make sure you're there, wherever you are. Daniel Sullivan While you prioritise getting things done above being occupied, you are fully present when you are working and fully absent when you are not. This gives you the opportunity to not

only be in the present but also to take the necessary time to relax and recuperate. Working at a high level is similar to being physically fit. You can't develop strength, stamina, or endurance if you don't take a rest in between sets. But not every "rest" results in recuperation. There are certain things that are more calming than others. Writing in my notebook, listening to music, spending time with my wife and children, making and eating delectable cuisine, or helping others are often how I unwind from work. These activities renew me. They not only enable but also enrich my work.

Many people are skilled in their fields. Some are even elite. Some people are simply unstoppable.

Do you have the mental fortitude to believe that "the universe will conspire to make it happen?" It's difficult to imagine thinking 10 times unless you try it. Once you've had it, you understand it's not only feasible—it could even be conservative. Within a few short years, moving from six figures to seven figures is possible. It's not so wild if you think large enough and are prepared to act bravely and shrewdly enough. In today's interconnected society, any tool is available. If not, then construct them. Many people are engaged in it. You have no other justification save the fact that you are unwilling to pay the price because you don't truly desire it.

Make ambitious goals that are much above your current capacity. You must set goals higher than your current abilities. You must learn to completely reject the boundaries of your potential. Make it your goal to work for the finest firm in its industry if you don't think you can. Make it a goal to be on the cover of TIME magazine, even if you believe you are unqualified. Make the place you aspire to a reality. Nothing is insurmountable.

Our capacity to advance and innovate depends critically on our capacity to learn and change. You must value education if you want to be unstoppable. You should continually endeavour to educate yourself and be an ardent knowledge consumer. Your mind is fed by being a voracious learner since it may make new connections and come up with fresh ideas.Those who are relentless in their pursuit of their objectives never stop trying to comprehend and learn more about the world they live in.

You should probably not do anything if you need permission. A very successful real estate investor is one of my mentors. Throughout his career, he has received hundreds of inquiries from people interested in "going into real estate." Every single one of them receives the same message from him: don't do it. In fact, he makes an effort to persuade the majority of them out of it. And he is often successful. What made him do that? He informed me, "Those that are going to succeed will succeed regardless of what I say." I know a lot of people who try to replicate what has been successful for others. They end up hopping from one thing to the next in an effort to find fast riches because they never really know what they want to accomplish. And time and time again, only a few feet from the gold, they stop digging and abandon the area. Nobody will ever permit you to pursue your goals.

People who are tenacious and unyielding never feel completely pleased with their accomplishments. Are you letting life happen to you, or are you using your strength of will and perseverance to create the life you want?

Unstoppable people build habits that help them stay focused and have an unquenchable desire to pursue their ambitions. You must identify your inner belief before feeding it and making it a fundamental aspect of who you are. Why do your objectives matter to you so much? Every day, ask yourself that question and tell yourself the response. On the other hand, extrinsic motivation is frequently focused on a reward from outside sources. You choose to accept a new position since the pay is greater.But external incentives lose their appeal with time. Those who are genuinely committed and unstoppable don't do it for the high pay or generous perks; they do it because they feel compelled to.

From this point on, your plan is to get everyone to your level; you're not going to lower yourself to theirs." You will never be in a rivalry with anyone again. They'll have to contend with you for business. From now on, just the outcome will be important. Timothy Grover You will ensure that you obtain what you desire when you are unstoppable. The knowledge you require is already within you. You only need to believe in yourself and take action.

Taking accountability entails two steps: You accept responsibility for your errors and shortcomings, but you also acknowledge your triumphs. Relentless individuals take pride in both their successes and mistakes equally. They are driven to keep moving forward and searching for the next great thing.

They don't allow themselves to get complacent or to bask in the glory of their prior successes. People that are unstoppable are always on the hunt. They continue to work towards the next level of greatness while maintaining their focus on the upcoming challenge. With ambition comes mental tension, which can occasionally feel like a heavy load. Many individuals break down under pressure, gripped by strain and worry. You must strengthen your mental toughness to deal with difficulty and failure if you want to become unstoppable.The ability to control your emotions when you need to be strong can help you stay strong, focused, and determined during the difficult moments.

Self-assurance and ego are quite different things. When you are aware of your value and have faith in yourself, you are confident. When your sense of self is exaggerated and you start to prioritise your own interests, that is when you have an ego. Jealousy and resentment are frequently intimately linked to ego and arrogance.Unstoppable leaders are aware that envy and ego are driven by fear. They understand that if these emotions aren't controlled, they will obstruct their own progress. In contrast, humility will encourage the greatest qualities in people around you. Time and energy are wasted on pride and bitterness. The success of another person does not jeopardise your chances of success, and vice versa. Quit being defensive and stop focusing on yourself. Focus on the end outcome while remaining open to new alternatives if you want to be unstoppable.

People who are unyielding do not flee from difficulty. They understand that confronting a challenging circumstance head-on gives them the chance to demonstrate their ability to cope with pressure and do well in it. The voice in your head that convinces you that although life is difficult, you are tougher than it is.

Nothing is more freeing than presuming response-ability, which I define as realising that everything—or at least 99% of "things"—is dependent on your capacity and desire to take accountability for your decisions and subsequent actions. By doing this, you put yourself in control and avoid becoming stuck in other people's traffic. Your reaction is in your hands. You're in charge of your actions. You have self-control. nothing else. Own it. Anything less would involve exercising fear, and who loves living in dread?

The desire for change and the ability to adjust are more crucial than ever in the modern world because change is continuous. We follow in the steps of those who change, and we lose relevance if we don't choose to change or choose to accept change. Rather than worrying about things you can't control, make the decision to not worry. Decide to wait and see rather than worrying about whether you'll make it to work on time. Make your next presentation successful rather than just hoping it does. Pick or don't choose, whatever you do. Simply avoid assigning blame.

There is nothing you can't do once you understand that you—and you alone—have the ability to control your ideas, emotions, and subsequent behaviors. Eleanor Roosevelt once stated, "No one can make you feel inferior without your cooperation," which is one of my favourite phrases. Whether we choose to view others' ideas, assessments, and behaviours as valuable or worthless determines the value we assign to them. Change your focus if the one you have isn't helping you in any way. You should only pay attention to the things you can influence and control. Ignore everything else. The problem is typically how you see it.

Being proactive means realising that you owe no one anything and that you are the only one who can assist yourself. It's crucial to remember that while things may "be as they will be," they are also "up to me." Consider yourself fortunate that you have a choice, alternatives, difficulties, and challenges because, well, how dull would it be if you didn't? Even if there were no obstacles in life and everything was perfect, you'd still have a problem because that's what people do. We resolve issues. And what about that? It is satisfying. You do indeed seek confrontation. You do desire a challenge. Yes, you want to feel uneasy and uncertain because when you do, you will be able to appreciate it when you don't because you will be able to tell the difference.

The ability to make decisions and have control over your thoughts and actions is a potential trait that has always been there in humans. It is constantly available and prepared for use. What we decide in the heat of the moment provides a window into the soul, clarifying what we want or need at that precise time. Choose your ideas wisely and benefit from them.

It soothes your anxiety, sadness, and grief. The adage "time heals all wounds" is untrue. Wounds do not heal with time. It won't get any easier ten years from now if you lost a loved one yesterday. Not all scars are healed by time. Option does. I say that without intending to seem judgmental or harsh, but rather as someone who has been there and who has lost a great number of friends. Making the decision to move on is difficult, but nothing worthwhile ever happens without effort.

The founding fathers of America made a decision over two hundred years ago. They made the decision to test freedom and opportunity in the face of inescapable uncertainty in order to follow their passions and goals. It goes without saying that it was a difficult decision, but it was one that stood the test of time, struggle, and every other impossibly high cost involved with such an endeavour. Choice is a potent tool. Both inspirational and self-defeating choices are possible. It may either set you free or render you a total prisoner to your own thinking. In a lecture I once gave to college students on choice, I said that it is the one and only right that every individual has in life. Human rights aren't involved.

When Chandubhai arrived back in Rajkot, he was either underwhelmed or dissatisfied by the offer. The inventor and director of Balaji Wafers assert, "I have never feared anything or anybody." If they thought their size would terrify me, they were incorrect. He was also experiencing sales momentum. Balaji has risen to become the top wafer brand in Gujarat and Rajasthan, and it was also listed in the top three in Maharashtra and Madhya Pradesh.

A lot has changed in the last six years. Balaji is currently in charge of a national campaign in India and is the clear frontrunner in four states. Additionally, he's in 11 additional states. Additionally, income increased by almost double to 2,374 crore throughout this period (till FY20). The only thing that lasts is Chandubhai's perseverance and determination to expand the company rather than sell it or even lower the family's ownership share. Why do an IPO? He muses. I have sufficient funds. I've never had a need for it.

All the Virani brothers sought was a "name" for themselves when they were forced to leave their Jamnagar village and move to Rajkot in search of work in 1974. "We never left our nation in search of fortune," said Chandubhai. Due to a lack of rain, his father sold the dry land and gave his sons 20,000 so they could leave the area and start a new life. The trio started a small business in Rajkot that sold farm equipment and agricultural supplies.

It failed after two years, and the brothers started working in the restaurant of the Astron Cinema. "My salary was $90 a month," says Chandubhai. "And in 2014, I had a $4 billion offer to sell my company," he chuckles.

When Chandubhai was in the Astron Theater, he had lofty goals. Two things happened that gave him the ability to see the bigger picture. The first step is to secure a contract to manage the movie theatre canteen. The second was how popular the theater's wafers were, with supplies always being insufficient. The Virani brothers decided to make potato chips in their little, one-room home. Customers were drawn to the Virani variety both inside and outside the theatre. The name Balaji Wafers was derived from a little glass figure of Lord Hanuman kept in the Viranis' chamber. There is no such thing as instant success, which is one of the most important lessons learned from living in the real world.

The merchants who either failed to pay them on time or duped them into believing the packets they sold were contaminated were the Viranis‘ first antagonists. Unfazed, the brothers chose to broaden their audience and appeal. The brothers started off riding their bicycles and, later, their motorbikes, lugging bags of wafers from one remote region to the next. Balaji's quality and flavour garnered enough attention over the next few years to become the talk of the town. Chandubhai was apprehensive about expanding abroad despite his early success. one empty place at a time. The 64-year-old said, "One argument at a time." The evolution has followed a predetermined pattern. Due to its enormity, "Fortress Balaji" development was prioritised above other projects for over four decades and spread across Gujarat, Rajasthan, Maharashtra, and Madhya Pradesh.

It is simpler to ask individuals to work late one night, or even every night for a week, rather than to demand that they do it constantly. Fix a finish date. Leaders don't ask followers to do something that they aren't willing to do themselves. If you're going to the spa this weekend, don't instruct your employees to work over the weekend. Put your hands to work and divide the workload. Fear may be a powerful motivator since it concentrates people's attention. If we don't do this immediately, we'll all be out of a job. But if you keep using fear to motivate people, it will have the opposite effect. Positive emotions like exhilaration, pride, a sense of belonging, and the rush of accomplishment are also powerful motivators for people, and they prefer them to negative emotions.

Why It's important to motivate and inspire others? Motivating and inspiring others brings out your best. Your self-esteem and degree of self-confidence increase when you are engaged in important work. More possibilities to inspire arise as a result of one act of inspiration. To put it another way, if someone approaches you and says that you were the reason for their success, you get so ecstatic and happy that you want to inspire even more people. Your life and your existence have value when you are inspired. You feel fulfilled knowing you made a difference by inspiring others throughout your time on earth. People who are inspirational are said to have higher degrees of spirituality and purpose.

As humans, we depend on interactions with others to accomplish important objectives. You are giving back to society through your motivating words and deeds. You are returning to others what you have learned from other people who have had an effect on your life. Leadership qualities are demonstrated when you directly or indirectly influence others. As a leader, you exert influence on others by inspiring sentiments of awe and admiration in them. When life is gloomy, knowing that you are inspiring and encouraging others might help you see the light. Knowing that you are an inspiration to others may dramatically alter your viewpoint just when you are about to give up on important goals because of too many hurdles.

Here is what we currently know about Ola's expected 2024 debut of electric vehicles. Ola's founder and CEO, Bhavish Aggarwal, said that the company will likely release its first electric car in 2024. What specifics about the automobile do we know? How have Ola Electric's vehicles performed on the market? After building an ecosystem for electric two-wheelers, Ola Electric, which is funded by Softbank, has its sights set on breaking into the market for four-wheeled electric cars. Bhavish Aggarwal, the company's founder and CEO, predicts the car will make its debut in 2024 and that it would have a 500-kilometer range on a single charge. According to Aggarwal, Ola plans to develop two vehicle platforms and six unique automobile types, all of which would be built in its expanding mega facility in Tamil Nadu. With incredibly affordable electric vehicles, Ola's founder confronts Elon Musk. Ola Electric unveiled concept images of its first electric car at the beginning of the year. The vehicle's prototype was publicly shown at the Mission Electric 2022 event, which was later on streamed online. By the summer of 2024, the unnamed electric car will be available for purchase and have a range of more than 500 kilometres on a single charge. Ola also made the S1 launch public. The S1 was momentarily put on hold after a variety of technical issues led Ola Electric to only offer the stronger S1 Pro model. There is still a lot of opportunity for conjecture despite the well reported and anticipated sequence of announcements' clues of a promising future.

How to use the power of words to your advantage?

Therefore, those of us who think negatively, such as "I hope I don't fail," are actually visualising failure in our minds. Also, the reverse is true. If we visualise ourselves overcoming obstacles, succeeding, or controlling a situation, it will eventually become our reality. The capacity to reorganise our brains is known as neuroplasticity. Choose words that will produce positive results. We must acknowledge that we frequently choose our words subconsciously, which might be problematic if we choose phrases that do not benefit us. There are some words that set us up for failure. Try is a significant one. Do or don't is the only option.

The death or empowerment of our habitual dictionary a technique to shift and transform our way of thinking and make our reality a more fulfilling experience in life is to replace the automatic, negative words we use in our regular vocabulary with more positive ones. Making words work for you to achieve success language is good. It will function regardless of how you use it. Because we do not choose our words carefully, we frequently choose terms from our default lexicon that are not helpful to us. They do not lead us to our desired destination.

The best approach to getting out of a rut is to speak in the past tense, like "I used to be no good at...." This frees up your mind so it can look for new resources and frame problems more positively. We reach a temporary period when we improve, saying things like, "I'm not excellent at this yet" or "I'm learning to. "Get rid of the negative and emphasise the positive. If we alter our negative pattern of telling ourselves we cannot accomplish something, our subconscious mind then finds the tools to succeed.

Everyone employs their own style of speaking to captivate the audience with their persuasive words, whether they are brilliant speakers, speechwriters, anchors, or content creators. Storytellers employ descriptive, accurate, and creative language. Marketing copywriters employ language to persuade readers to purchase their goods. Speech writers utilise language to guide their listeners through their own ideas. Everyone has their own special phrase that propels them forward to the point of emotional unanimity. As an example, we have restricted power words like "safety," "lust, wrath, and "greed" that are employed as needed.

Language is largely subconscious. We must intentionally choose linguistic patterns that will result in a more pleasant experience if we are to change. We may transgress and develop in the ways we envisage after we have mastered our habitual language in order to be more effective. This provides us with the ability to transform and achieve our goals. Looking for complete heart, mind, passion, and vision alignment? If so, our ground-breaking programme is for you. The vision, alignment, and strategy for the life you truly desire are created in design your life. Design your life is where it all starts if you're prepared to experience quantum leaps in your relationships, career, and life.

Watch what you say. Your speech can help you achieve your objectives.

Two frogs fell into a large pit while they were moving through the woods as a group. The rest of the frogs congregated close to the pit. They informed the two frogs that they were effectively dead when they realised how deep the pit was. The two frogs disregarded the criticism and made a valiant effort to leap out of the hole. They were repeatedly warned to stop by the other frogs since they were practically dead. One of the frogs finally gave up after listening to what the other frogs were saying. He died when he collapsed. The other frog persisted in doing his hardest jumps. The throng of frogs shouted at him to cease hurting and to simply die. He leapt even higher before making it outside. You see, the frog was deaf and could not hear the other people's cries. All along, he believed they were supporting him. The Lesson of the Story: A word of encouragement may lift someone who is depressed and enable them to get through the day. When someone is struggling, all it takes is one destructive word to kill them. Be Wary of Your Words. Speak life to everyone you come in contact with. It might be difficult to comprehend how far a supportive comment can travel.

Deciding whether to throw in the towel or do something different was the catalyst to their biggest wins.

After eliminating the unfounded rejections and placing the remaining rejections into perspective, you can now address the problems that are within your control that may be holding you back from achieving more rapidly. For instance, if you're having trouble finding the investors you require, have a professional analyse your company plan or look for a different role model to follow. Work on your script if your cold calls are constantly unsuccessful. Try a few other strategies. If you adhere to these guidelines strictly, you'll spend the least amount of emotional time and energy on experiencing rejection and the most on minimising the number of legitimate rejections you experience.

Sometimes what we learn from rejection ends up making us the best version of ourselves.

It's been claimed that disappointment just comes from absorbing the results too quickly. Being too quick to judge your success is taking the score too soon. If you've never heard it before, take this opportunity to write it down since it's a really useful idea. And it's true, you know. You've probably had situations where you initially believed you failed and were rejected but later realised you actually escaped serious harm. Or perhaps it turned out that, although you didn't receive what you desired, something much, much greater was taking place. So rejection may really serve as a type of defence, right? One of the most important things is to be patient when you are rejected.

Let's be clear: you grow via failure. One advantage is that you may use your errors, failures, and setbacks to forge better bonds with other people. Possibly the biggest advantage is how these trying circumstances will help you develop professionally as a person. Here, I'm speaking about your mental make-up and temperament, your basic everyday character, and how it will alter and develop as you start to learn how to view setbacks favourably. To methodically consider what led to a failure and what to do about it requires a lot of effort. The good news is that with practise, you'll pick up some helpful skills and your outlook on life will improve. I'll be more precise.

You'll gain more empathy, humility, bravery, and perspective if you can learn to accept defeat. Let's briefly consider each one. Compassion comes first. Humans are bred to evaluate and occasionally have haughty ideas. You'll be able to realise that others are just as flawed as you are and that they occasionally fail the more you choose to honestly acknowledge your shortcomings, own them, and learn from them. You'll be a little less judgmental and a little more understanding of what others may be going through. They'll most likely respond compassionately in return since you'll be acting more compassionately.

Don't get me wrong; any professional who wants to advance must be skilled at effective self-promotion. However, once the first disappointment wears off, a fresh feeling of humility appears.It's the awareness that, whatever how excellent your abilities or accomplishments may be, you are still only human, and as a result, you act a bit more modestly and kindly. Humility is admired and aids in establishing connection when it is genuine. How about bravery? You would anticipate that I would add passion to this short list. No, I'm assuming you have a strong interest and are watching this course to attempt to improve yourself. You need bravery, that's all. Oddly, passion may sometimes remain unused inside. It takes guts to allow passion to flow. Passion may encourage change and growth in your life when you have the guts to do so. You'll develop bravery as you fail more and succeed more.

Finally, gaining perspective via failure allows you to see things from a wider, more well-informed long-term viewpoint. When you start to accept the concepts taught in this course, you start to realise that a single failure is simply one statistic among millions that will define your professional or personal life. You realise that the average of all those data points, not just one particular endeavour or experience, actually defines who you are. That puts failure in perspective and serves as a reminder to keep learning so that your average is always rising. There are several avenues for you to advance personally and professionally. You may actively learn new things through books, mentors, degrees, projects, and promotions. You may actively learn new things through books, mentors, degrees, projects, and promotions. All of them are really helpful, but perhaps the most helpful one is to learn more from your mistakes than your triumphs. Applying the concepts we've covered can help you stop seeing failure as a personal failing and start seeing it as the most effective approach to get better.

Even if it's not always simple to get back up after an accident or failure, some people manage it and inspire others. When a horrific catastrophe or heartbreaking situation occurs, most people lose hope. However, some people never give up and go on to inspire millions of others. Yes, I'm referring to Muniba Mazari, a person who is confined to a wheelchair yet nevertheless motivates others and advances society. Let's examine Muniba Mazari's remarkable life story and how she came to be in this position.

Muniba claimed that her time in the hospital was the hardest time of her life since she had to rely on people for even a sip of water. She occasionally felt thirsty in the middle of the night, but she was forced to go the entire time without drinking anything since she didn't want to wake the others up. After spending two years in bed, she was given permission to use a wheelchair.

How to be grateful after difficulties, after a serious vehicle accident that left Muniba Mazari unable to walk, she chose to live her life rather than weep. There are many inspiring people in the world, and each one has a unique life narrative. This is the tale of a lady whose wonderfully flawed existence has shaped who she is now. This is the tale of a woman who holds the opinion that sometimes our issues aren't so large, but we're just not big enough to deal with them.

Muniba Mazari asserts that words have the ability to either make or ruin a person. They have the power to either restore your soul or irreparably harm it. Muniba Mazari has watched her life fall apart in front of her eyes since she was a small child, yet she has never given up. Many people have illnesses that render them permanently crippled, but the first thing they do is give up. One of them is this incredible angel who showed the world that everything is possible by rising from the ashes and standing higher. She served as an example for the rest of the globe, in addition to herself. Instead of running from her concerns, she faced them head-on and overcame them. In the end, we all come to the realisation that success, wealth, and celebrity are not the sources of true pleasure. It can be found in thankfulness.

Muniba exclaimed, "I was so thrilled when I sat in a wheelchair for the first time." What if I didn't have legs? "I now have two wheels," she declared. Her life then abruptly turned around. Doctors urged her to keep pursuing her goals and passion, which was painting. Muniba quickly made a reputation for herself in the art world and demonstrated that a wheelchair is no barrier to success. She is presently regarded as one of Pakistan's top painters and artists. She uses oil pastels as her medium, and her company is called Muniba's Canvas, with the tagline "Let your walls wear colours."

Muniba is now a recipient of several honours and often delivers inspirational talks at conferences all over the world. She is a representative of Pakistan on the coveted Forbes 30 under 30 list of the world's best young leaders, entrepreneurs, and game-changers. Her additional accomplishments include serving as the Body Shop's brand ambassador; being Pond's miracle mentor; being Tony & Guy's wheelchair model; and being one of the BBC's 100 Most Inspirational Women of 2015. Additionally, chosen as a U.N. goodwill ambassador in Pakistan, Muniba is promoting women's empowerment there. Many people find inspiration in her life story, and she also conducts several TED presentations.

India's most outstanding female batswoman, Mithali Raj, has accomplished a lot in her two-decade international career. She bowls right-arm leg breaks and bats right-handed in the opening position. The only female cricketer to cross the 7,000 run threshold in Women's One-Day International matches, Mithali is the leading run-scorer in women's international cricket. Mithali Raj became the top run-scorer in women's international cricket in July 2021 during the third women's One-Day International match against England. She surpassed the previous mark of 10,273 runs set by Charlotte Edwards.

"I hope my journey inspires young girls to pursue their dreams." -Mithali Raj

To become famous and successful, one must put in a lot of effort. Raj travelled to the India Women's Cricket Team's One-Day Internationals and Test matches. Because of the enormous skill pool, she was also rumoured to have played in the 1997 Women's Cricket World Cup at the young age of 14. Age wasn't included in the final selection, though.

Nevertheless, two years after she was left off the final list, Mithali Raj made her one-day international debut. Her 114 runs, which were too unbeatable, were what made her debut the most remarkable and unforgettable. The first test, played in 2001–2002 against South Africa, came shortly after. Since that time, nobody has turned back. On August 17, Mithali Raj successfully surpassed the record for the highest run in a women's test during the same season. She received numerous honours, including the Arjuna Award in 2003, the Padam Shri Award in 2015, the Wisden Indian Cricket Player of the Year Award in 2015, the Youth Sports Icon Excellence Award at the Radiance Wellness Conclave in Chennai in 2017, the Vogue Sportsperson of the Year Award at Vogue's 10th Anniversary in 2017, the BBC 100 Women List in 2017 and, more recently, the first Indian woman cricketer to be conferred with the prestigious Major Dhyan Chand Khel Ratna Award in 2022.

We must develop a love for the pursuit of goals and the sacrifices required in order to differentiate ourselves from the competition. Success comes to those who are willing to travel the difficult road and work toward difficult goals.

Without the so-called "work smart," I don't believe in luck or hard effort. It's not only about working hard; it's also about managing your time, resources, and thinking to get greater results."When it comes to things like team selection or job promotion, we will end up blending in with the herd if we choose the basic and straightforward routes in life.

There is no quick route to success; only steadfast labour may make one's life's goals and aspirations a reality. We frequently hear people's justifications for giving up. "It wasn't meant to be," "It wasn't enjoyable anymore," or "Life is all about having fun" are typical lines of speech that are used in response. It's important to note that our minds are capable of creating whatever mental state we give them. Instead, we should impose a commitment state that will enable everyone to realise their own goals.

A person who has expertise in a certain sector is more likely than others who lack experience to accomplish their life's goals and can operate shrewdly and effortlessly.

This is still, without a doubt, the most difficult part of achieving successful objectives. What drives some people to relentlessly pursue their dreams while other people give up when things become tough? We get experience via hard labour, which enables us to learn a lot of new things. We may use this experience to develop clever thinking skills to successfully address a challenging issue. A person's ability to solve problems is enhanced through experience.

Man needs his difficulties because they are necessary to enjoy success. Climbing to the top demands strength, whether it is to the top of Mount Everest or to the top of your career. Great dreams of great dreamers are always transcended.

"Your work is going to fill a large part of your life, and the only way to be truly satisfied is to do what you believe is great work. And the only way to do great work is to love what you do. If you haven't found it yet, keep looking. Don't settle. As with all matters of the heart, you'll know when you find it."- Steve Job

You can't just admit that you made a dangerous choice at some point. To achieve what you want, you must be prepared for the sort of ability that is actually required. You must, nevertheless, take chances in order to succeed in life. Being honest in life is crucial to you.

Every challenge you encounter has a single underlying question: how do you deal with yourself? An inability to manage what I refer to as the "You-Factor" is at the root of all of your stumbles, errors, and failures. &; The You-Factor is about managing yourself and your entire life properly, more so than self-worth or self-respect, even beyond character and sense of purpose.

No matter what your career, you must take challenges and come out of your comfort zone, and your humble background can't be an excuse if you fail. It is quite challenging to succeed in life if you don't respect others, whether they are your own or anybody else's. Let's imagine that when you enter any large building, you must treat everyone equally, from the first man you encounter to the managing director, for example.

Go through the challenging time; struggle through it, but if you can do it with a grin, I am giving those great examples of people, perhaps five people, who set examples through their lives and can truly pull it off. Because we sometimes complain about life and the difficult times, it's vital to remember that it's going through the difficult moments that will really help you become a better person. I hope it is the start of something amazing and mind-blowing for you. This chapter illustrates how your thoughts may impact your mental, emotional, social, and physical health. It also covers the subject of how your willpower and visions might help you achieve inner tranquilly. A step-by-step examination of overcoming the internal obstacles to achievement may be found in from passion to peace.

You must restrict or eradicate unproductive behaviours while imposing new habits that boost productivity if you want to have the desire and motivation required to consistently put out the level of effort required for productivity.

"Never give up on what you really want to do. The person with big dreams is more powerful than the one with all the facts."- Albert Einstein

Those who dare to dream frequently have a wider view of life and are able to transform the impossible into reality. Albert Einstein, a brilliant German physicist, is the author of this wise saying. He emphasised the value of being true to your goals, even if others may consider them to be "unrealistic." You will be able to notice how many chances are accessible that you might have previously overlooked when you strive higher and dream greater. Being more confident in yourself than ever before will also make it simpler for you to approach individuals and start a discussion with them.

To start thinking beyond the box, consider your goals in life and whether they align with your passions.

Additionally, you should learn as much as you can about the education and training needed for each job route so you can decide which one can provide you with the best chance at a successful future out of all those available. You need to stop worrying about what other people think of you and start thinking positively about yourself and your future. Stop worrying constantly about making mistakes, since doing so will make it more difficult for you to achieve great things in life.

Aiming high and having great dreams forces you to push yourself in ways you never could have before. Your chances of success rise when you always consider the optimal outcome because you can prepare and think more strategically. By setting high standards for yourself, you inspire everyone around you to do the same.

Keep dreaming until your dreams seem impossible to achieve.

When I mention Sundar Pichai, what comes to mind for you? The CEO of Google, who is Indian and headquartered in America, will be the obvious response. For additional information about the hip CEO of Google and Alphabet. Sundar Pichai, the CEO of Google, has joined the steadily expanding group of CEOs with Indian ancestry. Sundar

Pichai's ascent to the top wasn't easy, but it was an excellent affirmation of India's position in the global technology sector.

Since 2015, Google's CEO, Sundar Pichai, has been firmly in charge of the company. This straightforward CEO was born and raised in the southern region of India. Google CEO Sundar Pichai claimed that his father had to pay for his airfare to America in order to attend Stanford University, which cost him a year's income. He had never flown until that point, and he disappeared after that. He had a great deal of love for technology, and his open-mindedness encouraged him to succeed. He stated that since the beginning, computers have been his area of interest.

He advised the kids to be impatient, optimistic, and open-minded and to believe that they had the capacity to change.

Being fearless entails having confidence in oneself and the notion that, with enough willpower, everything is possible. In order to improve your mood and accomplish more in life, you must also harness the power of positive thinking. There will be occasions when you feel disheartened because you are having trouble accomplishing your objectives. Because it can often seem worse when those close to you don't support your actions, it is said that "misery loves company."

However, try to focus on finding answers and assisting people who feel like they are trapped at a dead end rather than focusing on all the unpleasant aspects of life and how they make things tougher for you. By doing it this way, even if some people continue to think you're crazy for pursuing your aspirations despite what occurs, you won't care as long as you can assist others in doing the same.

"A person who is happy is not because everything is right in his life; he is happy because his attitude towards everything in his life is right." -Sundar Pichai

Nothing short of inspirational can be said about the life of this former IIT graduate who is now the CEO of Google and the first Indian to hold that position. We all like the usual "rags to riches" tale, and there is something quite fulfilling about witnessing someone work hard and achieve success in life. Sundar Pichai, the CEO of Google, has led a life that is both inspirational and instructive.

"Let yourself feel insecure from time to time; it will help you grow as an individual. It is important to follow your dreams and heart. Do something that excites you."- Sundar Pichai

Never give up, says this son of a landless farmer who is now a billionaire and the owner of Thyrocare Technologies Ltd., the largest thyroid testing business in the world. One of the most clichéd things we've ever heard is probably that. But few people can maintain that level of commitment. Fortunately, there are others who will motivate you to press on. For instance, the son of a landless farmer from Coimbatore, who formerly struggled to eat twice daily, now controls Thyrocare Since setting off from the unremarkable village of Appanaickenpatti Pudur in Coimbatore, where he was born into a poor farming family and whose father couldn't afford to purchase him a pair of trousers or slippers, Dr. Arokiaswamy Velumani has travelled through some very challenging terrain.

According to Dr.Velumani, "My parents were not wealthy. They never had the money to treat me to a pair of chappals or pants. I was conceived at the base of the pyramid's ten segments. It wasn't simple. I am currently at the very top of the pyramid, though."

Suresh Vazirani's made it so big from a Rs 1 lakh loan to a Rs 1000 crore company. Actually, it's not really a secret; more of an untold story. Once leader Jayaprakash Narayan was hospitalised with kidney failure, Suresh Vazirani became aware of the condition in Indian hospitals and made the choice to enter the healthcare profession. The importing dialysis equipment malfunctioned, and there was a critical patient in the hospital. As an electrical engineer, Suresh stepped in when the hospital was unable to provide assistance. He became aware of the challenges patients might face in these situations and the potential fatalities brought on by medical equipment technical failures.

"Every two seconds, a Transasia gadget undergoes one test. On our apparatus, more than 150 billion blood tests are performed annually." -Suresh Vazirani, Founder, Chairman, and Managing Director of Transasia Biomedical Limited.

So, at the age of 29, Suresh vazirani launched his first business, Transasia Biomedicals, with the intention of improving the Indian healthcare sector. Suresh Vazirani contributed about Rs 250, and his buddy lent him Rs 1 lakh. The business targets pathologists, lab technicians, clinicians, and technicians. In order to guarantee that

Indian hospitals and clinics have access to the most modern technology, the primary goal is to offer items that are both inexpensive and made in India.

Motivation is fueled by passion. Having a passion makes you love the work you perform. Having motivation enables you to work efficiently. You must have the drive and responsibility to begin any assignment in order to finish it. One self-reflection question: Do you actually feel inspired to work? If the answer is yes, that's great; if the answer is no, you're not enthusiastic enough. If you are not passionate about what you do, it will just be a transitory life. You must develop a passion if you want to live over the long term. When you put your all into your job, it will undoubtedly help you accomplish anything in life. It will undoubtedly take some time, but your desire will help you maintain your patience till then.

Spend time honing your skills so they are even greater than they were before, rather than attempting to make up for your flaws. By doing this, you'll raise your market value over time while also being happier and more productive at work. Simply put, I'm asking you to commit internally.

CHAPTER FIVE

Stop Making Excuses

"The ultimate enemy of your dreams is excuses. Quit wasting time and stop blaming others. You'll be motivated to take action by these inspirational quotes about making excuses. People who are adept at finding justifications are rarely competent at anything else."

Being a victim affects more than just one person. It may also develop into a social gathering. In actuality, nothing unites individuals more than collective whining. Therefore, telling the victim's tale is not only addicting for us as individuals, but it is also a sign of our codependence. We enable others to suffer, which causes us to experience victimisation. In turn, they enable us to experience victimisation and show compassion for us while we do the same for them. We then experience friendship. I'm about to do something that is really risky. I'll show you how to ask the right questions to fully elicit the victim's narrative. I'm hoping that after seeing the questions, you won't ask them again.

However, despite how delicious they may taste, the victim's queries will ultimately lead to devastation because there will be nothing they can do to stop it. However, people will believe that you are a genuine buddy. Your true buddy is not the one asking you these questions. The first question concerns what happened to you.

So it's the feeling that something horrible happened to you; explain how circumstances outside of your control contributed to it. The second is: Who did you wrong? That person, who? Because there is always a responsible party—someone who acted improperly and thereby caused your problems—there is always someone to blame. What they should have done is the third question. Victims, you see, exist in a world of ought. What ought they to have done instead of what they did?

There is no right or wrong response in this situation, but you do need to decide for yourself whether you want to play it safe the majority of the time or decide to accept some of the risks involved in using mistakes as opportunities for tremendous learning. If you choose the latter, it will eventually benefit you to surround yourself with creative and learning-focused groups, leaders, and organizations. The try, fail, learn, and succeed approach ultimately calls for a little daring. Just keep in mind that there are advantages to numbers. You reduce your risks and quicken your learning process the more you network with other experts who support it.

Procrastination caused by excuses leads to zero productivity and frustration.

However, there is a manner in which you may still participate in that. When things go wrong, there is a method you may decide to use to react that can lift your spirits. They might not provide the outcomes you desire, but they will always give you the opportunity to express your values. Humans are moral beings, as you can see. Perhaps even more than achievement, we value our honesty. The most essential thing is that we all secretly want to feel good about ourselves. The main rule is that

What would you pick if someone offered you the option of choosing to succeed dishonestly or not achieving in a way that made you feel proud of yourself?

The ultimate redemption of any event is answering that question, for when you think in terms of expressing your beliefs, the worst-case scenario ends up becoming the best-case scenario. This is not a sentimental remark; rather, it is a profound philosophical assertion. What would you need, for example, to demonstrate that you are more than simply a fair-weather sailor? That being said, you need a decent storm because otherwise, you will only sail in fine weather and won't know what to do if a storm ever comes.

The best way to get over your fear of storms is to actually experience one.

You must, of course, be ready. You won't act with such an irrational display of arrogance. But you can't really demonstrate your mettle without the storm. When people remark, "You see who your friends are in the hard times," that is another way to look at things. When circumstances are good, everyone is your buddy. But who sticks with you through tough times? The true test is that. As a result, life has a way of putting us to the test by presenting us with difficult, upsetting, and challenging situations. While our minds are wailing, "Oh no, oh no, this is horrible; what am I going to do about this?" our souls are responding, "Oh yeah, this is my chance." This is my moment to demonstrate my sincere convictions. This is an opportunity for me to demonstrate my character and the principles I wish to uphold in the most trying of situations.

Now, a common occurrence that you may have witnessed at work is someone arriving late for a meeting. You wonder why you're late. What are the usual responses? Well, everyone on the globe is stuck in traffic, I guess. Oh, the traffic was awful. True, there was awful traffic, but the time of arrival also depends on the time of departure, and nobody ever talks about the time of departure. No one claims that I failed to permit traffic. They cite traffic. or another, yeah, the previous meeting ended early. You may have heard that. I was entrapped, I know that much. I was dragged into yet another meeting.

Alternatively, I was caught up in a phone call that felt like it had grabbed you by the neck and was holding you in place. It sounds like, "Oh, you know, I'm going to hold you by the neck so you can't go to your next appointment." That is untrue. Staying in the other meeting was your decision. You choose to stay on the call, but you don't want anyone to know since then you'll stop being innocent. We often engage in this behaviour, and if it were merely an excuse, it would be quite harmless.

However, there is an issue. The issue is that if you assert your innocence, you must also assert your incapacity. Why is impotence the price of innocence? Because being innocent requires that the determining factor for the issue be outside of your control, you must decide whether to concentrate your attention on the factors in this circumstance that are outside of your control, because if you have control, you are accountable. You are made innocent by that. But you're also conveying that there is nothing I can do by focusing on problems like traffic that are beyond my control.

Unless you were in charge of the other meeting, which would not be a good justification, you cannot change the other meeting. This individual hurried over to the other meeting, which was being led by someone else. That makes it simple to conclude that they did it. They are at fault; I am not. What I refer to as the victim's mindset is the tendency to place your emphasis on outside variables and things beyond your control in an effort to prove your innocence.

Just to be clear: We are all victims of circumstances beyond our control. Rain does, in fact, fall. There is traffic. Meetings go past schedule; terrible things just keep happening. The question is what you will do if this happens. And the victim is unaware of that aspect.

In order to feel guilt-free and good about themselves, the victim just concentrates on what is happening that is beyond his or her control. Only one person may be held accountable from the victim's perspective. What's going on with me, and why? I shouldn't be experiencing it. And as a result, the victim is in a state of justifiable fury. "It's not my fault" soothes the victim, who is then ecstatic and motivated by the righteous fury that this shouldn't have happened to her. They should pay since they messed up! They need to fix it since they broke it! And it is, in fact, the ideal medicine. It has both an upbeat and depressing side. You feel both energised and relaxed after using it, and you become addicted to it.

Most of us start taking this medication when we are very young. We go to our parents as children and exclaim, "Mommy, mommy, the toy broke!" The toy broke; take note of their cautious word choice. Have your kids ever said, "I broke the toy" to you? No, these are now normal ways of speaking and thinking that we learn as children, and when we become older, we say things like, "Oh, the project got delayed." Sorry, the file disappeared. Or perhaps this is the fault of the finance department; you know, the consumers aren't purchasing because the engineering department created a subpar product. We blame each other while narrating all these tales. And they may be true, for all I know.

Let's pretend for the moment that non-technical employees are not taken seriously by anyone at your firm. Is there a technical ally you can locate that you can get on board with to help you make your case and complete what has to be done? Consider the scenario where you have been thrust into a situation without any training and are suddenly expected to know what you're doing. Is there a course you might take online, a coach you could hire, or a coworker who would be willing to teach you the ropes?

Let's also assume that you don't have enough workers to complete your tasks. Is there a way you might persuade a few coworkers to offer their time to your project? They could get to put a useful new ability into practise or meet a significant decision-maker.

If not, perhaps you could concentrate on establishing expectations and inform your manager that you have tried every possible approach and this simply won't work. You've identified a solution that will allow you to satisfy your duties, such as if she agrees to extend the deadline a little. We may all think of several reasons why we shouldn't complete a task, but our success depends on our capacity to overcome these barriers and move on. You can accomplish that using these methods.

You must challenge for your self-improvement. Try, fail, learn, succeed is the success cycle. You, and everyone in between are all subject to that procedure. With a little retrospective analysis, you may jumpstart the process of applying your new viewpoint on failure. Consider your worst failures personally over the past five years and try to list the top two or three initiatives or circumstances.

Okay, now enquire as to why the top few failures occurred. Try performing some root cause analysis, like we talked about before. Contact a few important individuals who were also engaged to get their frank and open perspective on your part in the situation. Compare notes from those two or three instances now. It's possible that each failure has a similar component to its explanation. The idea is that if you see a pattern, you should start concentrating on it so that you may embrace the success cycle of attempt, fail, learn, and succeed.

Being a victim entails placing the blame for one's problems on other people or external events. This "it's not my fault" attitude may be applied to groups, companies, and whole communities. However, why assign blame when you can accept responsibility? In this chapter, I will guide you in making the decision to accept life's difficulties, to transform from victim to hero, and demonstrates how to encourage and teach others to do the same. Apple is currently the market leader in a number of product categories, but before the iPhone, there was the Apple Lisa and the Apple Newton tablet, both of which were abject failures from which they learned and developed.

Do you ever feel helpless in the face of uncontrollable events?

Do you feel helpless to change the situation since it's out of your control?

Simply put, it implies that you understand that everyone has flaws and makes mistakes and that you want to use this knowledge to motivate and push yourself to work harder. And it's a really easy process. It proceeds as follows: Sincerely try to comprehend how you contributed to the error. Admit it to everyone or any group that may be important. If necessary, give an explanation. Tell them what you've discovered or what you plan to do to make sure this error doesn't happen again. Then carry out your promise and do what you say. I'm done now.

Here are the advantages that will justify the effort: You'll first learn things more quickly and efficiently. because you are actively attempting to comprehend and correct your mistakes. Then, you'll be demonstrating to people that you have moral character and are capable of taking initiative and accepting accountability for your deeds. Because you can accept your flaws, you'll also be displaying a more real and genuine side of yourself. That enhances your perceived relatability from the perspective of other people. As a result of your decision to positively confront the reality we all face, it is possible that you may forge stronger bonds with others and gain their respect.

There is another approach. Since I've been coaching CEOs for ten years, I've discovered that one small adjustment may have a significant impact. The notion that you have the ability to react to whatever occurs outside is simple to understand but extremely challenging to put into practice. You are not required to suffer. Although you are subject to forces beyond your control, the situation is not yet over. You have a number of options for how to react to this that are within your power.

Those who are aware that they could bear some of the responsibility don't want to be identified with a mistake in front of others. So they keep quiet and don't own their part. In order to protect our self-esteem and our faith in our own abilities, we frequently unintentionally reject taking responsibility for our mistakes. That's unfortunate since, contrary to popular belief, taking responsibility for your errors might really help you grow professionally in the long term. You must acknowledge your flaws. All of us do. This should not imply that you are settling for subpar work or low expectations for yourself.

Recognising the victim mindset Not everything that is good tastes nice, and not everything that tastes good is good. We need a science of nutrition because we wouldn't live very long if we just ate what we thought tasted good. Similar to this, many things in life that we think are excellent for us but aren't actually beneficial do us no good, and vice versa. Feeling helpless in the face of external events is one of those habits that feels fantastic but causes us problems.

When something awful occurs, like if you're out enjoying a wonderful picnic and it rains and you get drenched, you know it's horrible. You and your buddies are now all soaked; it's unpleasant, and you're sad since it was such a wonderful day and you had everything planned. If someone were to ask you at that time, "What went wrong?" the usual response, the one that comes to mind right away and the one that makes you feel wonderful, is, "It rained; it was the rain." I mean, my picnic was destroyed by the rain. We don't recognise that it is just half of the tale because that is such a common way of communicating. Simply put, I'm saying that you won't be able to affect change if all you think about is how you're innocent and other people did it to you.

I'd like to suggest three different categories of failure. own mistakes, outside variables, and results of striving Okay, let's start with human error. These are errors that occur as a result of incapacity, lack of concentration, or an inadequate match between the person or team and the task at hand. This is the kind of problem that truly tarnishes failure. By optimising their hiring, job analysis, and training and development procedures, organisations may lower this well-known, straightforward type of failure by ensuring that the appropriate people are performing the correct duties. The category I call contextual factors comes next. These are things that are beyond your control.

Every process has flaws that result in lost time, extra expenses, or poor quality.

You just cannot foresee everything. Who will, for instance, leave or get sick? Which supplier will unexpectedly delay you? or if there is a sudden downturn in the economy. These problems are obviously out of your hands. However, there are two things you can do to try and lessen the hurt that comes with unanticipated failures. Develop your plan for any significant job before working on backup plans or contingencies. Planning for disasters is a crucial component of every endeavour. The second thing you can do is do an occasional audit to make sure your team and your company are putting the finest technology and techniques to use while implementing your plans.

"Try not to become a man of success, but rather try to become a man of value." - Albert Einstein

Being accountable means being ultimately responsible for your actions as well as being in charge of something. You must discover the will to carry out challenging tasks if you want to keep yourself accountable. You must emphasise the importance of your purpose, comprehend why it is important, and comprehend how accepting responsibility enables you to develop into the person you desire. In this book, I will help you develop a sense of responsibility. My outlines concrete, doable actions you can take to put accountability into practise. It's your duty to take care of things for which you are accountable. That report must be written, that client connection must be managed, and your receipts must be submitted within 15 days.

Accountability, though, is something very else. The difference between managing yourself and having someone watch your back to keep you on target is a state of mind, not what you have to accomplish. It's taking responsibility. One of the first things that comes to mind when we recall President Harry Truman is a sign that reads, "The buck stops here," which was posted on his desk. That is the accountability mantra. And since so few people adhere to that idea, it distinguishes you as a leader.

So why isn't everyone doing it if holding oneself accountable is such a terrific idea? It requires more of your attention, focus, and energy. You must use your motivation and truly understand at a visceral level why this is crucial for you in order to maintain it. Here are a few methods you can employ to enter the zone:

- Asking yourself what type of person you want to be will help. This is more than just saying, "Oh, I think I should be responsible here since it'll help my job." Yes, many things would, but we don't always do them. Consider your identity if you wish to maintain motivation. What kind of person do you want to be? How do you plan to arrive? What do you want people to say about you when you leave the room? Despite being intelligent, does he fudge his work? Most likely not. It has to do with character. Others respect you more if you keep yourself accountable. And maybe most significantly, you have self-respect.
- Consider the outcomes. What would happen if no one was in charge of the task or whatever you're working on? What is the most probable result? The probabilities are that development will be slowed or nonexistent, and that communication and implementation will be disorganised. You would be wasting your time and money. That might be disastrous, particularly if you're working on a project that is mission-critical for the business. Imagine the reverse now.
- What if you took charge of this, regardless of your position or title, and vowed to ensure that the pieces you can influence are completed on time and correctly? The project's future, and maybe even the future of your business, looks very different now. You have a lot of influence. Lastly, look for good instances. Every project or endeavour has periods when you're in the trough, where you feel like progress is stagnating and the future looks dark. At times like these, it may be tough to keep oneself accountable. But it's crucial to keep your attention on the big picture.

- Recall instances in which you have assumed a leadership position and succeeded. Again, the title is not the issue here. It has to do with your attitude and how you connect with your coworkers. Also, keep in mind successful instances of leaders holding themselves accountable and pulling their staff along that you've seen elsewhere in your organisation or sector. When you're struggling, it may seem that the project you're working on is insurmountable, but pausing to consider that something similar to this has succeeded in the past may be empowering. You can do it if they can.

In your excitement to hold yourself accountable, you could decide to take on a seemingly insurmountable assignment. However, that is actually a bad idea. You can't set your first goals so high that you're bound to fall short. Overpromising won't improve your reputation in the industry. Instead, it's crucial to have reasonable expectations for both you and other people. Let's discuss how to do it.

You must first be honest with yourself. It's easy to become excited and misjudge how long it will take to complete a task. This causes you to be behind schedule from the start, which is not a favourable situation. Don't start with wishful thinking. Start with the facts. Time tracking is something you can start doing right now and will be very helpful for your future project planning.

Simply note how you've been spending your time and how long things take, perhaps twice a day. Because your memory fades, don't wait; do it once a week instead. But after a few weeks, you may get an astonishingly precise sense of how long particular tasks take if you record them in a notebook or enter them into a spreadsheet before you leave for lunch and the day. Your ability to estimate what you can realistically take on will improve as you become a better estimator.

Next, consider how difficult or impossible the task is. It's excellent to aim for something challenging. It can inspire your team and you to think in new ways, but some ideas are just not achievable. In principle, it is entirely feasible to construct 1,000 client orders and deliver them in two days, but in practise, you will either require human labour or a robot of some sort. That would be a foolish endeavour if your supervisor didn't provide you with the necessary assistance to make it structurally impossible.

We now get to our final item, which is controlling other people's expectations. It's crucial to be forthright and clear about what's realistic. Saying yes at the time is simple. It's simple to say yes and think, "I'll work it out later," in the heat of the moment. It hurts to let your boss or coworkers down, and you could be concerned that if you refuse, they'll assume you're unmotivated or lazy. Yes, they are dangers, but a far bigger risk is making a commitment up front, then breaking it when it becomes evident that you won't be able to follow through.

Therefore, it's crucial to engage in some war gaming before going all in and accepting responsibility for this. Determine the potential difficulties and potential trouble spots, then have an open discussion about them. You'll be better protected even if you decide to attempt, and you may include crucial phrases like "I can promise the product will be ready if we have enough personnel at the plant to create it." That may make the difference between being viewed as a trustworthy leader or a person who keeps their promises. By establishing realistic goals for yourself and others, you dramatically boost your chances of success.

There are no outside enforcement mechanisms or observers watching you from behind. This is about you taking control of your career. Therefore, in order to facilitate accountability, you'll need to develop your own frameworks. Here are a few options for you to think about.

Leveraging a forcing mechanism is one technique that works especially well. Imagine that your manager has advised you to improve your public speaking abilities if you want to advance. You've made the decision to face this head-on and win. You will be held responsible! What is your process, then? What is your process, then? One strategy is to commit to something you know you can't back out of in order to force yourself to perform a difficult task. An example might be that you'll host your team's presentation next month, speak at a conference, or do an interview for the business podcast. The fact that you have that obligation scheduled is a forcing mechanism, and since cancelling would make you feel awful or seem bad, you are motivated to get ready and perform well.

Make a public promise, you may promise your buddies that you'll complete the Toastmasters programme by the end of the year and take the risk of seeming foolish if you don't. You may raise the stakes by making your commitment extremely public, such as through social media or your blog, or you can even place monetary wagers. If you don't succeed, the funds are donated to a charity that you fiercely oppose. So that's a good motivation. Making sure that you and your coworkers are constantly on the same page is another method to incorporate success systems into your life. For instance, it's quite easy to summarise the action items you both agreed on when wrapping up meetings or talks. Okay, Jigyasha will provide me with the client's contact details through email, and I'll send Deeter the latest advertising material. It takes two minutes, but it guarantees that the to-do list hasn't been lost or confused during the chat. It keeps us both responsible.

With a current valuation of over $37.6 billion, Flipkart outperforms all other Indian unicorns. In 2022, the firm raised over $3.7 billion. The pioneers who started Flipkart are Binny Bansal and Sachin Bansal. In India, the online shopping trend was radically transformed by Flipkart, a spectacular business that became a unicorn in 2012. With a current valuation of over $37.6 billion, Flipkart outperforms all other Indian unicorns. In 2022, the firm raised over $3.7 billion. The pioneers who started Flipkart are Binny Bansal and Sachin Bansal. The current subsidiaries of Flipkart include Myntra, Cleartrip, and PhonePe. Each of them has also caused disruption in their own fields.

A unicorn startup is any company that has a valuation of $1 billion or more. In the past, the phrase was used to describe exceptional and uncommon businesses that would establish valuation standards in their respective sectors. The unparalleled rise in the world's startup culture over the past two decades has helped many firms become unicorns. In order to put things into perspective, unicorn companies are businesses that have figured out how to disrupt the market. Without using IPOs and stocks, unicorn businesses generate greater financial returns than their rivals.

The most imaginative firms, those built on workable strategies, tend to be unicorn startups. These firms stand out for their focus on bringing about good changes in their target markets. In reality, a unicorn startup's long-term goal communicates to private investors or venture capitalists what makes it unique, making funding relatively simple for the founders. Previously, the term "unicorn" was connected to a startup to denote its stature and dominance. The number of unicorn businesses has dramatically expanded globally over the past ten years, and India has managed to climb to the third spot among the nations with the most unicorn firms.

"We were not thinking about numbers then, but we knew something big could be built out of e-commerce."Binny Bansal and Sachin Bansal, the founders of Flipkart One of India's leading e-commerce platforms is Flipkart. It began in October 2007 and has its main office in Bengaluru. The internet business, which was founded by Sachin and Binny Bansal, started off as an online bookshop, but as its notoriety rose, it flourished and expanded its activities. The Bansal brothers, Sachin and Binny, started Flipkart. Both individuals, who graduated from IIT Delhi in 2005, were formally introduced to the retail industry while employed by Amazon. The two connected at work and discussed their shared passion for transforming India's e-commerce sector. Due to this, both left their employment at Amazon in 2007 and started working on building a rival e-commerce business that catered particularly to Indian users. The two wanted to provide Indians access to an online shop that was developed in India, which is how Flipkart, as we all know it now, came to be.

The portal began selling a wide range of other goods, including music, cell phones, and movies. Flipkart rapidly expanded, continuously adding new product categories to its inventory as e-commerce began to transform the retail industry and gain traction in India. The company currently offers more than 80 million products in over 80 different categories, including mobile phones and accessories, computers, laptops, books and e-books, home appliances, electronic goods, clothes and accessories, sports and fitness, baby care, games and toys, jewellery, footwear, and more. According to Walmart, Flipkart set a record for monthly active consumers in the month of November 2020. The company now leases more than 1 million square feet of space in a number of locations, including Mumbai, Hyderabad, Bengaluru, Lucknow, Ahmedabad, etc., to ensure quick delivery to its customer base.

The first Indian business to achieve unicorn status was InMobi, which did so over 11 years ago. It began its journey as a mobile ad optimization firm and has now evolved into India's first unicorn business. The CEO of InMobi, Naveen Tiwari, stated in an interview that the company became a unicorn by continually applying improvements over time. InMobi has successfully provided the finest available services to its target audiences throughout the course of its 11-year history.

The CEO also stated that the idea of a startup unicorn was not well known at the time. InMobi went through a number of transformational stages before arriving at its current state. To assure greater improvement in the profit margins, the corporation also consistently changed its business strategy in response to market developments. According to reports, the firm received more than $250 million from a variety of investors, and the owners have been reaping substantial profits since 2016. According to reports, over 60000 new businesses were established in the previous five fiscal years, generating a whopping 333 billion dollars in capital. In 2021, 1584 financing agreements raised a total of 42 billion dollars in capital. In 2022, the fintech industry in India alone attracted the most gross financing of approximately $3.82 billion.The government's grand strategy to support Indian companies is the recently unveiled Startup India programme. Following the lead of a few early-stage unicorn businesses from India has helped early-stage entrepreneurs grasp the path to becoming unicorns.

In fact, India has added more unicorns to the economy in the last year than China has combined. For the Indian startup ecosystem, 2021 has been a successful year, as 44 businesses have achieved unicorn status.There are now over 900 unicorn startups in the world. The United States tops the list of nations with the most unicorn startups. There are around 625 startups operating in various US states, compared to about 312 businesses in China. On the list of nations with the most startup unicorns, the UK is listed just after India.

With a profit of more than INR 7 Cr in FY21, Physics Wallah produced INR 350 Cr in FY22. They have now raised $100 million at a $1.1 billion valuation. Let's see how they managed to do this! In 2014, Physics Wallah began as a straightforward YouTube channel. However, Alakh Pandey, the man behind Physics Wallah, had years of expertise instructing students in the subject. In reality, he relocated to work as a physics instructor in an offline JEE preparation centre after dropping out of engineering college in his third year. The maker of Physics Wallah, Alakh Pandey, is from a middle-class family in the Indian village of Prayagraj.

Alakh didn't have a stable financial foundation. It was up to Alakh to create a bright future for their family in light of his father's regrettable failed enterprises. He was put on the path to outstanding grades and a decent career after they took out a sizable debt to pay for his education. Alakh began tutoring students in Physics, his favourite subject, in the eighth grade and continued to do it in the eleventh and twelfth grades in order to assist his father. Alakh had the same aspirations of attending an IIT as many other 12th graders throughout the nation. But sadly, his wish was not fulfilled.

As mechanical engineering was "closest" to physics, he chose to enrol at a nearby engineering college to study it instead. Alakh discovered that college was not everything he had hoped for. The first year passed quickly. But after a few years, he realised he was not really learning anything. Alakh, who was very motivated to establish his future, made the decision to leave school in his third year of engineering.

It was this group that pressured Alakh to release his ed-tech app, dubbed PW, short for Physics Wallah, in 2020, when the COVID-19 epidemic struck. The software virtually crashed on the day of its introduction due to the overwhelming volume of downloads. The 300K download mark was attained in just 7 days! The software has over 5 million downloads, 3 lakh daily active users, and over 90 minutes of usage time as of right now. Physics Wallah has expanded from its one-man operations to a business with 50 lecturers, 250 faculty members, and 7 million subscribers.

Nothing inspires us to work harder than having a cause in mind.

Our finest efforts and accomplishments are fueled when we believe we are contributing to something greater than ourselves. Moreover, a feeling of significance what transpires, though, when your sense of purpose wanes? How is it renewed? It's actually simpler than you would imagine. You can workout in this way with a goal in mind. This is how it goes. Consider this question for a moment on those occasions when significance in your work seems to be lacking. What principles will I uphold today? The idea of fulfilling their potential or simply figuring out their mission frequently makes people feel scared. The easiest, most straightforward method to work with a sense of purpose is to simply choose to live by your most deeply held, non-negotiable principles. When I don't feel like I have much of a purpose on a given day, I've gone back to picking one of my core values to live out that day, such as compassion or persistence.

According to a recent study, only approximately 50% of people can state their essential principles with clarity when prompted. It's acceptable if you belong to the portion that cannot. Just take the time to consider and describe your beliefs in detail. Even so, note them down.

Great, let's go on to the next phase. Then, search for patterns. It's vital to consider whether the explanations you've provided seem "like an old story," as one of my colleague advises. Are you frequently thinking about something, or is there a lot of emotion surrounding it? If so, it's probable that what you're using as an explanation is really just a script that you've grown accustomed to telling yourself. Since I don't belong to the herd, no one pays attention to what I have to say. I don't want to self-promote the way other people do around here; you only get respect around here if you have a technical background. There could be some truth to this. But if it bothers you or seems to be a recurring pattern, it would be worth monitoring and considering whether you might be projecting your own worldview onto this circumstance. Start coming up with some solutions at this point. If there are difficulties, we must figure out a solution rather than just giving up. So, for each justification or defence, consider a possible solution.

Setting general boundaries is something I strongly support. Think for a moment about the things you do in your life that make you the most successful and, on the other end of the spectrum, the things that hold you back or make you less successful. What if you could condense your decision-making process into a list of "I always" and "I never" statements? I always exercise, for instance, on Mondays, Wednesdays, and Fridays. You find a way to do it regardless of whether you're on a business trip since the choice has already been made. Similar to this, you can opt to establish a policy that states, "I never check social media during work hours," if you've previously squandered a lot of time on it. Period! Done! Setting boundaries enables you to develop guidelines that keep you on course.

Finally, while getting your technology correct will undoubtedly take some effort and trial, it will be worthwhile when it comes to deploying systems. Although some individuals definitely flourish when they have digital reminders beeping on their phones and online note-taking systems, when I mention "technology," it doesn't always imply something technological.

However, if your method consists of notebooks, binders, and planners, that's good too. The secret is to experiment with various applications, tools, and items until you discover the set that enables you to work as productively as possible. A system that enables you to prioritise, track, and keep track of all the things you need to do is what you desire. And it may be a paid system or something as inexpensive as a legal pad. The important thing is that it functions for everyone. Better systems provide better outcomes. Therefore, investing the time to do this correctly will pay off greatly in the long run.

Think of a situation. You hired a new employee, but they didn't work out. Your presentation was heard by the leadership team, who swiftly rejected it. All of us have been there. every person. Even when you put forth a lot of effort and hold yourself accountable, failure still happens. The important thing is to get back up after it. That's obviously easier said than done.

Let's discuss how to get back on track after failing and the three things you must do. It's crucial to first comprehend what caused the failure. Of course you want to prevent something from occurring again, but if you don't know what caused it, you can't prevent it from happening again. So why did the launch not succeed? Was there a timing mishap? Was it something you could have managed, or was it maybe because the stock market plummeted the day before and people were in a panic? It's possible that the messaging wasn't thoroughly tested or that there was a technical problem that caused you to believe that everyone was receiving three follow-up emails when they actually received only one.

The first task is to determine what actually happened. They advise getting back up and trying again as soon as possible after falling from a horse or a bike. Otherwise, you'll gradually develop dread and be unwilling to repeat the experience. In a similar vein, you need to move immediately to get back on track. It would be simple to flee and hide for a time. You may feel ashamed, let down by others, or like they don't want to see you, but the reality is that you cannot withdraw from the game. There isn't any free time for pouting. Instead, resolve to take a concrete step that demonstrates you're accepting responsibility for the failure and changing the script.

Elaborate goal setting is the first step in the journey of success. Define your approach and plan for achieving your objectives, aspirations, and visions. Remember that success is the result of a string of achievements, so be careful to break down your goals into more manageable subgoals.

Excellent books! Everyone is curious about what it takes to achieve long-lasting success in both business and life. It all boils down to having a firm understanding of the principles of business and life skills, the same ones that successful people are taught at many of the most prominent schools in the world, together with useful life lessons. As you read the book, it will subtly assist you in finding personal happiness in your own way, which is always the best course of action for you.

Create a learning mindset. One of the wisest moves you can make while facing personal mistakes and losses is to take a step back and attempt to obtain a larger perspective. You must keep in mind that you are not alone when you fail. You belong to a sizable group. I want you to keep in mind that everyone who is successful fails a lot, then learns from their mistakes, becomes better, and eventually succeeds. It's unavoidable, and if you learn to like learning, it can even be enjoyable.

Remember that everyone is affected by this reality, even myself. Prior to being a well-known professional speaker, I was a lousy professional speaker who was unknown. I needed to learn how to get better. This truth holds true for both people and organisations. For instance, take a look at these well-known instances of failure followed by tenacity that led to success.

The objective is to gain new knowledge and abilities. An openness to possibilities forms the basis of this mindset. Although personality plays a role in how open you are, you can also choose to be open. You see, some people mistakenly believe that applying your knowledge to a problem is the only way to solve it. The true secret is to look for something fresh.

So keep in mind that being open is best seen as a decision. Here's something fascinating right now. Sometimes looking behind is necessary in order to move ahead. New possibilities are at the heart of a learning mindset, but they are frequently produced by drawing lessons from the past.

Because of this, you must perform a root cause study after a setback. That is a methodical approach to moving past focusing on a problem's symptoms and beginning to explore for the root cause of the issue you are experiencing. Starting with your presumptions, do this.

I want you to consider all the important factors at play in the issue, including the primary expenses, individuals, resources, and procedures. Are you making the assumption that someone or something cannot change, won't change, or won't cooperate? In conclusion, you must be prepared to laugh, grin, and learn the next time your flaws are exposed. Because you are aware that for a clever individual, they are only learning catalysts.

When did you most recently truly fail? Let me put this to you: If it has been a while, you could be taking unnecessary risks and wasting part of your potential. Now it's your responsibility to exploit the success cycle such that, over time, your failures will only cause minor discomfort while the triumphs they enable will provide you with a tremendous amount of happiness. There is a superior option. You see, our primary mental error is to excessively concentrate on one failing instance rather than taking a step back to see the larger picture, or to examine our average selves rather than just one data point.

You must keep in mind that every setback is only one frame in a very lengthy movie. It is sad and true, but it does not define who you are. You start a predictable failure cycle when you give a failure too much weight and let it define you like a label rather than allowing it to spark learning. We try not to fail. If it does happen, we try to avoid dealing with it. Your mind becomes overburdened by the failures, and eventually you suffer a breakdown and start to doubt your value. However, things don't have to be that way. Your perception of failure will change once you read this. You simply need to keep in mind one fundamental concept of reasoning.

When we talk about the word Gucci, we often think of celebrities, vast amounts of money, glamour, etc. This brand has a lengthy history of being connected to class and luxury. 2017 marked the 100th anniversary of Gucci, one of the most sought-after brands in the world. Guccio Gucci founded the business in Florence in 1921, and it rose to fame for its luxurious, handcrafted travel bags from Tuscany. Following a number of family disagreements, court fights, and other challenges, the name Gucci was in the news. When a group of investors began to take over the management of the company, everyone in the family was excluded.

In the late 1990s, Gucci hired Tom Ford, a well-known new boss. By betting on the re-release of prior blockbusters like bags and loafers that still bore the Gucci logo, the young designer totally altered the business. By changing the sorts of advertising campaigns, models, and alluring new collections, Tom gave Gucci a more modern air during his time there. After managing Gucci for a while, Tom Ford founded his own business, which is still extremely successful today. Despite several ups and downs, Gucci remains one of the most significant businesses in the world. Gucci is the best brand for people who want to constantly be fashionable since it innovates with stunning releases for each new collection.

The Success and Failure of a Lift Boy Who Founded Gucci, One of the World's Most Expensive Brands Some people put in years of hard work, while others are simply lucky. Some people have a mix of the two. Gucci's remarkable "rags to riches" story is all about relentless perseverance, which has brought the business to its present level of international renown.

Prepare your calendar and planner! Pick one or two from the list, set a goal, and check in on it once a week or once a month. Then, by choosing to take action, you will significantly alter this environment. As an illustration, a SMART objective is linked to each of the tactics. It will be your responsibility to create the action plans to hold yourself accountable in a methodical, orderly, and effective manner in order to achieve the objective.

Consider the kind of picture you are projecting when people see your mannerism, facial expressions, and general appearance. For instance, your appearance and actions could inspire people to regard you as someone they want to strive to be! Remind yourself to share your experiences, problems, and triumphs with your children, grandchildren, or other family members at family gatherings and events. Let them hear about your tenacity and ability to overcome challenges so they will get inspired and realise they can do the same!

Would you like to start motivating others or making a difference in their lives?

Are you seeking some methods and suggestions for motivating others?

Would you like to be a source of inspiration more frequently?

Do you want a plan in place in your life to continuously uplift and encourage others?

Being connected to the human spirit or soul as opposed to material or physical objects is what is meant by the term "spirituality." Have your family members, acquaintances, or coworkers ever referred to someone as "deep" or "shallow"? It is the idea of being able to comprehend the complexity of the human spirit and engage in dialogue with others while keeping in mind that you are not the only one involved. Many "shallow" individuals struggle to establish genuine connections with others because they fail to understand that relationships are mutually beneficial. Being a competent salesperson has a lot to do with being personable, so spiritual growth is quite important in the field of sales. Good salespeople can empathise with their customers and not only comprehend but really care about their problems, which gives them more reasons to push the customer to buy from them.

Simply defined, business is about helping people with their issues. Sales are the interactions between those who have problems and those who can solve them. You will have trouble succeeding as a salesperson if you haven't grown spiritually and are just concerned with your own issues rather than those of your customers. The fiscal year ends as the calendar is turned. reviewing the last 12 months. Time to pause, think, and consider the future. Of course, performance and success are also important considerations.

Having big goals but only taking small steps success does not appear to develop gradually. It isn't a myth or magic. At first, only small, barely detectable steps are taken until a tipping point is reached, at which time success becomes inevitable. We may not be aware of how long someone's trip was since the majority of us are not aware of how many small activities were required to bring about their great accomplishment. The biggest online retailer in the world was founded by Jeff Bezos, who first focused on selling books. The largest social network in the world was created by Mark Zuckerberg, although he initially only used college students. As the Chinese saying goes, "The journey of a thousand miles begins with one step." And after that, plenty more followed. (Since it's a distance, start walking early.)

My research revealed that many successful people used a variety of small successful routines to achieve their life goals: I believe the to-do habits (lists) mentioned above will help you lead a fulfilling life of excellence. I sincerely appreciate you taking the time to read my post on LinkedIn. It's true that I used to write self-help essays for the benefit of others. Stay inspired, stay hungry, and remain upbeat no matter what. I just discovered that you have a moral obligation to share valuable things with others when they are shared with you and you benefit from them.

Nobody can stop you if you are willing to learn and succeed, both for yourself and others.

What do you want? If you really want something, you should battle for it and put in long hours of labour to get it. Desire should always motivate you. "DESIRE" is the driving force behind all accomplishments. Remember this at all times. The same way that a little fire produces a limited quantity of heat, weak desire produces poor outcomes. Make a decision on what you want to achieve this week, this month, this year, and throughout your entire life. Run toward it after writing down your work or to-do lists. First, resolve not to put off doing something. Apply the "Do It Now" guideline and complete the task immediately. Concentrate solely on "Results." "Once YOU make a decision, that's your vision." Let's face it, persistence will be necessary to bring out the best in you. Never consider failures, discomfort, or barriers; they are all feedback. Stay persistent until you succeed. Never forget the saying, "No Pain, No Diamonds."

No one can assist you if you are unwilling to study and take chances in order to accomplish great things.

It's not simple, but it's also not difficult. I'm referring to the fact that 80% of the people you travel with are critics, toxic, negative, time-wasters, energy-drainers, destroyers of lives and careers, etc. Show them that you are different, powerful, brave, humble, thoughtful, etc. Post some motivational sayings at your office or other frequented locations. My favourite song is "Stay Positive," in particular.

Use phrases like "Only Positive Allowed Here" or "No Negativity Allowed Here." Make them feel as though you are guiding them differently than other people.

Never waver in your commitment to excellence. Excellence is a journey, not a destination. Be prepared to sacrifice everything except persistence, commitment, enthusiasm, diligence, tenacity, self-belief, appreciation, and motivation in order to achieve your goals. Most importantly, commit to lifelong learning and make learning your top priority. As a result, you are now a "student of success." Spend all of your time, effort, money, and resources achieving what you desire in life.

Be a Big Dreamer. Every successful person is a big, big dreamer all the time.Make a list of your goals, then take one step at a time. Review yourself twice daily (imagine that you have already accomplished your goals), but retain "focus" on your progress and work toward it every single day. "A goal is a dream with a deadline," always keep in mind. Set your goals, dreams, and deadlines at this point. It would be a "sign of success" if you did it.

Of all the Ds, discipline is the most crucial. "Discipline is the link between objectives and success." Self-control is the secret to all success. From now on, YOU must discipline your choices, desires, resolve, goals, dreams, and anyone or anything that is important to YOU.

"There are multiple rewards for every disciplined effort."

Your first key to accomplishing anything meaningful is self-discipline. Always keep this in mind, and if feasible, make it your phone or computer's background. Place it in your living room. "You are the major key to a better future,"

I have no idea what you are going through or what your desires, determination, dreams, or goals are, but I do know that you are a miracle in your own life. It is possible, yes.

You are a born winner. You were meant to be radiant, joyful, at ease with yourself, self-assured, and prosperous. To do so is to share in life's pleasures. You weren't sent on this earth to live a life filled with illness, fear, worry, loneliness, poverty, or any kind of failure. Continuous failure is the actual purpose of a rich, joyful, healthy, and creative existence for you. Living in poverty, being unhappy, and having poor health means that you are not in harmony with life. To be in sync with life means to be successful, healthy, and joyful. You should advance mentally, spiritually, and financially as you get older.

When attempting to figure out how to succeed at work, this quotation is a great one to keep in mind and give some thought to. Think about the potential success you may have in your current role. In the end, you'll probably discover that you have to put in a tonne of effort and time into it. Being successful in your career may just imply that you will have to do more of the things you detest. What purpose does this serve?

People usually think that in order to succeed, they must commit their entire lives to achieving their goals. People who are confident in their ability to succeed at work may put in long days and frequent late hours. However, this comes at the sacrifice of enjoyment of life, health, and leisure. They can ultimately become exhausted and lose their professional effectiveness. If their social life and friendships are the foundation of their success, their work may deteriorate and they may lose their job, which would prevent them from going out with friends. In a statement made by Nike Inc. CEO Phil Knight, he pointed out, balance promotes success in a number of ways. Think of it as a careful balancing act between leisure, effort, or work, and enjoyment. Are you still unsure about your passion?You must first get to know your motivational engine.

Why not pursue your interests? Once you've found your passion, you'll have more drive to keep moving forward. If you achieve this, your dreams will come true. There is a story, and even if it's not certain whether it really occurred, the lesson it conveys about success is still relevant. The lightbulb was invented by Thomas Edison after several unsuccessful efforts. He was interviewed and asked, "How do you feel after all of your fruitless attempts?" Every "failure" taught him something. That lesson taught him what wouldn't work and what might work in its place. Every failed attempt was an essential step on his path to success. It's easy to feel like giving up after a setback, but perhaps it would be the worst decision. Every failed attempt was an essential step on his path to success. It's easy to feel like giving up after a setback, but it could be a good idea to look for a lesson in that failure.

The successful guy is aware of the meaning behind his existence and makes positive use of his creative thinking abilities to shape and direct his future. Failure-type people struggle through life without knowing their actual calling, and they fail to make good use of their creative abilities. Knowing your actual inner self and comprehending "why" and "how" your mind functions and what it is capable of in your life is being successful on the side.

In the west, men's worldview is oriented toward material luxuries. He has a propensity to disregard his spiritual self. According to eastern philosophy, only the spirit residing in this transitory body is immortal; the physical body is insignificant. Man should thus consider his raison d'être in order to better comprehend himself, his environment, and other people.

You must express your true self if you want to succeed creatively.

Free your mind from the restrictions of superstition and ignorant, negative thinking that prevent you from achieving your actual potential. You are here to creatively convey all that is "good." Determine your degree of creativity and use it. Nobody in the world is quite like you. No one else can do the same things as you in the exact same way, despite the fact that others may try to mimic and copy you. You have unique thoughts that inspire unique behaviors. Most importantly, you possess distinct abilities that are just waiting to be presented in a manner that is original and special.

Don't be an imitator; be a creator.

It's critical that you completely comprehend how unique you are compared to everyone else in the world. Others cannot produce or express their skills and ways of expressing them in the same manner as you. However, they may be replicated. You are now in a unique situation since there are no rivals, just copiers. In this environment, you compete with yourself by erecting barriers in the shape of unfavourable beliefs and attitudes about what you can and cannot do. Put an end to rivalries. You are you. You are psychologically, spiritually, and physically distinct from others. Instead of copying, try to create.

Everyone has untapped talents. It's your responsibility to find and nurture them. Due to your failure to develop latent skills, you may be wasting away in life and missing out on important possibilities. When you use your mind's power in an affirmative manner and acknowledge that your thoughts, feelings, and beliefs are the only things standing between you and success or failure, miracles will start to happen in your life. Every day, when you "think" and "believe," success or failure seeds are automatically planted in your subconscious. These seeds are nurtured by your regular thought patterns to either produce success or failure. having the belief that you can succeed. Recognise it!

Numerous intrinsic abilities of yours are ready for development. Identify them. Foster them. If you truly believe your abilities are up to par, you will succeed. Often, a struggle is won by having faith in winning. Here are five suggestions to help you plan your life in an organised manner.

"Even though a dream seems unachievable, you may still make it come true by dreaming it."- Dr. A P J Abdul Kalam

Steve Jobs was well known for being in quest of excellence constantly. His approach to product development was straightforward: only flawless items needed to be in the hands of consumers. Simply expressed, this kind of thinking may be used in all facets of business: don't sell something you wouldn't want for yourself. Steve Jobs was once expelled from his business and might have retired wealthy, but he persisted in creating and finally returned to Apple. Only because of his innovative and risky business strategies could he return to Apple. This lesson in life advises us never to give up seeking larger and better things. The life lessons Steve Jobs picked up along the road, such as how to persevere through adversity and discover passion in adversity, can be credited for his success. Even now, businesses still rely on his counsel since Steve's successes have become a how-to manual for aspiring business owners.

In order to be as effective as you can be, it is crucial to be enthusiastic about the task you are doing. Steve lived this out every day. Never content with less than the best, he worked tirelessly to achieve excellence in all facets of his profession with the goal of building a company he could be proud of. To sum up, Steve Jobs was a role model and will be missed. He accomplished a great amount of work each day he lived on this planet, mostly as a result of his outstanding work ethic and desire to make the world a better place. He was, in our opinion, among the best motivational speakers of all time, and his modest teachings will endure for all time.

What you desire could well come true, so use caution.

Therefore, have a positive outlook and tell yourself encouraging things so that your subconscious mind might assist you in achieving your goals. Your internal thoughts and the affirmations you tell yourself have a direct impact on the outcomes that emerge in your life.

Everything in life starts with the mind.

Positive affirmations and positive thinking in general are based on this principle. If you want to genuinely embrace the idea that using positive affirmations will enhance your life and bring success, you must come to terms with this concept.

Be cautious when you think, since you could just get.

The simplest method to confirm this claim is to take a quick glance at you right now. Everything you can see, with the exception of nature, began as a human notion. Everything you own, including the clothes you wear, the car you drive, the street you travel on, the house you live in, the TV you watch, the books you read, the computer you use at work, the phone you never leave home without, the chair you sit in, and the business you work for, all began as an idea.

Your ability to think creatively and accomplish goals is almost boundless. You may achieve anything in life if your head is filled with optimistic thoughts and opportunities. Being upbeat and at ease with oneself inspires creativity. You must say a positive affirmation each day in order to nourish your mind.

"If you're trying to create a company, it's like baking a cake. You have to have all the ingredients in the right proportion." —Elon Musk

Elon Musk has lofty goals and has accomplished them in his life. To achieve great things, you must have faith in your goals. It's only a matter of time before his vision of autonomous electric vehicles and passenger aircraft comes true. He did what seemed right. When he was 17 years old, he forced himself to live off $1 a day in order to follow his business drive. He dropped out of college to pursue his commercial interests, and he was successful. So, don't chase after money. If you follow your passion, money will come after you.

People should pursue their passions, he said, with a valid point. That will make them happier than anything else. He is a leader with a vision. His goal is to settle Mars soon. He is now working on realising an ambitious set of goals. When he succeeds, he will go down in history as the person who started the entrepreneurial movement that other people followed. He is a driven businessman who knows how to break new ground. People are motivated by ambition to achieve the impossibly difficult. He goes off the beaten path. I always have optimism, but I'm practical," he said. I did not launch Tesla or SpaceX expecting to be extremely successful. just because I believed they needed to be done in any case. He first had a number of failures during the rocket launch and gained knowledge from them. Even though he ran into several difficulties throughout the design and testing phases, he kept going. He said that failure is an option here.

"People can choose to be, not ordinary... yes, I think ordinary people can choose to be extraordinary."-Elon Musk

You are not inventing enough if things are not failing. Success has a price. A lot of sacrifice and effort are required for success. Due to a shortage of funding, Elon Musk originally faced several difficulties. His entrepreneurial journey began with volatility, unpredictability, intricacy, and ambiguity. He once faced bankruptcy when Tesla Motors was in a bad financial situation. He did, however, manage to survive by acting swiftly to fix things. You must go through hardships today in order to achieve success later in life.

"Trying to start a business is similar to making a cake. All the elements must be present in the proper ratio. Mr. Elon Musk, Elon Musk is a model businessman who sets the standard for innovation throughout the world. By venturing outside the globe, he raised the bar for the populace. He will be remembered for his inventiveness and entrepreneurial endeavours. His ingenuity, entrepreneurship, and leadership are examples that other aspirational businesspeople should follow. In conclusion, Elon Musk is a leader with a broad vision and a transformational mindset.

For all generations, he serves as an inspiration.Numerous businesspeople and entrepreneurs have been inspired by Elon Musk's success. Elon Musk's journey of achievement includes a number of obstacles. But Elon always managed to fulfil his goals for the business he founded and bring forth a great conclusion. "Life can not just be about solving one miserable problem after another, that can't be the only thing," he says. "There need to be things that inspire you, that make you glad to wake up in the morning and be part of humanity."

"When you try different things, a lot of things aren't going to work, and that has got to be okay."- Elon Musk

Be aware that affirmations may not always produce immediate results. Your hopes of acquiring wealth quickly are false unless you are a lottery winner. You could have to wait days, weeks, months, or even years, depending on the outcome you want from your assertion. Success is yours if you are patient, persistent, and optimistic in your approach to your objectives and aspirations.

Those who wait will receive good things.

Success always comes after focus, which is impossible without a distinct focus on what matters most. And this crucial fact is something that leaders must continuously remind themselves of. The pursuit of a purpose and vision is necessary for focusing.

Be tenacious. Entrepreneurship and business development should be founded on a foundation of love, and any great love necessitates tenacity and perseverance to achieve your goals. You will encounter disappointments and setbacks, but you will also discover success. "You may have numerous setbacks, but you must not give up." According to Maya Angelou, to know who you are, what you can rise from, and how you can still overcome failures, it can even be important to experience them.

Whether you realise it or not, you have the capacity and power to make remarkable, life-changing contributions right now. Often, all we need is the knowledge of how to begin, maintain consistency, and seek achievement throughout our lives in order to be successful in life and act on that potential. You may learn how to succeed in life, whether it's your personal or professional life, and become unstoppable in attaining your objectives, by forming a few crucial habits.

I make a commitment to you that all of these behaviours apply to all of your goals, regardless of how you approach achievement. Spend time reading and learning in order to better yourself. They read a tonne of books, much like successful people like Bill Gates, Warren Buffett, Mark

Zuckerberg, Mark Cuban, and others did. Extraordinary individuals are aware that they must get fresh and improved information in order to reach a higher degree of perception.

"We can't fix problems by using the same sort of thinking we used to create them," Albert Einstein reportedly observed. What Einstein is saying is that we can only solve an issue when we improve and think more intelligently. As a result, resolve to educate yourself and lead a better life every day. Regularly read books and take advice from others. Always look for methods to do things better and improve your performance.

"It's not whether the glass is half empty or half full, it's who is pouring the water. The key in business and success at any endeavor is doing your best to control your destiny. You can't always do it, but you have to take every opportunity you can to be as prepared as-and ahead of-the competition as you possibly can be."

You are in charge of your own destiny. You have undoubtedly heard this a lot in your life. Maybe this resonates with you, or maybe you feel that the sentiment condescendingly oversimplifies the difficulties of life that might restrict your alternatives. Whether or not you feel like you have complete control over your destiny, the truth is that you do. Controlling your ideas is a key component in shaping (or influencing) your future. The viewpoint that you have influence over what happens rather than feeling as though something is happening to you is created by viewing problems as opportunities. Because of this, you may take action and affect change as opposed to just accepting your circumstances.

You can leave a legacy because you control your destiny.

You ought to take into account how you view yourself. Remind yourself that you are never a passive victim of your circumstances since pride is something to exercise. You have the power to control your circumstances and alter your course. A life with meaning is abundant when you operate from the level of the soul. Please bear with me as we go a little deeper into this. Living from the soul level entails letting go of our ideas about how life ought to be. You have a more profound understanding of your spiritual existence. It necessitates focusing on your actual essence, independent of your worldview. These are ideas you developed to help you make sense of your surroundings, but they serve no more purpose than a motorcycle's training wheels.

When things do not go as planned or as we had hoped, we frequently blame it on fate. The opposite is also true in that some individuals frequently blame others' success on their fate rather than recognising the effort they put into their accomplishments. In other words, we associate our choices with our future.

We frequently believe that destiny, a great power, governs our lives rather than ourselves. What one should understand, though, is that a man's fate is determined by his mind and the thoughts he puts into action. Thank goodness Walt decided to ignore all of his detractors and pursue his ambitions instead of listening to them, as a result of which we now have the Disney corporation. A determined intellect might lead you to destinations you never imagined. That is why the phrase "It's all in the head" is so popular. Only the choices we make will determine our future.

"All success in life, whether material or spiritual, starts with the thoughts that you put into your mind every second of every minute of every day. Your outer world reflects the state of your inner world. By controlling the thoughts that you think and the way you respond to the events of your life, you begin to control your destiny."

Successful individuals handle situations differently. They just alter their reactions to the occurrences until they get the desired results. You have the power to alter your behaviour, communication style, mental representations of the world, and way of thinking (the things you do). You essentially just have control over it. Unfortunately, the majority of us are controlled by our routines. We become mired in conditioned reactions to our partners and kids, our coworkers, our clients and customers, our students, and the rest of the world.

"No matter how profound a loss, time always cures the agony, even though the scars remain," writes Arunima Sinha in her book Born Again on the Mountain: a narrative of losing everything and finding it again.

Arunima Sinha has received several honours for her courageous example. She was involved in a railway accident in 2011 and lost her left leg as a result of a fight with robbers. Arunima was unfazed by the conditions as she used her prosthetic leg to ascend Mount Everest.

The first amputee from India to climb Mount Everest is Arunima Sinha. When she encountered a catastrophe on the train, it was reported by the media that she attempted suicide by jumping off the train. Later, her mother rectified the statement and clarified the situation with the media. Patients who have lost their legs often require 4 to 5 months to learn to walk again. Arunima Sinha, however, walked for two days. She did that because of her courage and drive. She raised the Indian flag for photos at the peak of Mount Everest. When she was taking photographs, she had less oxygen available. When the opportunity to quit shooting pictures presented itself, she decided to do so anyhow, even if it meant risking her life. Due to a lack of oxygen, Arunima Sinha believed she would not make it to sea level. But it just so happened that she ran upon a British climber who had turned back in the middle of their ascent. He provided her with oxygen, which let her survive until she returned to the camp.

"By conquering all the seven summits I will prove that physical disability can never be a hindrance in achieving your life's goal if you have mental strength, strong willpower and firm determination."- Arunima Sinha

Arunima Sinha is a role model for young people, demonstrating her determination to pursue her dream of proving herself to the world. In 2015, the President gave her "The Padma Shri," the fourth-highest civilian honour. She also discussed the "Ted Talk" platform, which broadcast her success and motivated young people all over the world.

Our ideas are the embodiment of our minds, and our actions are the result of those thoughts. One just cannot sit back, fold his arms, and claim that everything in his or her life is the result of fate. Our way of thinking and the way we see the world directly affect how we live. Only the choices we make will determine our future. For instance, if a person has a strong will and a determined attitude, the decision-making process and how the choice is carried out will eventually establish that person's fate, which will finally determine their destiny.

You must learn to regulate your ideas, pictures, dreams, daydreams, and actions. Your thoughts, words, and actions must all be deliberate and in line with your mission, beliefs, and objectives. Sometimes you come up with a brilliant concept right away that you can develop and run with. Everything seems to be going great until you have a setback. You get punched in the gut by failure, leaving you with aching wounds and no choice but to whine about what might have been. Change your replies if you don't like the results.

We are solely responsible for our own destinies. Whether things turn out better or worse depends entirely on how we perceive and respond to the events that occur in our lives. One's fate is decided by the way they think and behave. Our thoughts have a major role in how we behave, and our actions play a major role in how we are seen by others. Therefore, a man with control over his thoughts has power over his actions, which in turn gives him control over any circumstances in life that may eventually determine his fate.

Considering that everything is temporary, try to avoid being attached to people, places, or events. Dread is the source of clinging, which breeds more fear.

Change your thoughts to more powerful ones so that you can easily allow what is required to flow into your experience. Don't hold onto things you don't need anymore.

Consider repurposing it if you haven't used it in the past three months. Less tangible possessions free us from having to handle more. I'm not advocating leading a simple existence; rather, you shouldn't look to worldly items to bolster your sense of identity.

When compared to the effort we put into achieving success, we frequently have higher expectations and hope that it will arrive sooner rather than later. If it does not, we tend to become upset and eventually sink farther into the pit of inferiority. The majority of individuals have observed this circumstance, when regular and committed efforts are neglected and only failures are celebrated. Such instances may be found anywhere in the world. The majority of famous people have had significant setbacks in their battles with life. Nevertheless, they persisted in their paths to success and eventually experienced enormous success in their specialised industries. They never let their race, religion, or any other distinction stand in the way of their achievement.

Whatever you choose to call it—destiny, fate, karma, serendipity—the notion that life is predetermined by forces outside of our control is an age-old one. It exists in every culture on earth, including ancient Chinese narrative and

Greek mythology. But what if fate wasn't actually real? What if you had influence over your future? You have acknowledged your internal centre of control if you think you are in charge of your own destiny.

It means that you accept responsibility for your thoughts, actions, and results. This method of thinking can help you become unstoppable. You may learn to take charge of your future. You must first embrace who you are and where you are right now in order to take control of your future. You'll run out of things to do if you trick yourself into thinking that you're further along in your goals than you actually are.

Don't delude yourself into thinking your life is worse than it is, though. Take a step back and consider your situation differently. Increase your awareness of yourself and embrace the truth. If you don't know where you're starting from, you can't develop a strategy to control your fate. Accepting reality does not entail passively accepting your fate without taking any action. It entails taking responsibility for the things you can alter and letting go of the things you can't. You have no influence over what people believe or do. You have no power over the market. Your own mentality is the only thing you have control over. To do that, you must challenge the self-talk you believe in and replace it with an empowering one.

Everyone is aware of Michael Phelps' exceptional athleticism. Few people are aware that he suffers from Attention Deficit Hyperactivity Disorder (ADHD), and swimming is how he manages the excess energy his body produces. Many people think ADHD is a bad affliction, but Michael used it as motivation to swim. He recognised his primary weakness and channelled it into his greatest strength. You can take inspiration from him and use your flaws as motivation to strive harder or smarter. Michael Phelps is constantly in top physical shape to pull off his victories. He keeps up excellent levels of fitness and has a fantastic body. He puts a lot of effort into his exercises and attributes his general skill to strong genetics.

More than most people, Michael Phelps is aware that success does not come easily. The most decorated Olympian in history, while becoming a standout at a young age, put in the necessary effort over the duration of his career. He is aware of the impact of perseverance and hard effort as well as the places that these qualities might lead. Nothing else is getting in the way of our achieving our objectives and desires. Continue to be inspired, hungry, and driven. He is renowned across the entire world for becoming the most decorated Olympian in history. Olympic swimmer Michael Phelps is one of them. He has won 28 Olympic medals in total. There are 23 gold medals among them. The most incredible part is how he managed to accumulate all of these in only five Olympics. Michael is widely recognised for using the butterfly as his preferred swimming stroke. At the age of 31, he made the decision to stop competing in professional swimming after many Olympic victories. However, he won 5 gold medals and 1 silver medal, bidding the Olympic pools a happy farewell. He has a brave, tenacious, and resolute narrative.

Last but not least, the Phelps comment that is unquestionably the most well-known of all time and a favourite among fans. Given how frequently we have heard it (and read it) during our swimming careers, it may now feel like a cliche. But that is absolutely true. Michael Phelps points out that we are the only ones who have real limits.

When you are aware of the specific reason why your performance fell short of expectations, you get a particular feeling in the pit of your stomach. Give your best effort in order to avoid these emotions and all of the "what ifs" in order to do yourself a favour. Focus on the tasks you know you should do. Later on, you'll appreciate yourself. It's easy to occasionally go into a type of funk. It's simple to allow how your body feels to take control after a particularly challenging training session. You're feeling worn out and hurt, and you're unsure when the taper will start.

But it's important to remember your initial motivations while you go through this unavoidable period. You set a goal for this season at the start of the year, whether you wrote it down or just had it in the back of your mind. It's not the right moment to stop pursuing it right now; instead, intensify your efforts.

Successful individuals spend a lot of time considering what and how they should act, and it is this way of thinking that has enabled them to change their fate and achieve better things in life. A strong and capable intellect is capable of great things. A man's ability to regulate his thoughts and use willpower is what enables him to achieve so much in life. The mindset that "it was destined to be" brings about disaster because it causes us to give up on our efforts to continuously work toward success and instead to use this as a justification for our failures.

Limiting beliefs, or the unfavourable things we tell ourselves about who we are and how the world operates, only prevent you from having complete control over your future. The motivation behind your actions, or your driving force, may also be gleaned from your connections. Six human needs certainty, importance, diversity, love/ connection, development, and contribution—are what motivate each of us. We all require these things on some level, but each of us has a primary need that dominates all others.

You'll be able to better manage your destiny if you see your life in this light, since you'll be able to identify and meet your needs in healthy ways. Although it is a survival mechanism, fear doesn't always help us, just like in relationships. Living in fear prevents you from ever learning how to master your destiny. You must learn to control your fear rather than allow it to control you if you want to reach your full potential and become the best version of yourself. Be open and honest with your spouse. Take action to launch the company you've always wanted. Enroll in a public speaking course. Do whatever it is you're terrified of right now.

We've all used justifications in the past, and some of us still do, despite our reluctance to acknowledge it. Whether it's to avoid having to do something we don't want to, to attempt something new (maybe a new martial art?), or just because we won't leave our comfort zone, we choose the easy option of making excuses.

Even though some justifications can seem innocent, the fact is that every justification you offer keeps you from realising your full potential. Also, you risk missing out on chances that may never come your way and failing to develop the qualities and skills that may help you advance.

Absolutely, we are aware that it can be challenging to get past your previous mistakes, especially when they still have a significant impact on you. The truth is that criticising yourself and dwelling on the past will only make you feel worse. Moreover, rather than analysing what went wrong and attempting to correct it, you can find yourself coming up with excuses in an effort to defend your shortcomings.

You'll be able to take action when you learn to be present and concentrate on what is happening at any particular time. You'll therefore quit creating excuses and concentrate on reflecting on your prior errors.

You'll wind up making excuses about not having "good luck" or, worse, blaming other people or things in order to avoid taking ownership of your mistakes if you don't accept responsibility for your deficiencies and errors. This is a pretty unhealthy way to live, to be perfectly honest. When you think about it, there are some things you can control—in this case, owning your mistakes. Instead of blaming external factors, why not exercise control over what you can?

As you develop the ability to accept responsibility for your mistakes, you'll be better equipped to concentrate on not making the same errors again and, more significantly, learning from them. Once you realise that you have control over certain things, you'll also feel more empowered to take command of your life.

The next step after accepting responsibility for your errors is to get back up, decide to improve as a result of the experience, and go on. You'll be able to discover a lot more about life and yourself once you've done that. Knowing this allows you to go on instead of making the same excuses over and over again out of a lack of courage to get up and try again.

We don't recognise that using excuses makes us more pessimistic since they make us dwell on our flaws and/or how inadequate we are. As a result, we experience failure and discouragement. In order to change this, it helps to concentrate on your strengths and keep in mind all of your potential so that you may hone them and use them to make the most of any circumstance.

You should be honest with yourself about your shortcomings (instead of making excuses!) so that you may work on transforming them into strengths. It's crucial to concentrate on and develop your strengths. You'll learn to love imperfection and realise that it's acceptable to not be flawless by embracing your defects. You are, after all, a singular person on a singular path.

You are a unique person, and your path is unique as well. Because of this, it is harmful to judge yourself against others and provide reasons for "not being good enough" just because you believe your accomplishments fall short of theirs. Keep in mind that you are the only one to whom you should compare yourself. By doing this, you'll put your best self in focus, and you'll naturally succeed in doing so.

It could be difficult to stop making excuses, especially if they have developed into a nasty habit. The truth is, however, that bad habits can be broken! Be patient, maintain your optimism, and, most importantly, keep moving forward even when it seems like you're not making any progress.

You'll soon be slapping all your justifications in the face and becoming the best version of yourself. Try it; you can do it!

Jessica Cox, a pilot with no arms who learned to fly with her feet. Due to a rare birth abnormality, Jessica Cox was born without arms. She has continued to live her life to the fullest despite this. Ms. Cox has really accomplished and experienced more than most individuals do in a lifetime. She started her pilot training after earning her degree from the University of Arizona in 2005. According to CNN, Cox, a motivational speaker who can play the piano, drive a vehicle, scuba dive, and even hold a third-degree black belt in karate, wants to inspire individuals with disabilities and has visited more than 20 countries. She frequently considers what her life would be like if she could turn back time and be born with arms. Not only would her life be drastically different, but she would also understand how powerful it is to live one's life in a way that has such a profound effect on others.

She has had leaders and role models. And now that she has experienced it, it's her duty to provide the same for the next generation of arms. She told the CNN news channel. Despite her initial dread of flying, Cox quickly overcame it and concentrated on obtaining her licence. Cox told the media outlet, "I had multiple flying instructors and contributed to my training to find this out." Therefore, determining what would work through trial and error took three years.

The You-Factor offers the secret to living the life of greatness you were meant to live by weaving together personal experiences, useful ideas, and profound biblical truth.

Everyone wants success in their lives. However, we all define prosperity slightly differently. Some people interpret it as having plenty of money and being wealthy. Others believe that happiness begins with perfect health or freedom. The Prosperity factor is your road map to achieving your goal and personal dream of success.

Nick Vujicic was born with phocamelia, a rare congenital disorder characterised by limb deformity. He has overcome the odds despite having very little foot by becoming a motivational speaker, getting married, and becoming a new father to Kiyoshi. Nick shares that he was fortunate to be born without limbs and legs, showing remarkable humility and sensitivity. For him, coping entails finding out how to live without something they have always known, which is a far more difficult task. How was this all made possible?

I watch in awe as Nick tells tales that highlight significant events in his life. He is very grateful for a small foot (or chicken drumstick, as he fondly refers to it), which allows him to do a lot of things, like wash his teeth, drive a car, use a computer, and more. With what he has, he has been able to lead a self-sufficient existence, produce four books, and inspire others. He says that comparing oneself to those who are better, richer, or more attractive all throughout one's life would only lead to unhappiness.

When coming up with justifications, people may be quite inventive. We frequently used them to escape challenging or unpleasant circumstances, as well as those that gave us anxiety and worry. Sometimes we make excuses just because we don't want to do anything, or perhaps it's because we're lazy and prefer to put off doing something. In some way or another, in every sphere of our lives, we have all been engaged in it. None of us have it easy in life. What, then, is that?

We need to be persistent and, most importantly, confident in ourselves. We have to think that we have a talent for something, and that this talent must be developed.

CHAPTER SIX

Unfurl Your Boundless Potential

"If you believe you are not capable of anything, your mind will provide you with all the evidence that you are not."

You'll start to see answers and breakthroughs if you change your perspective and convince yourself that you can do anything. Ignore the negativity within and around you and make the decision to only think of good ideas. Do that repeatedly, despite your feelings of helplessness, dejection, and lack of motivation. By giving yourself encouragement, you may direct your inner energy toward good expectations and look forward to the results of your work. It is essential to have a development attitude in order to push your boundaries.

It is essential to have a development attitude in order to push your boundaries. When you adopt a development mentality, you clearly communicate to your subconscious that nothing is out of your reach. You can learn anything you're enthusiastic about, develop your talents, and become whatever it is you want to be. There are no restrictions of any kind. Your mind starts to see the bridges instead of the streams, the solutions instead of the issues, and the road ahead instead of the hurdles with the appropriate sort of programming.

The fundamental shift in how you view yourself that the growth mindset causes is what makes you unique and unlocks the doors to your future success. You must push past your limitations and leave your comfort zone in order to achieve your objectives and become the person you desire. Eleanor Roosevelt once stated, "You must do the things you believe you cannot do." You only become aware of your potential when you push past your limitations.

What does it mean to "put boundaries in place"?

Why do we take them upon ourselves, exactly? When we create limits for ourselves, we determine that there are some things we are only capable of, certain distances we may travel, and certain things we only have a limited set of abilities. Why did we make this decision? Where did these concepts come from? Frequently, we create them without any tests or evidence. They stem from feelings of dread or failure, from messages we received as children, or from the fact that we have allowed the limitations of others to affect us. Your mind is what you feed yourself, just as your body is what you consume. All facets of your life are affected negatively by your thoughts.

Nothing can prevent you from succeeding and evolving into your greatest self if you train your mind and harness its immense potential. Have faith in your own potential, skills, and abilities. All of your hopes and dreams are attainable for you.

Things only seem challenging before you try something new or start working toward a goal. When you overcome mental obstacles, you feel at ease performing tasks and discover that they are simpler than you had believed. The human mind is hard-wired for simplicity and takes the easiest route to keep you safe from harm. It would always pick comfort over unfamiliarity, pleasure over pain, and leisure over hard work.

The human mind is hard-wired for simplicity and takes the easiest route to keep you safe from harm. It would always pick comfort over unfamiliarity, pleasure over pain, and leisure over hard work.

The You-Factor offers the secret to living the life of greatness you were meant to live by weaving together personal experiences, useful ideas, and profound biblical truth. Everyone wants success in their lives. However, we all define prosperity slightly differently. Some people interpret it as having plenty of money and being wealthy. Others believe that happiness begins with perfect health or freedom. The Prosperity factor is your road map to achieving your goal and personal dream of success.

Limitations only exist when you impose them on yourself mentally.

As a result, you must flip the narrative and prepare your mind, teaching it to do what you desire. It's all in your head in the end, whether you succeed or fail, fight or give up, or live an ordinary or remarkable life. You must make the necessary effort.

However, you must first let go of any mental restrictions and have confidence in your ability to bring your aspirations to reality. Your world is created by what you think and visualise in your head. When you have confidence in yourself, you'll start to attract opportunities, your skills will advance, and your chances of success will dramatically improve.

You must understand that your inner world determines what you manifest in your outer environment. Since your inner world determines what you manifest in your outer environment, you must plant the seeds of positive thought if you want your efforts to have a positive result. Despite all of the opposition, justifications, and weak arguments, you must be proactive and take action. Just get going. Any worthwhile goal must be pursued with zeal.

"If four things are followed - having a great aim, acquiring knowledge, hard work, and perseverance - then anything can be achieved."- A. P. J. Abdul Kalam

How often have you heard that success comes from hard work? Undoubtedly a great deal, and it's true! Success is mostly dependent on effort, and this is true for many different reasons. Let's first discuss why working hard matters before we go into our arguments for why it's essential for success. Working hard enables you to gradually improve your level of self-discipline.

Even though procrastination may make even the simplest chores more difficult to complete, we occasionally nevertheless self-destruct. Sometimes we don't even know why we do it! But if you are committed to working hard, self-control will come. This is another another example of why perseverance is essential for success.

"I've missed more than 9,000 shots in my career. I've lost almost 300 games. 26 times, I've been trusted to take the game winning shot and missed. I've failed over and over and over again in my life. And that is why I succeed."- Michael Jordan

There will always be challenges in our path to achieving our objectives. They shouldn't, however, prevent you from making the initial move. Obstacles are there to be overcome. The fact is that if you do nothing, nothing will ever change, and there is no other option except to try. Behavior is contagious. You'll succeed if you take the initiative and are consistent in your efforts. He was the first to understand that fear was a myth, which allowed him to work more and dream greater. The biggest barrier to success is the fear of failing.

Humans are so afraid of failing that it prevents us from taking any action, yet the irony of life is that if we do nothing, we are destined to fail. Isn't that contradictory?

It's crucial to understand that the only limitations are those we impose on ourselves; in this case, the limitation is the delusion of fear. But you don't have to let challenges stop you. Do not turn around and give up if you hit a wall. Find a way to scale it, get through it, or go around it. Avoid wasting your time and energy by worrying when you encounter a bottleneck. One solution exists — take a moment to collect yourself. Use this as motivation to be tough rather than allowing the pressure of the moment to bring you down.

Remind yourself of why you must succeed and use that motivation to follow your ambition, which is what truly counts. The game has its ups and downs, but you must never lose sight of your own objectives, and you must never allow yourself to lose out of indifference.

A person with discipline, devotion, and resolve to succeed in life is someone who works hard enough. We've all heard the sayings, "There is no quick fix to success" and "Nothing worth having comes easily," but how many of us have actually lived by them? Sometimes in life, our goals and ambitions appear insurmountable, and we begin to lose patience.

As a result, we start looking for shortcuts since we are exhausted and believe that our efforts are going in vain. Although the road to hard work is not always easy, the end result will be worth all the challenges, so trust me when I say that it will eventually pay off. Everyone must demonstrate a dedication to consistent hard work that will take them to the pinnacle of accomplishment if they are to accomplish anything in life.

"The three ordinary things that we often don't pay enough attention to, but which I believe are the drivers of all success, are hard work, perseverance, and basic honesty." -Azim Premji

Hard labour cannot be substituted for Take a look at these inspiring sayings about hard work from some of history's greatest performers if you or your team are feeling worn out, overworked, or just "not in the mood" to work. You'll undoubtedly become inspired and get back on the road to success! A person who has expertise in a certain sector is more likely than others who lack experience to accomplish their life's goals and can operate shrewdly and effortlessly.

This is still, without a doubt, the most difficult part of achieving successful objectives. What drives some people to relentlessly pursue their dreams while other people give up when things become tough? We get experience via hard labour, which enables us to learn a lot of new things. We may use this experience to develop clever thinking skills to successfully address a challenging issue. A person's ability to solve problems is enhanced through experience.

In order to realise your dream, you must first take the first step in that direction. You must give your all, regardless of where you are in the process of creating yourself or if you already have a life purpose.

According to a report, four out of ten people are leading unhappy lives. In all honesty, we have no idea what will occur tomorrow or a year from now. Many people have been heard expressing, "I wish I had done it before." due to the passage of time. They only wish they had put in more effort when it was necessary. You can live a life without regrets if you work hard. You won't ever have to regret not doing something since it will provide you with the foundation for a brighter future. Images, ideas, and literature are what people in the twenty-first century need to continually push themselves in a positive direction. While doing this, we fail to remember that drive and optimism result from effort. With hard effort and the sensation it brings, you'll be able to maintain your optimism for a longer time with hard effort and the sensation it brings. All of us have fallen head over heels for someone, whether it be a person with a lovely personality, someone we admire, or someone we aspire to be.

We must, therefore, give our lives significance while we are living them. Without putting up effort and striving, nothing is possible.

Having a single objective is the best way to make the most of your life. Having a goal is crucial, regardless of how large or small it is. And when you set a goal like that and work hard and dedicate yourself to it every day, you can achieve it and become the person you were meant to be. At this point, I believe that you have an understanding of how hard work and perseverance enable you to maximise your potential and turn your efforts into both monetary and non-monetary advantages that steadily grow over time.

"If you always out limits on everything you do, physical or anything else, it will spread into your work, and into your life. There are no limits. There are only plateaus, and you must go beyond them." – Bruce Lee

It takes time to increase your self-awareness. There is no magic bullet. We know that people who are very successful in both their personal and professional lives have one thing in common: they are self-aware. Building self-awareness is essential, whether you want to focus on your personal growth, advance your profession, or improve your leadership abilities. And you can do so by taking a few simple steps.

"The only limit to your impact is your imagination and commitment." – Tony Robbins

Sean Diddy Combs, who has a $700M+ net worth despite losing his father when he was 3 years old, believes that "Positive Attracts Positive." You receive what you put into anything. A positive attitude may produce bad results just as easily as a negative mindset can provide good results. In addition, Henry Ford is credited with saying, "Whether you think you can or you think you can't, you're correct." Helping others seems to be a regular behaviour among successful people, and this habit promotes their success. Some could refer to it as karma. Some people can completely miss the link.

But in actuality, relationships are the foundation of success. We create the world around us. Helping others achieve success and happiness will make you happier and more successful. There is no way to do this wrong. If you desire happiness for one hour, the Dalai Lama says to take a nap. Go on a trek if you want to be happy for the day. Win the lottery if you want happiness for a year. But if you want lasting satisfaction, do good deeds. By assisting others in their success, you will also be assisting yourself in their success.

People who are successful must consume a lot of lemonade. We've all heard the proverb, "When life gives you lemons, make lemonade." They are masters at transforming challenges into chances. In fact, it could be one of their most admirable character attributes. When the Dalai Lama was still a child, he was banished from his homeland. He said that his exile had given him the chance to travel the world and make every place he went his home when asked how difficult it must have been to never have a home. He credits that with enabling him to broaden his horizons and develop into the well-known leader he is today. Nelson Mandela spent a large portion of his life in jail, which he describes as an "extended vacation for 27 years." He made the most of it by reading and writing, which helped him develop into the powerful leader that he was. "I am inherently an optimist," he said. Keeping one's feet going ahead and one's head pointing toward the sun is a necessary component of optimism. Successful, productive individuals have a lot of similar tendencies.

How might we surpass our targets for the upcoming year, furthermore? What primarily drives and inspires us is our desire for higher and greater things. However, I believe that it's important to put things into perspective in addition to simply examining the numbers. When considering the previous year, this becomes especially valid. None of us wanted 2020, yet that was the year that we received. Due to constraints caused by the coronavirus epidemic, we were compelled to behave flexibly and work online throughout that year. Putting this into perspective, I can state that we devised fresh ideas, overcame difficulties, and achieved success. I'm quite happy with what our international sales and marketing team has accomplished.

How to determine which behaviours will best help you achieve your goals?

Success, therefore, also involves individuals. The human traits most essential to commercial success are appreciation, openness, accountability, and honesty. The appropriate mindset is also the secret to all of our success. But as a leader, you must also take stock of your own leadership accomplishments. What drove you to your breaking point and produced the best leadership outcomes for you personally? It's not just the stats that matter—challenge yourself, reflect on your leadership successes, and make it a point to improve each time!

Meeting your requirements is the key to success. Before helping someone else, put on your own oxygen mask. If you want to make a real difference in the world, you must take care of yourself. Success is understanding when you need to say no. Only a balanced existence can lead to success. Learning to say no is a necessary component of balance. Saying "no" does not suggest selfishness; rather, it only indicates that you have priorities and are aware of what requires your focus at any given moment. Realising how abundant your life is is a sign of success. Life is abundant with love, health, friends, and family. Understanding this is a crucial step in developing gratitude for what life has provided you. If you can sense this, your journey to achievement has already begun.

Success is realising that what you don't give away, you can't retain. Only by assisting others in their success can you achieve it. A part of constructing the society we all want to live in is learning to give rather than constantly taking. By helping others, you will also foster an atmosphere where people desire to assist you. Getting through fear is success. You feel invincible when you overcome a fear. It's definitely something to be proud of, even if it's just facing one minor fear each week. Greater concerns will take more time to conquer, yet any effort you make will be successful.

Success is acquiring new knowledge every day. Successful people are aware that learning is a lifelong process. Make time every day to chat to someone who holds a different opinion than your own, read an intriguing article on a subject you don't know much about, or watch a TED lecture on cutting-edge research. Learning doesn't take long, so begin right away. Success is realising that you can win a war by losing a few battles. People that are successful pick and select their conflicts. You will be successful when you realise which conflicts will eventually aid you in achieving your objectives. Loving and receiving love is success. It might be scary to open your heart to other people. A vital step toward a successful life and fulfilment is having the guts to love and receive love from others.

Success is sticking up for what you believe in.

Research indicates that roughly 40% of our everyday actions are truly habits, which is sort of frightening to consider. There are the obvious ones like taking a shower or brushing your teeth, but there are a lot more routines in your life than you may think, such as the route you take to travel to work or reading the news online when you sit down at your desk each day. When it comes to developing and attaining objectives, that's really excellent news. This is due to the fact that if you can create the appropriate habits, you won't need to exert as much effort or be as deliberate about acting in accordance with your moral obligations. Instead, you develop automatic behaviour and follow a predetermined route to success. So how can you develop those success-enhancing habits?

How daily, modest acts add up enormously to make you an action warrior! This chapter is devoted to helping you stay inspired to succeed every day! Everyone immediately conjures up something bad when someone mentions habits, such as smoking, drinking, or using illegal substances. They believe the word "habit" connotes something negative, degenerative, or fatal. However, habitual behaviour isn't always bad. Just as you may develop bad habits, you can also develop positive ones. Bad habits like smoking or healthy ones like cleaning your teeth might be the culprit.

God gave us the gift of habit, which enables us to achieve. "Habit is a suitable term. Habit simply implies that anything gets simpler the second time you do it. It's how God wants to see you prosper. Is habit a good thing, I wonder? Yes! Habituation can be advantageous. Most people frequently misunderstand the word "habit." Every time people hear the word "habit," they misinterpret it. Apply simple techniques to improve your life. Less than 10% of people stick with their resolutions from the previous year. Would you like to be a part of that 10%? If so, you should read this book. You've taken the first step in realising your objectives by choosing to read this book. Why choose this habit book when there are so many others available?

"We repeatedly become what we do." by Aristotle "Success comes from modest disciplines done every day; failure comes from minor faults repeated every day." Habits have a compound effect as well as a rippling effect. Charles Duhigg uses Lisa Allen as an example, who made the decision to give up smoking in order to go on a desert walk in Egypt despite being overweight, in debt, and unable to hold down a job for more than a year at the time.

A new habit or a change in an existing habit can have a cascading effect and lead to the emergence of new behaviours in different contexts. You stopped smoking and started running as a result, which changed her eating habits, sleeping habits, ability to save money, and organisational skills. So, take some time to think about it and acknowledge the influence habits have on your life. So, take some time to think about it and acknowledge the influence habits have on your life. What positive behaviours contribute to a happy or healthy life? What routines do you have that are bad for your health? What routines are holding you back from moving forward?

You must first ask yourself: What habits do you wish to develop? You can't choose 20 new behaviours and expect to adopt them all at once, as we've already explained. Start with one foundational habit instead—something you know will benefit you and make your life smoother overall. Even though it will take some effort and time to develop into a true habit, going to the gym every morning before work will be well worth the effort since you'll have more energy for all of your other responsibilities as a result of your improved physical health. Be patient with yourself next.

It's a common question to wonder how long it takes to develop a habit, yet everyone is different in this regard. Some people rapidly develop bad habits. That could be advantageous, like going to the gym, or detrimental, like developing a drug addiction. Others require far more repetition, so you must be patient, but keep in mind that each time you do an action, you're building stronger brain pathways that will make it simpler the following time. Finally, be aware that undesirable behaviours are difficult to completely break.

Your mind does more than simply forget them. Instead, your brain has to be retrained and rewired. Finding the trigger for your habit is the best approach to doing it. In other words, what motivates you to act in a certain way? For instance, you could start browsing social media to unwind after a stressful day at work. The next step is to choose a replacement behavior.

The next step is to choose a replacement behaviour. The key is that in order for the new behaviour to satisfy the same demands and become habitual, it must also feel rewarding. For example, it's unlikely that you can substitute Instead of checking Facebook, I'll just do my taxes, but you might come up with another incentive that would be more significant to you. You might attempt two minutes of deep breathing to help you relax and reduce some stress.

Alternately, you may take a little break to talk with a coworker, which is equally sociable but might promote deeper teamwork at work. Because human willpower is limited, we must use it wisely. Being aware of habit creation is one of the finest methods to save our mental resources and accomplish more. This is because the more we can do automatically, the more effectively we can use our willpower to accomplish even greater things.

Many individuals have had the experience of making resolutions for the new year and then not following through on them. There aren't any requirements for taking this course. You may start right now. But maintaining an open mind is crucial before you begin viewing. Based on prior experiences, you could be concerned that you don't do well with objectives or that making an effort to follow a plan would only lead to failure. All of us have been there. But in reality, no one succeeds in their endeavours only through willpower.

What separates a goal from a to-do list? Most likely, you have a to-do list. I am aware that I have them, and research conducted by LinkedIn indicates that 63% of professionals do as well. To-do lists are a terrific way to keep track of your obligations and ensure that nothing is overlooked, but they aren't really that efficient. In fact, a firm with to-do list capabilities looked into the behaviours of its customers and found that 41% of tasks entered never got finished. That success rate is not particularly high. So, can to-do lists be used efficiently, and how do they relate to our goals in any case? Let's begin by defining and differentiating certain terms.

A to-do list is a written or electronic list that you may use to keep track of particular things that need to get done. You'll be miserable if you confuse it with your aspirations, since they are not at all the same thing. High-level strategic priorities are your objectives. Your goals should be in line with your to-do list—those annoying daily duties—rather than the other way around. There are three categories of tasks that are often added to your to-do list.

I refer to the first group as maintenance activities. Unfortunately, these aren't strategic goals, but they must be completed. Making an appointment with the dentist is one of the items on my current to-do list. Even if it's not precisely a big-picture task, it must nevertheless be done. The key is to do these silly, insignificant duties as soon as you can. Use the extra 10 minutes in your day if one of your meetings finishes early. What I refer to as manifestations of strategic priorities make up the second group of items on your to-do list. These are the specific steps that turn your strategic goals into reality.

For instance, I'm about to launch a new programme, which is a major area of concentration for me, and right now, editing video testimonials and updating the sales page are on my list of things to accomplish. These are specialised jobs, yet they are of the utmost importance since they help me achieve my main objective. You ought to spend the majority of your time on these activities. Your third category of tasks is those that are top of mind for other people. These pursuits do not correspond to your strategic goals, nor do they even represent pursuits that are just essential, such as visiting the dentist.

Instead, it involves demands from others to include you in activities such as editing a report, conducting an informative interview with a relative, or attending a meeting that you don't actually need to attend. You must fervently avoid doing these things. Not all of them can be avoided. Even if it doesn't correspond with your highest and best usage, you must endure and carry out the request since you may owe the individual a favour in some circumstances or because your supervisor may be the one asking. But whenever you can, question the request.

Check to see whether it's actually essential or if there's a quicker or simpler way to handle it, such as emailing someone a useful article rather than scheduling a meeting or simply bowing out since you're focused on a huge project. To-do lists are a fantastic tool that, for me personally, provide a lot of comfort in knowing that nothing is getting missed, but the trick is to make sure you're looking at your to-do list through the lens of your main priorities. Your to-do list cannot control you.

Success does not come easily. It requires preparation and effort on your part. We've been talking about the methods you may use to decide on, carry out, and accomplish your goals. Your career will only benefit if you are able to become one of the most productive and effective people you know. Here's how to start bringing something into being right away. Get very clear about your priorities first. Describe how you see your life in one, five, and ten years. This gives you the ability to understand where you're going as well as the skills and knowledge gaps you have, allowing you to develop a more effective plan of action to get there.

Next, choose just two objectives to concentrate on during the following six months. Check if this matches the future vision you have for yourself by looking back. For instance, you could understand that you need to develop your management abilities if you want to get a promotion before the end of the year. Perhaps you should enrol in a course over the next six months, either in person or online, to help you learn more about best practises and improve so you're ready for the opportunity.

Every three to six months, it's crucial to reassess your goals. Make time for this today by pulling out your calendar. This may really be configured as a recurring calendar reminder. Get out your goal review worksheet since it will be useful at this point. You cannot choose your objectives once and believe they will always be important. Every few months, make it a point to review them to make sure they align with your current goals.

Consider how you will celebrate your victories lastly. Too frequently, even when we accomplish a goal that we have been working toward for a while, we have already adapted and have lost interest in it. Include time in your schedule for celebrations and reflections on your accomplishments. You put a lot of effort into your career, so when you reach a milestone, be sure to celebrate it. Additionally, it will keep you more driven to keep pushing forward and make further advancements.

Did you learn how to build your self-awareness in this chapter to advance your profession and help you personally? By now you must have learnt how to become more self-aware so you can comprehend how people see you and more effectively match your actions to your objectives. You must have gone through how to use a self-awareness action plan, identify beliefs to increase self-awareness, go outside of yourself to acquire a fresh perspective, and more. Now you make the decision to share your knowledge and wisdom through your lives of narrative that demonstrate: accepting full responsibility for your life; behaving in ways that will help you; and using visualisation to help you achieve your objectives. Take action to have a prosperous life.

While there are many things that might contribute to someone becoming successful, almost all people who succeed both personally and professionally have a strong sense of self-awareness.

We have a lot of things to do, but we don't enjoy them. Everything is based on an individual's needs. When we enter, we are delighted. When we take a tour with our friends and family, we are excited. With our loved one, we are content. When we do something very intriguing, we get excited. But have you ever considered how you feel when working? Do you actually feel content, ecstatic, or happy? Ideas are created out of passion. Being enthusiastic about something encourages the creation of fresh ideas. Because when we love someone, we always work to keep them shining, and this encourages us to think of new and inventive methods to improve the quality. These will spark the development of fresh concepts for solving that problem.

Having a good attitude involves more than simply having a grin on your face. It involves keeping a positive outlook and attitude even while everything around you is in complete disarray. Positive and negative ideas are considered to have a similar effect on your mind as a healthy or unhealthy diet has on your physical health. Positive ideas will help you witness great improvements in the world around you.

Life is always equal parts positive and negative if you look at it as it is. When you see things for what they are, neither the good nor the bad can overwhelm you. Everything is happening the way it is because they are equal. Both must be controlled so that you may create what you can. Because electricity has both positive and negative charges, a light turns on. We are getting a good outcome, therefore we don't mind the bad. If there is a man and a woman, we don't mind who they are as long as they are happy.

All that ever occurred to you—darkness and light; agony and pleasure; joy and despair—happened within you.

Every aspect of existence is a struggle between two dualities. Male and female, light and darkness, day and night, are what you mean by positive and negative. Without it, how can life exist? It would be like declaring that you just desire life and do not want death. Life exists only because death does. There is light only because there is darkness. Just don't let the bad beat you down. Let them both be present and consider ways to make them both productive. It is crucial that we tell the truth about where we are right now if we care about this life. If they were to start producing a lot of undesirable effects, we might start to view them as a concern. The issue is with the outcome you generate, not with the good and bad.

You only need to use it to your advantage to produce a favourable outcome; resisting either the positive or the negative is not necessary. It is crucial that we tell the truth about where we are right now if we care about this life. Then, and only then, can we go. Many opportunities for people have been destroyed by positive thinking. There is a poem composed by a thinker who is optimistic:

There is no way to change life if you are unable to accept it as it is. There is nothing you can do about it. You can only perform amusing mental feats, which may amuse you briefly but won't get you anywhere. There is a lot of information available regarding how positive thinking may change your life. Can you avoid accumulating more karma by using positive thinking, or can it even help you get rid of it?

Change your negative self-talk to a positive one.

Whatever you observe in this world is something you are witnessing within. You are able to see a pen on the table because light strikes it, reflects off of it, travels through your eyes, and then passes through your mind, where it is recognised as a pen. Actually, what happens is that you are perceiving internal events with your eyes and intellect. And you alone are the solution.

If you control what's occurring within you, you alone will define your whole experience of life. Even if the incident in your life may not have been planned by you, how you perceive it, how you feel about it, and how you respond to it are all up to you. Therefore, if you want to succeed and have a better life today, you must learn to be self-reliant. According to best-selling author Jack Canfield of the Chicken Soup for the Soul series, your outcome is influenced by the incident and your response.

How much time are you willing to devote to honing your abilities in order to raise your worth per hour and advance in your career?

How much time, specifically, besides your regular working hours People frequently believe that they should only work during the hours for which they are getting paid. While performing your duties and receiving a fair salary are undoubtedly crucial, you should also invest in your career by frequently enhancing your abilities outside of your usual work duties. Spending time in this way can help you develop your strengths, which will increase your worth per hour and work stability. By following a straightforward four-step procedure, you may make this investment in yourself. Identifying the time commitment you're willing to make is the first step.

I advise budgeting at least an hour each week and blocking out time slots on your schedule. Give it a name that is specific, such as "your strength investment." It will be simpler for you to keep your promise if you schedule time in advance on your calendar. Gathering your resources for the short course you are designing for yourself comes next. You must now locate your own classes, books, and other resources in order to improve the most important strength you choose to concentrate on.

Practicing gratitude increases your likelihood of achieving happiness and contentment in life. True happiness can only be attained by being grateful for what you have.

I may take online classes regarding my favourite apps if I want to strengthen my computer skills. Books, periodicals, websites, blogs, and community classes are other sources of information. Decide to deliver something that plays to your strengths as the following phase. Inform your supervisor, a peer mentor, or a colleague about this strong investment you are making. Inform them that you'll be giving them an assignment to show them what you've learned.

If I'm a writer, for instance, I may promise them that I'll finish the first draught of one chapter in a month. To ensure that you are held accountable, request that they mark that day on their calendar. This will make you more devoted to your goal and enable the other person to be your supporter. They will want to help you and provide you with any resources they can since they have been actively involved from the beginning. Finally, adhere to the schedule you made.

Consider the positives, no matter how minor.

Remain true to your word to yourself. Stop doing whatever you're doing at the appointed time and concentrate on building your strength. Your use of information is considerably more useful than just knowing it. Your strengths will develop as you stick to your training plan and complete the assignments assigned to you by your accountability partner. This will allow you to advance consistently in your profession.

Eliminate and overcome the inability to plan well due to a lack of drive and willpower.

The founder of Air Deccan, Captain Gopinath, who revolutionised air travel in India, comes from a modest background. The second of eight children, Captain Gopinath's father was a schoolteacher. Gopinath joined the Indian Army after completing his education and was given a commission for an eight-year term. He started a sustainable farm, developed an Enfield dealership, and operated an Udipi hotel after leaving the military. Captain Gopinath started Deccan Aviation, a helicopter charter service, only after several attempts, failures, and hardships; this business subsequently served as the foundation for Air Deccan.

I will explain practical techniques that will show you precisely how to make excellent plans that are effective with habits, break poor plans, throw out ineffective plans, and master the small actions that produce amazing outcomes. It's not you; it's your regular plans that need to change, not you. Your system architecture is the issue. The reason why terrible plans, sluggish plans, dispersed plans, and bad habits keep happening isn't that you don't want to change; it's that your change management strategy is flawed. You fall short of reaching your objectives.

Your plans may be used to design your environment and make success simpler. They can also be used to get back on track when you get off track and make up lost time. The complete guide to planning your everyday in 30 days, whether you are a team trying to win a championship, an organisation hoping to redefine an industry, or simply a person who wants to stop smoking, lose weight, reduce stress, or achieve any other goal or anything at all that envisions long-term and successful outcomes, will reshape the way you think and work about your very own progress and success, and give you the tools and strategies you need to transform your habitual plans. The key to transforming your life is in realising how important imagination is in shaping your awareness.

Discover how to use the law of attraction and the power of positive thinking in your life to start attracting more money, a new profession, improved health, or meaningful relationships. How I found the key to unleashing the full force of the law of attraction: wealth from the inside out; the soul of language; prosperity and the body, mind, and spirit connection; the gifted heart; overcoming adversity; you were created to be healthy; the prosperity factor is your road map to completely embracing the life you wish to live.

The reasons why most people struggle to change for the better and how to avoid making the same mistakes. How to incorporate a new routine into an existing one? How to make changing your behaviour easier. What do you anticipate? ? Are you prepared to change?

Can you train your brain to become faster, stronger, wiser?

During the past few decades, we've discovered some straightforward yet effective guidelines for how the brain regulates energy from the top down and bottom up. The brain is the supreme controller of the human system from the top down, and whatever we focus on absorbs our energy. For instance, even though your big right toe is likely receiving blood and oxygen right now, if you were to pay attention to it right now, you'd likely begin to notice how it feels.

Our awareness delivers new feelings or sensations when we pay attention to anything, and it can alter both the quantity and quality of our energy. You could notice a change in how you are now feeling physically and emotionally if you think of someone in your life for whom you are thankful and focus on the area surrounding your heart. Top-down processing occurs when you deliberately think about something, focus on it, and then notice a change in how you feel.

In addition, a very potent bottom-up process is at work, much like when your body takes control when your brain perceives a potential threat in your environment. Your brain may detect a possible threat in your environment when you begin to feel worried and breathe shallowly and quickly. Most of the time, we try to stop these bottom-up processes by telling ourselves things like, "You shouldn't be stressed," "Others have it worse than you," or "I'll take care of it tomorrow."

But consider this: Everything changes when our bottom-up feelings indicate a threat to our survival. Because this sensory information is given priority by the brain initially, this is why you've felt that your thoughts are diverting your attention. The brain's mission is to keep you safe at all costs, even if doing so prevents you from achieving your objectives. So consider what can undermine your sense of security during the day.

Maybe eating the incorrect meals or going too long without eating. Going too long without breathing or moving in a stressed-out manner. concentrating excessively on analytical and logical work without pausing to be contemplative or creative. Being truly present is impossible when we begin to feel overextended. We can only direct the energy we require to the upper area of the brain, where we enable these more logical, reasonable, and deliberate actions, when we feel comfortable and have the capacity to handle all of the demands in our lives. You can rely on your brain to feed you more efficiently and assist you in achieving your most significant goals when you learn how to be in control of it and provide it the things it actually needs to feel safe.

Every living organism, including the human system, has some type of rhythm or pattern. Everything, including your heartbeat, brain waves, and blood sugar levels, should fluctuate. Your energy is no different. You want a rhythm or pattern to the way your energy rises and falls throughout the day. The fluctuation of energy will support your peak performance and make you feel less stressed. Before I give you some helpful advice on how to do that, I want you to take a moment to consider your own day. Or do you wake up and go and go and go and then be astonished when you can't unwind at night?

Do you expend energy and then invest it back in yourself to recharge? an energy flatline, in my opinion. Now, while it might sound a little excessive, my argument is just that. You're effectively taking over your own system and wearing yourself thin if you don't follow the normal course of stress and recuperation.

How do you ensure that your energy fluctuates in a normal pattern each day?

Here are a few straightforward tactics you may use. First, if you drink coffee in the morning, take your time drinking it and read a few pages of a motivational book or listen to some motivating music to make it a conscious and perhaps even inspirational experience. In this way, your energy comes from more than simply coffee. Taking regular breaks during the day is definitely something I'd advise, especially if you find yourself spending a lot of time sitting down.

Setting a timer to remind you every hour is the best course of action. Then stand up and go outside for five minutes. Your body receives an immediate boost from the activity and fresh air, and your mood may also be lifted.

Additionally, it will unquestionably sharpen your focus and attention for when you go back. You should also make an effort to obtain a full night's sleep each night. Although you've probably heard of it before, it's really important to refresh your body and mind. Good sleep helps you wake up feeling more awake and decreases stress and inflammation. Sleep offers the brain the time and energy to evaluate your day and draw crucial connections between the significant events that occurred, which can help your memory. Nature follows these predictable rhythms, much like day and night, to keep us alert enough to be productive while maintaining a healthy balance with adequate rest, relaxation, and restoration.

Furthermore, as we strengthen our ability to handle whatever life throws at us, the more we can really use the stress and problems in life to drive achievement. Consider how a baby uses their time and energy if you've ever been around one.

Now consider your day. How frequently do you give your all to the things that are most important to you at the time? Are you easily distracted when you receive a new email, message from a friend, or text from a coworker? When you're driving, do you ever check your texts? Our mental and emotional well-being may be completely destroyed by these distractions, especially if they start to form thinking and behaviour habits.

Because the brain isn't made to continuously multitask, be stimulated continuously, or do anything continuously at all. In the same way that eating only vegetables is equally harmful as eating only pizza, continual stimulation can cause our energies to flatline, which is always negative. At least, that's what I tell myself. But in all seriousness, the plague of distractions is dangerous, whether it's the accelerated ageing process that causes illness and disorder to develop more quickly in our bodies or the fact that individuals cause automobile accidents when they multitask while driving or even just crossing the street. This trend must be broken.

You may do this by establishing guidelines and limitations for your behaviour in each situation. Here are a few things I recommend you do. First and foremost, always strive to prioritise energy over time. To do this, pay attention to your body, monitor your energy levels, and take breaks throughout the day to rest and recharge.

Keep in mind that the important thing is to ensure you have the energy necessary to complete the necessary tasks in the proper manner, not how quickly you complete them. Use those frustrating small pauses, such as traffic lights and long lines, to genuinely breathe and be grateful rather than feeling upset or agitated, is a specific guideline I've started to follow that has been extremely helpful.

While you wait, you might want to check your phone or send one more email, but by seeing downtime as an investment in yourself, you'll be able to recharge more frequently. You may begin to teach your brain to stop multitasking over time to make it less alluring to try to pass the time whenever you get a minute to yourself. You could forcibly restrain yourself from reading your email while speaking to a friend or a member of your family. You could even come to the realisation that you don't have to act on every notion you have because it is only a thought. These methods will assist you in revitalising your energy so that you are prepared and able to take action once more.

There are easy things we can do at work and at home to revitalise others around us in addition to replenishing our own batteries. Making rules and setting boundaries for our time is one of the most effective methods to do this. and truly combine energy management with time management, putting more of an emphasis on the value we derive from the time we have available and not promoting the unhelpful notion that we must constantly be running and stressed.

There are numerous other approaches you may take, but I'll only mention the two that I believe would be most beneficial. More meaning-making and less multitasking. We manage our energy considerably better when we stop attempting to accomplish too many things at once. This keeps the brain's more primitive, sensitive regions calm, adaptive, and flexible. And it spreads easily. Consider this.

When someone's phone rings when they are near you, their mood and focus are affected. However, it can also cause you to think about things you might or ought to be doing in the present rather than concentrating on the discussion or work at hand. On the other side, when we provide more possibilities for meaning-making, we activate the pre-frontal logical cortex, which supports higher-order abilities like creativity, curiosity, and teamwork. This improves our ability to think effectively and allows us to do a great deal more in less time.

Simple actions like asking others to share something for which they are glad or anything amusing that occurred to them today might serve as meaningful-making chances. Alternatively, it might be more extensive and continuous, such as assisting individuals in making connections between their own missions and values and those of the business so that everyone is aware of how the work they are doing contributes to the overall success of the whole team.

If you're like most people, you've had nights when you were so exhausted that you couldn't get your brain to shut off and really let you sleep, leaving you wired and exhausted at the same time. You'll be able to work at your best and genuinely switch off your energy when you need to relax and recharge if you develop better habits throughout the day. Following what I refer to as a "High Five" is a fantastic approach to going through these new rhythms.

If you're unsure of where to begin, think about including a few seconds of appreciation in your daily stroll or cup of coffee. Consider an amusing event that happened to you during the day when it's time to go to bed. Both of them are quite quick and easy to accomplish, yet they help you channel your energy in a more useful way. The following three tactics are focused on how you eat, move, and take breaks, and we're going to pay extra attention to how you do these things even more than what you do after you have routines to start and finish your day appropriately.

Everyone is aware that what and how much they eat affects their energy levels, for instance, but you might be shocked to learn that how you eat matters just as much. Everyone knows we need to exercise during the day, but what may surprise you is that how often you move may be more important than how much time you spend at the gym.

When you take a moment to really appreciate your food, you put your brain in a more positive state that actually enables you to digest food more effectively. Regular movement is a crucial component of energy management.

Finally, it actually matters when and how you take breaks. This is the hardest habit to form for most people since we have a tendency to feel as though we must always be creating. However, we all know that producing poorly when we are always working makes it crucial that we take frequent breaks to recharge.

Now, if you feel that self-care is selfish or if you're concerned that if you slow down, you might not pick up speed again, it might be difficult to prioritise it. Remember that everything is normal. With just a few easy steps, you can begin to rewire these thought and behaviour patterns, making it easier for you to incorporate them into your daily routine. As you begin to feel better and receive encouraging comments from those around you, you'll be even more inspired to continue on your current path.

How much energy do you now have?

We actually don't notice the majority of the time since we are so preoccupied with getting things done. Gaining more awareness of our energy levels during the day gives us insightful information that enables us to decide what needs to be changed in order to recharge most efficiently. Then I'll lead you through a brief energy audit after we discuss the five main forms of energy we have and how they are related. First, the body's supply of nutrients like glucose and oxygen determines how much physical energy we have at any one time.

Our emotional energy therefore determines the type of energy we have and whether we are concentrating on possibilities or possible threats in our environment or on good or negative things. We focus thanks to the power of our minds. It's our capacity to focus attention on the things we decide to pay attention to. Then, our morals and beliefs serve as the source of our spiritual vitality. It is what propels us towards the people and things that are most important to us.

Finally, the kinship we experience with others is what we refer to as our social energy. When we feel connected and protected, both our bodies and minds flourish. Let's consider the degree of connectivity between these energy systems now. Like when you skip meals for an extended period of time, it affects more than just your physical vitality.

Like most people, you can start to feel angry or lose your temper more frequently than you'd like. Then, because your emotions are diverting your attention, you probably won't be able to concentrate properly or think in a creative or flexible way. There really is a mind-body link. The brain processes information and energy in a two-way process to calculate how much energy you have to use in the time that is available.

Understanding your capabilities in each of these areas will thus enable you to develop more focused and planned recharge strategies. Now is the time to print the energy audit guide from your workout files. Right now, we're going to assess your energy. An easy approach to achieving this is to rank each energy domain from zero to ten, with zero representing complete emptiness and ten representing full fuel.

What are your current feelings like?

Write down your results for each of the five categories on your handout. Add up your numbers after you're done, then multiply the result by two. This will provide you with a total number out of 100, which will also show what proportion of your overall energy you have charged at this time. For instance, if you sum up the five domains and receive a score of 40, you'll be charged 80% of that amount after multiplying it by two. You are at 50% if you tally up your points and obtain a total of 25.

As a result, if you're not feeling as energised as you'd like, consider doing something right away to recharge in one of those energy regions, such as going for a short walk. Consider something or someone for which you are thankful, or read something motivational. Focusing on the energy domain where you need it most will yield a substantial return, even if it doesn't take much time.

Let's not go too personal here, I think. I'm simply curious to see what goes through your head when you first realise it's time to begin the day. Do you feel motivated, eager, or inspired? Or do you feel worn out, overextended, or exhausted? If you're like most people, your alarm jolts you out of sleep and makes you anxious enough to get you out of bed quickly. This implies that what you do immediately after you get up is a crucial step in determining whether your day will be good or bad.

Your brain's task is to assess whether you need to remain in this high-stress state or whether you can switch into a more peaceful, focused, and productive mode.It's crucial to attempt to delay reading your email, social media, or any other type of media, when you first get up. Although it may be tempting to check in straight soon, please resist the urge and wait until you have given your mind something uplifting, motivating, or invigorating. Bad news and additional tasks to add to your list before you've refilled your own tank just don't sit well with your sensitive brain.

You can do this by reading a few pages of an uplifting book or listening to a guided meditation. You may play a brief podcast or a few upbeat tunes while working towards your daily objectives. Depending on how I feel when I wake up and how I want to feel, I have a few different playlists that I listen to. I put on some soothing music when I'm feeling pressured or anxious. But if I'm more down or discouraged, I turn to music that inspires me or makes me feel like I'm part of something greater than just trying to serve another day. Another fantastic technique to boost your energy is through physical activity. You may take a stroll, practise some mild yoga, or resolve to work out for for five minutes.

You could discover that once you get going and feel the energy flowing, you wind up accomplishing more than you anticipated and even like it. You could also want to inject some healthy humour into your morning by finding a hilarious movie to watch or telling a funny tale to a friend or relative. Instead of laughing at what's wrong, you should train your brain to see the lighter side of things more frequently. This will strengthen your resilience and improve your problem-solving skills. What will it be for you then? Take a moment right now to jot down two or three morning routine ideas that you think you'd want to try, and you may as well attempt one of them right away to get yourself ready for the rest of the day.

We can exercise our brains to help us manage energy more efficiently, just as we can train our physical muscles at the gym to help us move through life more successfully. I like to see this as being similar to brain exercise. Our capacity to use our brains to help us be the best versions of ourselves in the situations that are most important to us Similar to physical fitness, there are three distinct sorts of capabilities you might consider: your strength, flexibility, and endurance. And just as we need a solid plan to ensure that our workouts at the gym are effective, it's crucial to bear in mind certain analogous ideas when considering how we exercise our minds.

Anything that is going to generate a big change must first be difficult enough to require the brain to adjust.

It is obvious that just repeating the same actions day after day won't make something different occur just because we want it to. The difficulty of forming new habits should be just severe enough to make us strive for them without being too stressful. We may increase the level of difficulty as we gain strength and find it easier to keep up the habit in order to get better over time. Second, repetition of the new habit must be made frequently enough for adaptations to begin to accumulate if anything is to result in long-lasting change. Consider visiting a gym. Even if going once a year can seem amazing at first, it won't be enough to prevent your fitness level from rising. Or if you started taking vitamins, it would be excellent if you did so every day for a week, but that wouldn't be enough to strengthen your immune system for a whole year.

So keep in mind that if you want to teach your brain to help you manage your energy more successfully, you must challenge it by doing something new that just barely pushes you outside of your comfort zone. Don't try to run a marathon on your first visit to the gym, but do ensure that your exercise is at least somewhat painful. Then, practise the new habit consistently and often until it begins to naturally drive you in that direction. One new habit can be added at a time as you develop momentum to ensure that you can maintain your drive.

When you wake up, what is the first thing that comes to mind?

We work better both individually and in groups when we focus on the things that are most important to us rather than attempting to achieve too much at once. This is because the energy we bring to the task at hand is so much more useful. Because our surrounds and feelings of safety occupy a significant portion of the brain's attention, it is crucial to consider how our environment affects our energy. This is something to consider both in your own space and the spaces of those around you, both at home and at work.

Even though it may not seem rational, between 95% and 99% of your brain's energy is really directed towards subconscious environmental cues that make you feel comfortable or endangered. For instance, even while we are aware that common city sounds like traffic, sirens, or construction are not always signs of danger, the brain still needs to filter these sounds and form opinions about them, which may be extremely taxing on a brain that is already overworked.

Even while hearing natural sounds like birds tweeting or waves crashing doesn't always put you near the beach or a dense forest, research has shown that these rhythmic sounds can make individuals feel more at ease.T hey even boost immunological response while lowering blood pressure and inflammation. Therefore, it could be worthwhile to consider how you might enhance natural patterns in your surroundings while minimising those that are disruptive, such as doing your best to replace harsh lighting with more natural light. or turning on a sound machine to block out commotion.

The brain and body can be relaxed by just altering the sort of artwork or paint colour in a space.

According to studies, being around nature—whether it's genuine plants and water features or just photographs of nature on the walls—makes individuals feel more at ease. You might even use aromatherapy or a candle, depending on the environment, to assist you change your mood. You might feel more at ease and grounded by inhaling earthy aromas like clove and lavender. While energising scents like citrus or vanilla might support the improvement of motivation and vitality.

Last but not least, although it may seem trivial, having pictures of your loved ones around gives your mind something uplifting to think about while switching between jobs. Inspirational sayings, upbeat colours, and even upbeat music may all be deliberately employed to refuel and shared with others for special occasions that are mutually beneficial. As they collect during the day, these seemingly little changes to your surroundings might result in considerable energy benefits.

In addition to assisting us in keeping our promises, social support is an essential component of boosting energy capacity as a strategy in and of itself. According to a recent study, feeling lonely is really worse for one's general health than being inactive, eating poorly, or even smoking. Being alone in the world is a terrifying concept that puts a lot of stress on our bodies since the brain's largest dread is running out of resources.

Unfortunately, one of the first things we often do when we start to feel worn out or overcommitted is to put off social responsibilities. The last thing we want to do when we're feeling bad is ask for help because we don't want to put anyone else through it. However, when we do ask for help from others, the brain releases Oxytocin, a highly useful molecule that actually increases both the body's and brain's resistance to stress.

When we face stress with individuals we care about, the brain actually becomes even stronger rather than tearing us down. Thus, something that ordinarily harms us suddenly turns to benefit us just because we are with someone we care about. I could list several studies that show the significant benefits of social connections, but I'd like to nudge you to consider how you might make fostering and forming relationships with others a top priority both at work and at home.

To actually feel comfortable, it's first necessary to take your time and give each other your whole attention. We refer to this as psychological safety, which calls for a sense of being seen and heard. Rushing about and juggling many tasks all the time sends the message to others that they aren't as essential as anything else, which not only renders the time we spend with them useless but also dangerous. The good news is that connecting and being completely present in the moment don't need a lot of time or effort.

However, it does require some work to educate your brain to be able to do this more frequently. Turning off your phone at the door or leaving it in the car can help you focus on the here and now. You can also try deliberately listening to music while sitting in the driveway to help you change your vibe and leave work at work when you enter the house. As you practise these small adjustments over time, you might start to wonder how you ever allowed yourself to live your life without putting all of your energy into the time that you have. These small adjustments help to prime your brain to be able to show up fully in the moments that matter most to you.

Why are you unable to simply be present, without any sort of attitude?

Just mindful. simply conscious. It is critical that you accept the situation as it is. You don't make any denials. Grief will come if it does. Sadness is inevitable. Joy is what comes. Ecstasy appears immediately. You are not trying to deny or halt anything when you do this. Everything is occurring all at once, but you are not a part of it.

Let's think of a situation where individuals have become frivolous by concentrating all of their attention on what is easy for them, which they refer to as positive, which is why their lives have lost substance. They want rapid response times for everything. There isn't any commitment to anything. Imagine if someone had to train to be a scientist. He has to spend years studying. He forgets everything and gives himself, so perhaps he will forget his wife and kids. Only after that does he experience something, even in the physical realm. Because of the overabundance of instruction that says, "Do not worry, be joyful," this type of continuous attention is mostly lacking in our society. The situation is fine. Enjoy yourselves, please!" This type of bliss will unavoidably end, and people will experience mental illness.

Be cheerful and live in the now is a particularly well-liked adage I hear in the West, and it's starting to catch on in India as well. Please show me how to live somewhere else. Where else could you be right now, wherever you may be? Everyone mentions this because books have been written and programmes have been run by people who lack knowledge or experience.

The people who are constantly telling you to "be joyful" eventually get depression. Because your energies are allocated for various possibilities based on your karmic framework, they will always hit you extremely hard. There is something available to ease your suffering, sadness, pleasure, and love. The term for this is prarabdha karma. Not just in your head, either. Data is karma. According to this information, your energy is working. Prarabdha resembles a wounded spring. It must discover a way to let go. If you suppress and deny those feelings, they will take root in unexpected places.

Who do you believe should decide what is occurring around you if everything that happened to you happened inside of you? Even though you may occasionally experience negative things, how you choose to respond to them will influence how things turn out for you. You have a choice in how you respond to company failure or financial challenges. And the crucial factor that will determine your outcome and, eventually, your life is your response.

Never forget this saying: "I can't control the wind's direction, but I can modify my sails to always get there.

Focusing on the positive aspects of life and expecting good things to happen is known as positive thinking. A positive attitude is a way of thinking that resists giving in easily and is not deterred by challenges, problems, or delays. True optimism involves anticipating challenges and thinking about failure in addition to just asserting that everything will be fine. A positive attitude has to become your daily default mental attitude if you want to make good adjustments and improvements in your life. It needs to develop into a habit and a way of life. Although it can seem difficult, doing this is a slow and fun process.

What you do, not what occurred to you, is what counts most. And exactly like my advises, in order to achieve more success and have a happy life, you must learn to take command of your life.

True optimism involves being realistic about potential setbacks while still maintaining the belief that things will work out for the best. A positive attitude has to become your daily default mental attitude if you want to make good adjustments and improvements in your life. It needs to develop into a habit and a way of life. Although it can seem difficult, doing this is a slow and fun process.

This chapter discusses a few techniques for cultivating a positive outlook in order to achieve a healthy physical and mental condition. True optimism involves anticipating challenges and thinking about failure in addition to just asserting that everything will be fine. The tone of the day is determined by how we begin each morning. Even if you think it's stupid, say things to yourself in the mirror like, "Today will be a fantastic day" or "I'm going to be amazing today." These encouraging words will get ingrained in your subconscious mind, guiding, inspiring, and motivating you to think more positively and productively.

There's never going to be a flawless day; you're going to face challenges almost all day long. When faced with a difficulty like this, keep your attention on the advantages, no matter how minor or insignificant they may seem. Find humour in difficult circumstances: Give yourself permission to find humour even in the grimmest or most stressful circumstances. Try to get a laugh out of this scenario by reminding yourself that it will likely make for a wonderful tale later.

Learn from your mistakes.

No one is flawless, and we frequently make errors and fail in various situations, at various occupations, and with other people. Turn your failure into a lesson by considering what you'll do differently next time rather than dwelling on how you failed.

Be careful to replace any unfavourable ideas with positive and joyful ones. Start paying attention to your ideas, and as soon as you notice any negative ones, calmly and naturally replace them with helpful, joyful, and optimistic ones. Always work to keep your mind's door closed and prevent any bad thoughts from entering. We can stop our negative thoughts from arising and having an impact on us by keeping our attention in the here and now. The majority of sources of negativity are based on memories of recent events or overly optimistic predictions about prospective future events. Therefore, it's crucial to remain in the present.

You'll hear positive perspectives, nice anecdotes, and positive affirmations when you're surrounded by positive individuals. Their encouraging comments will stick with you and influence your own way of thinking, which spreads to others. Avoid being among folks who could make you feel inferior or discouraged.

Read success-related tales that will inspire and motivate you.

You will be motivated and inspired by this, and you will learn what they actually accomplished so you may copy them. Use the power of vision to see yourself performing and reacting favourably in various scenarios. One of the most effective ways to change your attitude and your life is to visualise the results you want to attain or the way you want to act or behave. Be proactive by taking initiative on both little and major issues. If you keep yourself busy, you will be more likely to be optimistic and less likely to become negative.

Before becoming one of the wealthiest people in the world, Kenny Troutt supported himself while attending Southern Illinois University by doing a side job selling insurance. Troutt, a bartender's son, was raised in a low-income household. He would go on to create Excel Communications, a long-distance phone firm, nevertheless, after earning his undergraduate degree. Twelve years after the company's founding, in 1996, he decided to go public. In a $3.5 billion agreement, Kenny Troutt sold Excel Communications to Teleglobe in 1998. He used the gains from the transaction to buy more stocks, bonds, and racehorses. Currently, he is the owner of WinStar Farm in Versailles, Kentucky, which produced a Kentucky Derby victor. Troutt's current net worth is $1.4 billion.

"He who is not courageous enough to take risks will accomplish nothing in life"- Muhammad Ali.

There is no way to do this wrong. If you desire happiness for one hour, the Dalai Lama says to take a nap. Go on a trek if you want to be happy for the day. Win the lottery if you want happiness for a year. But if you want lasting satisfaction, do good deeds. By assisting others in their success, you will also be assisting yourself in their success.

Creating opportunities out of obstacles people who are successful must consume a lot of lemonade. We've all heard the proverb, "When life gives you lemons, make lemonade." They are masters at transforming challenges into chances. In fact, it could be one of their most admirable character attributes. When the Dalai Lama was still a child, he was banished from his homeland. He said that his exile had given him the chance to travel the world and make every place he went his home when asked how difficult it must have been to never have a home. He credits that with enabling him to broaden his horizons and develop into the well-known leader he is today.

How networking works for those who are successful (and what success entails!) A short-term transaction is not what networking achieves. Creating relationships that benefit both parties is key to networking success. Similar to learning a language, it is a continual give-it-first process that demands an ongoing time commitment.

As a result, it is not a series of acts you perform only when you need something; rather, it is a continuous process since you never know when someone could need you. Disseminate knowledge, provide pertinent information, and assist others in achieving success in life. Do it since you enjoy it. Authenticity is essential.

Helping others achieve success and happiness will make you happier and more successful.

Nelson Mandela spent a large portion of his life in jail, which he describes as an "extended vacation for 27 years." He made the most of it by reading and writing, which helped him develop into the powerful leader that he was. "I am inherently an optimist," he said. Keeping one's feet going ahead and one's head pointing toward the sun is a necessary component of optimism. Successful, productive individuals have a lot of similar tendencies.

Can you tolerate pain, pressure, stress, interaction with nasty people, and unfavourable conditions while being joyful, committed to your purpose, successful, and persistent? What it means to be unbeatable is this. Mindset, skills, and habits that must be developed if you want to become invincible. These part was chosen based on the author's research over the previous ten years and his work with a variety of people, including students, senior professionals, and celebrities.

One thing all successful people have in common is that they did not come up with the solution on their own. They adopted the strategies used by coaches, mentors, and other prosperous individuals before implementing what they had learned in their own lives.

Find the temperament is the amount of activity that ensures that businesses and individuals achieve their objectives and fulfil their desires. "Your Action," which enables you to break beyond business clichés and risk aversion while taking actual action to achieve your goals.

Additionally, how to proceed through the first three steps and establish the rule as a discipline. To get massive action outcomes, learn exactly where to start, what to do, and how to follow up on each action you take with additional action.

Focus is the deliberate selection of what merits the most of your time and attention. However, the majority of individuals use their time and attention in a disorganised manner. They only sometimes focus on what is most important. They essentially look at anything on social media, on their phone, or in the news for the remainder of the time. Instead, you should carefully select your areas of emphasis before scheduling time to ensure that you don't lose them. What should you pay attention to? That's simple. You will have determined your greatest strengths if you have finished the previous chapters. These are the pursuits that not only suit you well because of your talents, interests, and abilities but also have a high market value.

Are you ready to concentrate on them now?

More significantly, are you prepared to begin declining offers to change your professional weaknesses? That's a scary question, huh? But it's a crucial one to think about since every time you say "no" to one thing, you say "yes" to another. Declare to yourself that you're not going to divert your attention to less important qualities or even shortcomings. Decide right now to concentrate on strengthening your strengths. Once you've decided on your area of concentration, you should look into particular actions you may take to strengthen that skill.

Sometimes there just doesn't appear to be any way to make your abilities fit with your current employment, and there just isn't a match at all. Maybe there aren't any positions available at the company where you work that fit your particular set of skills. Maybe you're a freelancer, and you've come to the conclusion that your present line of work isn't really a good fit for you. So, what should you do? Firstly, a general observation Avoid making the mistake of confusing job unhappiness with job mismatch.

Numerous leaders I've worked with have expressed burnout and a desire to leave their positions. Then, as we dug more into the issue, we discovered that it was an odd present scenario, not the work itself, that was making them burn out. Their job satisfaction increased again when we found a solution. Changes in careers are only essential when our jobs are genuinely incompatible with our personalities. This is similar to when a socially awkward individual who is great with statistics and definitely belongs in accounting attempts to create sales and connections with people, or the other way around. These scenarios are rarely successful.

So, if you still feel there is a complete mismatch after some reflection, start to consider what employment or line of work outside of your present one would be a better fit. Which occupations closely match the combination of a couple of these skills working together? Refer to your list of your most useful strengths. You shouldn't expect the solution to be simple for you.

I suggest discussing this with a dependable friend or mentor who might provide you some insight you would not otherwise have. Simple web searches that include your area of expertise and the terms "careers" may potentially turn up some possibilities. Start compiling a list of prospective professions that you believe would better utilise your talents. If you can, contact those who are currently employed in such fields. Inquire specifically about the role that each of their strengths plays in their day-to-day activities.

How much of your day, for instance, is spent conversing with others? How much room do you have for original ideas each day? so on. If you eventually determine that a switch is required, take care. Although a profession that plays to your skills is preferable in the long run, we don't want to forfeit your capacity to support yourself and others in the near term, so please be patient. You are much more likely to succeed if you can find a job that allows you to use your talents, makes you happy because you enjoy going to work every day, and allows you to grow and advance your skills.

Productive people have productive habits.

It's crucial to consider how we recharge throughout the day to maintain our energy levels once we've established the proper daily routines at the beginning and end of the day. Nutrition is one of the main ways we do this. It's crucial to remember that what you eat is probably extremely personal and ought to be. All diets, according to studies, are effective, but only when they are practical, fun, and realistic.

If you're serious about improving your eating habits, I advise consulting a nutritionist who can create a plan specifically for you based on your particular body type and mental makeup. How we should eat is something that applies to everyone, which is where mindful eating comes in. We can exercise our brains to help us manage energy more efficiently, just as we can train our physical muscles at the gym to help us move through life more successfully.

I like to see this as being similar to brain exercise. Our capacity to use our brains to help us be the best versions of ourselves in the situations that are most important to us Similar to physical fitness, there are three distinct sorts of capabilities you might consider: your strength, flexibility, and endurance. And just as we need a sound plan to ensure that our workouts at the gym are effective, it's crucial to keep certain analogous ideas in mind as we consider how we train our brains. Anything that is going to generate a big change must first be difficult enough to require the brain to adjust. It is obvious that just repeating the same actions day after day won't make something different occur just because we want it to. The difficulty of new habits should be just severe enough to make us strive for them while not being too stressful.

We may increase the level of difficulty as we gain stronger and find it easier to keep up the habit in order to get better over time. Second, in order to produce changes that stick, we must repeat the new behaviour frequently enough for adaptations to begin to take hold. Consider visiting a gym. Even if going once a year can seem amazing at first, it won't be enough to prevent your fitness level from rising. Or if you started taking vitamins, it would be excellent if you did so every day for a week, but that wouldn't be enough to strengthen your immune system for a whole year.

So keep in mind that if you want to teach your brain to help you manage your energy more successfully, you must challenge it by doing something new that just barely pushes you outside of your comfort zone. Don't try to run a marathon on your first visit to the gym, but do ensure that your exercise is first painful. Then, practise the new habit consistently and often until it begins to naturally drive you in that way. One new habit can be added at a time as you develop momentum to ensure that you can maintain your drive.

As it happens, excellent leaders have a lot of the same behaviours. Developing good habits involves both doing and avoiding the appropriate things. The most productive habits practised by the most successful and productive people in the world are listed below. This list is intended to inspire you to create your own habits that will improve your effectiveness and productivity in daily life.

Prowess of the intellect and body are what you essentially need to succeed in the world. Equanimity is one of the most crucial traits if you wish to master the mind. You can enter several mental realms while you are centered. You have far less mental capacity if there is no serenity. Another crucial characteristic is your degree of energy; you must be vigorous on the inside as much as on the outside. You can only overcome challenges in daily life and progress toward achievement when your energies are vivacious. Success will come to you much more readily if you bring serenity and joy into your mind and body.

You are well aware that no matter how quickly or persistently you run, you will never arrive at your destination if you are running in the wrong direction. While diligence is essential, success requires a combination of intellect and diligence.

About The Author

Dr. Amit Das, is a renowned executive advisor, consultant, educationist, author, speaker, counsellor, and coach whose 25+ years of business experience provides high-impact, practical solutions that support his clients' leadership development and organisational transformations. He worked for fortune 500 companies and left rich leagacy of organising transformational learning workshops.

He has transformed more than 5000+ working executives through his path breaking capability building learning workshops. Dr. Amit Das is recognised as an innovative, principled thought leader who combines intellectual rigor and discipline with an ability to translate theory into practice. His operational skills are coupled with a strategic ability to analyse, develop, and implement successful strategies for profitability, growth, and sustainability.

Dr. Amit Das has a successful track record in aligning learning and training solutions to key business strategy with a strong focus on flawless execution excellence to facilitate individual, business divisional, and organisational performance. He keeps relentless focus on measuring training impact and ROI, people capability building graphs, training process governance, performance coaching, and strategic thinking. These have been some of his key individual success traits. His core capabilities include performance coaching, designing training and development frameworks, psychometric assessment and analysis, competency framework development and assessments, content design and facilitation of soft skills and leadership programmes, Learning Management Systems, Learning Impact Measurement, Talent Analysis, and Performance Coaching and Counselling.

Dr. Amit Das has authored multiple management and self-development books, like Toxicity at the Workplace, Akrasia to Enkrateia, You Are Born To Succeed, Reinventing and Redefining You, Change Your Perspective Change Your Life, 90 Minutes Mindfulness, The Alchemy Of Resilient Leadership, Redefining Organisational Excellence, High Impact Leadership, A Divorce-Free Married Life, Redefining Corporate Spectrum, Create Your Leadership Edge, Love-Laugh- Live With Happiness, SMART Parenting @ Zero Cost, Redefining HRM, Building Organisational Capability, Ethical Road Map, Attomic Attention, BYPB, Redefining The Power Of Mentoring, Making The Most Future Fit Organisation, Redefining Talent Management, Defining Your Success Factors, Lead or Plead, Make The Most Of Your Life, Better Half or Bitter Half, Psychology Of Learning And Development, The Transformative Mind & Soul are few of them.

He has a Ph.D. and a Fellowship in strategic learning, along with his first class degrees in Human Resource Management, Marketing Management, International Business, and Corporate Laws from the top business schools in India. He is a certified Psychometric analyst, HR Analyst, OD Interventionist, Human Psychologist, Lifecoach, Leadership Developer, Black Belt (LSS), Strategic Thinker, Talent Analyst, certified professional trainer and certified behavioral coach.

Dr. Amit Das teaches courses related to Organisational Development, Human Resource Management, Self-Management, and Leadership Coaching. He regularly engages in consulting and training work for organisation and leadership development with organisations across industries and with many institutions of higher education. He has published many research articles in the fields of human resource management, business compliance at the workplace, mindfulness, the business-society interface, and the best practises in management in reputed journals.

Dr. Amit Das likes googling, reading books, writing articles & books, cooking, listening to old melodies, and counselling people to unleash their true potential to build a strong nation. He is married and blessed with a son. He would love to hear about your experience after reading his books. You can email him and share your thoughts, or you can use his services for life coaching, positive behavioural counseling, educational support, and mentoring for young, promising students pursuing their B.B.A. and M.B.A. degrees.

Dr. Amit Das, a leadership consultant by training and occupation, is passionate about writing. He is a firm believer in giving top attention to resolving covert social and psychological goals at work. He aspires to foster a positive workplace atmosphere and uphold improved mental wellness. In order to raise awareness, he plans to write more about these subjects in his next projects.

He enjoys travelling, watching Bollywood & Hollywood movies, and researching a variety of subjects in addition to writing on the aforementioned themes. His insightful, funny, and brutally honest writings about success and failure, self-awareness, and interpersonal relationships have established him as one of the top personal brands. He is an authorpreneur and content producer. The main concepts that have driven his journey—which started with him wanting to be an IIM professor and concluded with him producing material that has been viewed and read by millions—are collected in his book.

His opinions cover a wide range of topics, including the value of forming habits for long-term success, the cornerstones of self-management, embracing and accepting failure, and the unvarnished truth about developing empathy.

References

- *Smarter Faster Better: The Transformative Power of Real Productivity, March, 2017 by Charles Duhigg.*
- *Tuesdays with Morrie: An Old Man, a Young Man, and Life's Greatest Lesson, 25th Anniversary Edition Kindle Edition, June, 2007 by Mitch Albom.*
- *Good Vibes, Good Life: How Self-love Is the Key to Unlocking Your Greatness Paperback – January 2019 by Vex King.*
- *Life's Amazing Secrets: How to Find Balance and Purpose in Your Life | Inspirational Zen book on motivation, self-development & healthy living Paperback –October, 2018 by Gaur Gopal Das.*
- *Thriving Hacks: Simple Hacks For a Richer, Healthier and Fulfilling Life Paperback –October 2021 by Ravikummar M.*
- *Directed by Purpose: How to Focus on Work That Matters, Ignore Distractions and Manage Your Attention over the Long Haul (Six Simple Steps to Success Book 5) Kindle Edition, July, 2021 by Michal Stawicki , Anthony Smits.*
- *The Happiness Tree: Grow Your Happiness by Cultivating a Healthy, Creative and Purposeful Life Paperback – December, 2015 by Shane Eric Mathias.*
- *Who Do You Want to Be? Paperback – May, 2021 by Alina Shahnazari.*
- *Finding Purpose Beyond Oneself: How to Live a Fulfilling Life & Find Your Life's Work by Focusing on Others Instead of Yourself (15 Minute Life Series Book 1) Kindle Edition by Sean Bobby Maximilian, Nov, 2016.*
- *Finding Your Purpose: How to Find Your Purpose In Life*

and Make the Most of Your Time Here on Earth, a Non-Religious Perspective - (What is the Purpose of Life ?) Kindle Edition by Kathleen Rao, June, 2014.

- *Finding Your Passionate Purpose: In Life, Leadership, and Love, November, 2016 by Heidi McKee.*
- *Finding Your WHY: Discover Your Life's Purpose, February, 2015 by Mike Rodriguez.*
- *Know What You Want: The Simple Step-By-Step Guide to Finding Your Passion And Living On Purpose Kindle Edition by Pearce Lee, Aug, 2015.*
- *Discovering Your Personal Potential: Finding God's Will and Purpose for Your Life, December, 2007 by Tobenna O Ebubechukwu.*
- *Man's Search for Meaning Paperback – May, 2006 by Viktor E. Frankl.*
- *The Element: How Finding Your Passion Changes Everything, December, 2009 by Ken Robinson , Lou Aron.*
- *12 Rules For Life, January, 2018 by Jordan B. Peterson.*
- *The Untethered Soul: The Journey Beyond Yourself, Oct , 2007 by Michael A. Singer.*
- *Find Your Passion: 25 Questions You Must Ask Yourself, Oct , 2013 by Henri Junttila.*
- *Do the Work: Overcome Resistance and Get Out of Your Own Way, March, 2015 by Steven Pressfield.*
- *Miracles Now: 108 Life-Changing Tools for Less Stress, More Flow, and Finding Your True Purpose, April , 2015 by Gabrielle Bernstein.*
- *The Crossroads of Should and Must: Find and Follow Your Passion, April , 2015 by Elle Luna.*
- *The Happiness of Pursuit: Finding the Quest That Will Bring Purpose to Your Life , April , 2016 by Chris Guillebeau.*
- *Unwrapping Your Passion: Creating the Life You Truly*

Want, July, 2017 by Karen Putz

- *The Life You Were Born to Live (Revised 25th Anniversary Edition): A Guide to Finding Your Life Purpose, August , 2018 by Dan Millman.*
- *I Could Do Anything If I Only Knew What It Was: How to Discover What You Really Want and How to Get It, August , 1995 by Barbara Sher.*
- *The Art of Work: A Proven Path to Discovering What You Were Meant to Do, March , 2015 by Jeff Goins.*
- *How to Achieve Immortality: 100 Ways to Create Your Own Legacy for Future Generations Paperback – November, 2004 by Lloyd Silverman.*
- *Make Your Own Luck: How to Increase Your Odds of Success in Sales, Startups, Corporate Career and Life Paperback –October, 2019 by Bob Miglani & Rehan Yar Khan.*
- *The Purpose Driven Life: What on Earth Am I Here For? Paperback –June 2016 by Rick Warren.*
- *Provisions For Your Purpose Kindle Edition, May,2022. by Adetola Balogun.*
- *Purposeful: A Step-by-Step Guide to Finding Clear Direction in a Chaotic World Paperback – September, 2016 by John Carroll.*
- *On Purpose: The Busy Woman's Guide to an Extraordinary Life of Meaning and Success Kindle Edition, October,2021 by Tanya Dalton.*
- *On Purposeful Systems: An Interdisciplinary Analysis of Individual and Social Behavior as a System of Purposeful Events Paperback –July, 2005 by Fred Emery.*
- *Living a Purposeful and Fruitful Life : The 33 Principles Kindle Edition,January,2021. by Michael O. A. Asenso , Nana Amma Oforiwaa Sam.*
- *Incredible Power of Inspiration: Creating the Life You*

Yearn for Paperback – October, 2017 by Jenifer Zetlan.

- *Wise Mind Living: Master Your Emotions, Transform Your Life Paperback –January, 2017 by Erin Olivo Ph.D.*
- *What Is Your Legacy?: 101 Ideas On Getting Started to Create and Build One Kindle Edition by Anca Iovita, July 2021.*
- *Your Legacy In A Book: How to Create a Memoir Your Family Will Cherish For Generations Kindle Edition, February,2022 by Travis Cody.*
- *9 Tips To Take Your Life Back - Simple and helpful tips on organizing your life, melting the stress away, and living a more happier, healthier, & purposeful (Simple Ways To A Stress Free Life Book 1) Kindle Edition, July,2016 by Rich A. Williams.*
- *Finding Purpose Beyond Oneself: How to Live a Fulfilling Life & Find Your Life's Work by Focusing on Others Instead of Yourself (15 Minute Life Series Book 1) Kindle Edition, November,2016 by Sean Bobby Maximilian.*
- *Living A Life Of Purpose: A 10 week study focusing on ways to live a purposeful life Kindle Edition, October,2021 by Marni Ausenbaugh devotional.*
- *The Power of Positive Thinking, March, 2003 by Dr. Norman Vincent Peale.*
- *High-Hanging Fruit: Build Something Great by Going Where No One Else Will, July, 2016 by Mark Rampolla.*
- *Choose Yourself! June, 2013 by James Altucher, Dick Costolo.*
- *Mindset: The New Psychology of Success, December, 2007 by Carol S. Dweck.*
- *Man's Search for Meaning, June , 2006 by Viktor E. Frankl.*
- *You Are a Badass: How to Stop Doubting Your Greatness and Start Living an Awesome Life, April, 2013 by Jen Sincero.*

- *Make Your Bed: Little Things That Can Change Your Life...And Maybe the World, April, 2017 by Admiral William H. McRaven.*
- *The Alchemist, 25th Anniversary: A Fable About Following Your Dream, April, 2014 by Paulo Coelho.*
- *The 5 Second Rule: Transform your Life, Work, and Confidence with Everyday Courage, February, 2017 by Mel Robbins.*
- *Unfu*k Yourself: Get Out of Your Head and into Your Life, August, 2017 by Gary John Bishop.*
- *Hustle: The Power to Charge Your Life with Money, Meaning, and Momentum, September, 2016 by Neil Patel, Patrick Vlaskovits, and Jonas Koffler.*
- *Think and Grow Rich: The Landmark Bestseller Now Revised and Updated for the 21st Century (Think and Grow Rich Series), January, 2005 by Napoleon Hill , Arthur R. Pell.*
- *Now, Discover Your Strengths: The revolutionary Gallup program that shows you how to develop your unique talents and strengths, February, 2020 by Gallup.*
- *The Gifts of Imperfection: Let Go of Who You Think You're Supposed to Be and Embrace Who You Are, October, 2010 by Brené Brown.*
- *Finding Your WHY: Discover Your Life's Purpose, February, 2015 by Mike Rodriguez.*
- *Know What You Want: The Simple Step-By-Step Guide to Finding Your Passion And Living On Purpose Kindle Edition by Pearce Lee, Aug, 2015.*
- *Discovering Your Personal Potential: Finding God's Will and Purpose for Your Life, December, 2007 by Tobenna O Ebubechukwu.*
- *Man's Search for Meaning Paperback – May, 2006 by Viktor E. Frankl.*

- *The Element: How Finding Your Passion Changes Everything, December, 2009 by Ken Robinson , Lou Aron.*
- *12 Rules For Life, January, 2018 by Jordan B. Peterson.*
- *The Untethered Soul: The Journey Beyond Yourself, Oct , 2007 by Michael A. Singer.*
- *Find Your Passion: 25 Questions You Must Ask Yourself, Oct , 2013 by Henri Junttila.*
- *Do the Work: Overcome Resistance and Get Out of Your Own Way, March, 2015 by Steven Pressfield.*
- *Miracles Now: 108 Life-Changing Tools for Less Stress, More Flow, and Finding Your True Purpose, April , 2015 by Gabrielle Bernstein.*
- *The Crossroads of Should and Must: Find and Follow Your Passion, April , 2015 by Elle Luna.*
- *The Happiness of Pursuit: Finding the Quest That Will Bring Purpose to Your Life , April , 2016 by Chris Guillebeau.*
- *Unwrapping Your Passion: Creating the Life You Truly Want, July, 2017 by Karen Putz*
- *The Life You Were Born to Live (Revised 25th Anniversary Edition): A Guide to Finding Your Life Purpose, August , 2018 by Dan Millman.*
- *I Could Do Anything If I Only Knew What It Was: How to Discover What You Really Want and How to Get It, August , 1995 by Barbara Sher.*
- *The Art of Work: A Proven Path to Discovering What You Were Meant to Do, March , 2015 by Jeff Goins.*
- *The Gifts of Imperfection: Let Go of Who You Think You're Supposed to Be and Embrace Who You Are, October, 2010 by Brené Brown.*
- *How to Achieve Immortality: 100 Ways to Create Your Own Legacy for Future Generations Paperback – November, 2004 by Lloyd Silverman.*

- *Make Your Own Luck: How to Increase Your Odds of Success in Sales, Startups, Corporate Career and Life Paperback –October, 2019 by Bob Miglani & Rehan Yar Khan.*
- *What Is Your Legacy?: 101 Ideas On Getting Started to Create and Build One Kindle Edition by Anca Iovita, July 2021.*
- *Your Legacy In A Book: How to Create a Memoir Your Family Will Cherish For Generations Kindle Edition, February,2022 by Travis Cody.*
- *9 Tips To Take Your Life Back - Simple and helpful tips on organizing your life, melting the stress away, and living a more happier, healthier, & purposeful (Simple Ways To A Stress Free Life Book 1) Kindle Edition, July,2016 by Rich A. Williams.*
- *Finding Purpose Beyond Oneself: How to Live a Fulfilling Life & Find Your Life's Work by Focusing on Others Instead of Yourself (15 Minute Life Series Book 1) Kindle Edition, November,2016 by Sean Bobby Maximilian.*
- *Living A Life Of Purpose: A 10 week study focusing on ways to live a purposeful life Kindle Edition, October,2021 by Marni Ausenbaugh devotional.*
- *7 Divine Laws to Awaken Your Best Self Paperback – 30 December 2020 by Swami Mukundananda.*
- *Rule Your Day: 6 Keys to Maximizing Your Success and Accelerating Your Dreams Hardcover – Import, 8 March 2022 by Joel Osteen.*
- *Success A Few Steps Away Book by J C Chaudhry, Your Daily Dose of Success and Motivation Paperback – 1 January 2020 by J.C. Chaudhry (Author).*
- *How to Live Your Best Life: Transform your mindset and manifest real success Hardcover – 2 September 2021 by Maria Hatzistefanis (Author).*

- *Your Ultimate Success Plan: Stop Holding Yourself Back and Get Recognized, Rewarded and Promoted Kindle Edition by Tamara Jacobs (Author).*
- *Cultivate Your Emotions: How to Stop Feeling like Sh*t, Build Empowering Emotions, and Turn any Fear into Success (Cultivating Greatness) Kindle Edition by Giuseppe Ferraro (Author).*
- *Make Your Own Luck: How to Increase Your Odds of Success in Sales, Startups, Corporate Career and Life Paperback –October, 2019 by Bob Miglani & Rehan Yar Khan.*
- *The Purpose Driven Life: What on Earth Am I Here For? Paperback –June 2016 by Rick Warren.*
- *Provisions For Your Purpose Kindle Edition, May,2022. by Adetola Balogun.*
- *Purposeful: A Step-by-Step Guide to Finding Clear Direction in a Chaotic World Paperback – September, 2016 by John Carroll.*
- *On Purpose: The Busy Woman's Guide to an Extraordinary Life of Meaning and Success Kindle Edition, October,2021 by Tanya Dalton.*
- *On Purposeful Systems: An Interdisciplinary Analysis of Individual and Social Behavior as a System of Purposeful Events Paperback –July, 2005 by Fred Emery.*
- *Living a Purposeful and Fruitful Life : The 33 Principles Kindle Edition,January,2021. by Michael O. A. Asenso , Nana Amma Oforiwaa Sam.*
- *Incredible Power of Inspiration: Creating the Life You Yearn for Paperback – October, 2017 by Jenifer Zetlan.*
- *Wise Mind Living: Master Your Emotions, Transform Your Life Paperback –January, 2017 by Erin Olivo Ph.D.*
- *What Is Your Legacy?: 101 Ideas On Getting Started to Create and Build One Kindle Edition by Anca Iovita, July*

2021.

- *Your Legacy In A Book: How to Create a Memoir Your Family Will Cherish For Generations Kindle Edition, February,2022 by Travis Cody.*
- *9 Tips To Take Your Life Back - Simple and helpful tips on organizing your life, melting the stress away, and living a more happier, healthier, & purposeful (Simple Ways To A Stress Free Life Book 1) Kindle Edition, July,2016 by Rich A. Williams.*
- *Finding Purpose Beyond Oneself: How to Live a Fulfilling Life & Find Your Life's Work by Focusing on Others Instead of Yourself (15 Minute Life Series Book 1) Kindle Edition, November,2016 by Sean Bobby Maximilian.*
- *Living A Life Of Purpose: A 10 week study focusing on ways to live a purposeful life Kindle Edition, October,2021 by Marni Ausenbaugh devotional.*
- *The Power of Positive Thinking, March, 2003 by Dr. Norman Vincent Peale.*
- *High-Hanging Fruit: Build Something Great by Going Where No One Else Will, July, 2016 by Mark Rampolla.*
- *Choose Yourself! June, 2013 by James Altucher, Dick Costolo.*
- *Mindset: The New Psychology of Success, December, 2007 by Carol S. Dweck.*
- *Man's Search for Meaning, June , 2006 by Viktor E. Frankl.*
- *You Are a Badass: How to Stop Doubting Your Greatness and Start Living an Awesome Life, April, 2013 by Jen Sincero.*
- *Make Your Bed: Little Things That Can Change Your Life...And Maybe the World, April, 2017 by Admiral William H. McRaven.*
- *The Alchemist, 25th Anniversary: A Fable About Following Your Dream, April, 2014 by Paulo Coelho.*
-

- *inding Purpose Beyond Oneself: How to Live a Fulfilling Life & Find Your Life's Work by Focusing on Others Instead of Yourself (15 Minute Life Series Book 1) Kindle Edition by Sean Bobby Maximilian, Nov, 2016.*
- *Finding Your Purpose: How to Find Your Purpose In Life and Make the Most of Your Time Here on Earth, a Non-Religious Perspective - (What is the Purpose of Life ?) Kindle Edition by Kathleen Rao, June, 2014.*
- *Finding Your Passionate Purpose: In Life, Leadership, and Love, November, 2016 by Heidi McKee.*
- *Finding Your WHY: Discover Your Life's Purpose, February, 2015 by Mike Rodriguez.*
- *Know What You Want: The Simple Step-By-Step Guide to Finding Your Passion And Living On Purpose Kindle Edition by Pearce Lee, Aug, 2015.*
- *Discovering Your Personal Potential: Finding God's Will and Purpose for Your Life, December, 2007 by Tobenna O Ebubechukwu.*
- *Man's Search for Meaning Paperback – May, 2006 by Viktor E. Frankl.*
- *The Element: How Finding Your Passion Changes Everything, December, 2009 by Ken Robinson , Lou Aron.*
- *12 Rules For Life, January, 2018 by Jordan B. Peterson.*
- *The Untethered Soul: The Journey Beyond Yourself, Oct , 2007 by Michael A. Singer.*
- *Find Your Passion: 25 Questions You Must Ask Yourself, Oct , 2013 by Henri Junttila.*
- *Do the Work: Overcome Resistance and Get Out of Your Own Way, March, 2015 by Steven Pressfield.*
- *Miracles Now: 108 Life-Changing Tools for Less Stress, More Flow, and Finding Your True Purpose, April , 2015 by Gabrielle Bernstein.*
- *The Crossroads of Should and Must: Find and Follow Your*

Passion, April , 2015 by Elle Luna.

- *The Happiness of Pursuit: Finding the Quest That Will Bring Purpose to Your Life , April , 2016 by Chris Guillebeau.*

Printed by Libri Plureos GmbH in Hamburg,
Germany